Gender and Mobility

Gender and Mobility

A Critical Introduction

Elina Penttinen and Anitta Kynsilehto

ROWMAN & LITTLEFIELD
London • New York

Published by Rowman & Littlefield International Ltd
Unit A, Whitacre Mews, 26–34 Stannary Street, London SE11 4AB
www.rowmaninternational.com

Rowman & Littlefield International Ltd.is an affiliate of Rowman & Littlefield
4501 Forbes Boulevard, Suite 200, Lanham, Maryland 20706, USA
With additional offices in Boulder, New York, Toronto (Canada), and Plymouth (UK)
www.rowman.com

British Library Cataloguing in Publication Data
A catalogue record for this book is available from the British Library

ISBN: HB 978-1-78660-267-1
          PB 978-1-78660-268-8

Library of Congress Cataloging-in-Publication Data Available

ISBN: 9781786602671 (cloth : alk. paper)
ISBN: 9781786602688 (pbk. : alk. paper)
ISBN: 9781786602695 (electronic)

♾™ The paper used in this publication meets the minimum requirements of American
National Standard for Information Sciences – Permanence of Paper for Printed Library
Materials, ANSI/NISO Z39.48–1992.

Printed in the United States of America

Contents

Abbreviations

CCM	Civilian crisis management
CEDAW	Convention on the Elimination of All Forms of Discrimination against Women
EU	European Union
EULEX	European Union Rule of Law Mission in Kosovo
EUROPOL	EU's law enforcement agency
FDI	Foreign direct investment
FGM	Female genital mutilation
FIFA	World Football Federation
FRONTEX	European Border and Coast Guard Agency
FYROM	Former Yugoslav Republic of Macedonia
GBV	Gender-based violence
GCC	Global care chain
GDP	Gross domestic product
ICCPR	International Covenant on Civil and Political Rights
ICTs	Information and communication technologies
IDP	Internally displaced person
IGO	International governmental organization
ILO	International Labour Organization
IOM	International Organization for Migration
IPTF	International Police Task Force
IPV	Intimate partner violence
IRB	Immigration and Refugee Board of Canada
LGBTQI	Lesbian, gay, bisexual, transgender, queer or questioning, and intersex
LOC	Line of control
OFW	Overseas Filipino worker

OPTs	Occupied Palestinian Territories
PRC	People's Republic of China
PRS	Protracted refugee situation
RLI	Regime of labour intimacy
RPV	Reproductive, productive and virtual
RSD	Refugee status determination
SAR	Search and rescue
SCO	Shanghai Cooperation Organization
SFOR	Stabilisation Force in Bosnia and Herzegovina
SOGI	Sexual orientation or gender identity
3D	Dirty, dangerous and demeaning
TIP	Trafficking in Persons Report
TMC	Technomuscular capitalism
UN	United Nations
UNHCR	UN Refugee Agency, United Nations High Commissioner for Refugees
UNTAC	UN Transitional Authority in Cambodia

Acknowledgements

From the start of the writing process of this book on gender and global mobilities, we were clear that our primary responsibility was always towards the people who are on the move. Our purpose has been to provide a wide enough range of theoretical perspectives and practices of feminist research to gain insights to and understanding of how gender, global and mobility intersect and co-constitute each other. In the process of compiling the materials for this book we have been aware of our own responsibility as authors in terms of how we represent, and indeed re-create, the lives of the people travelling through these pages and into the lives of the readers, hopefully touching them.

During the writing process, the number of refugees on the global scale has increased considerably. Meanwhile, the political climate has become all the more violent against racialized and gendered "Others." With this book, we invite the readers to care about the lived realities of real people who make hard choices, embrace opportunities, sometimes trust the wrong people, and hopefully most of the time connect with others who are kind and helpful. And like everyone, people on the move live and learn throughout this process, grow and are changed by it. Therefore, we want to acknowledge that we are indebted to all the people on the move, and we wish that we have been able to represent these lives fairly. We have aimed to convey the message that life in the midst of global mobilities is never either-or, good or bad, constricted or free, but it is all of these at once, like life usually is, and it never stays the same.

We have sought to create a book that satisfies some of the curiosity of the new generation, who are eager to ask the hard questions and look for out-of-the-box solutions for persistent problems in the world we share. Yet, in doing so, our strategy has been to provide tools, theories and approaches with which to embark on a journey and imagine new ways of knowing and asking questions, which can lead to more ethical policies. Therefore, we want to express our gratitude to all the students we have had the joy to work with during the process of this book and whose relentless desire for knowledge has inspired us into creating this book.

We want to express our heartfelt gratitude to our colleagues worldwide who have been there to instil faith in us during the writing process and cheer us on. We are grateful for the support and encouragement we have received for this project from our institutional settings at the University of Helsinki and the University of Tampere. We want to express our gratitude to Marjut Jyrkinen, Johanna Kantola, Tuija Pulkkinen and Julian Honkasalo at Gender Studies in the University of Helsinki for their support, encouragement, useful comments and resources. We want to give thanks to Risto Heiskala, Eeva Puumala and Tiina Vaittinen at the University of Tampere and the seminar participants at the Cresppa-GTM in Paris for their encouragement and valuable advice. We are also grateful for the anonymous reviewers and their comments that enabled us to finalize the chapters in the form that they are presented here.

We want to express our heartfelt gratitude to editor Dhara Snowden for comments and assistance and for helping us with all the practical details. We also want to thank Michael Watson for helping us with the final details and making sure that this book turns out beautiful.

We want to, of course, thank our spouses and children and acknowledge the sense of humour and flexibility required from family members, as we have intensely focused our energies on this book.

This book is dedicated to all the people on the move, and to those who stay put.

Chapter 1

Gender and mobility:
A critical introduction

A regular workday is to begin and I open my computer. The first thing that catches my attention is a message I have received from a Nigerian man. We met a month earlier at the detention centre in Korinthos, Greece. He has now been detained for irregular presence in Greece for a year, and as the recent legislative change that was extended in line with the maximum time defined in the EU Return directive from 2008 permits, he is likely to stay detained for a half a year longer awaiting deportation to his country of origin. He had filed his asylum application from detention. Now he has received a negative decision to his claim. Desperate for help, he has sent me the decision asking whether I could find a lawyer to help him. I look at the documents, all written in Greek. I don't understand a word except for his name and nationality that I'm able to guess. I wonder whether he understands anything more of the decision than I do. I doubt it.

Just a few weeks earlier, in October 2013, I was in Greece and Turkey as a member of an inter-associative team enquiring after the current migratory situation in these countries, and the context of push-backs at the Greek-Turkish border (Frontexit 2014). Now I think of the people met and those with whom I have been in contact afterwards. As a researcher in social sciences, I don't have much else to offer this Nigerian man other than my contacts.

When I return home from the field, it takes time to adjust my pace to the rhythms of the academia, as it is my job to work toward analytic distance and write in terms of theoretical generalizations. But, what is one supposed to do when the "field" gets back in touch? In other words, when making contact becomes easier in general, how does one manage the daily assignments and routines and long-distance relations, and maintain a balance between different personal and professional spheres?

(Extract from Anitta's research diary, November 2013)

The above story brings forth the very complex relations between academic research as a knowledge production and an activist practice towards enhancing the awareness of inconsistencies and harmful outcomes of migration policies in contemporary world.

These encounters, situated in places such as the immigration detention centre and communication beyond field research setting, crystallize our multiple positionalities as academics and co-producers of knowledge with research participants, and as activists seeking to influence migration policies and practice. The narrative highlights how our personal hopes, desires and gendered bodies are not somehow separate but influence research relationships and indeed create often unanticipated tensions.

In this particular story, the tension is situated in the interaction between an academic researcher/activist and a migrant detainee seeking for help in an acute crisis. These two positions are literally located on the opposite sides of the barbed fence of detention infrastructure. How would one proceed in such circumstances in relation to a research participant? And how would one proceed with creating an academic text about migration policy for academic audiences in ethically sustainable ways?

The purpose of this book is to explore the complexity of gender and mobility in the contemporary globalized world. Our objective is to compel the readers to *question* how gender and global mobility come to matter in diverse lived experiences and to *think* critically about the practices and politics that shape these trajectories based on the range of feminist theorizing.

This book sets out a multidisciplinary and multi-perspectival approach to explore *gender*, *global* and *mobilities*. When we set out to explore *gender*, *global* and *mobility*, we are dealing with a complex issue that combines gender-specific choices and subjectivities, changes in the global labour market and migration policies as well as politics of representation of gender and culture.

Therefore, gender analysis of global mobilities is about recognizing not only how gender matters in terms of what kinds of choices or possibilities are available for individuals and families but also how migration policies and global market direct and channel migration. The politics of cultural gender representations concretize and produce mobilities, in turn producing and reconfiguring new representations. Yet asking questions about gender in the context of global mobility is really about understanding the lived realities of people on the move in the complex globalized world.

Our hope is, in line with Enloe (2004), to inspire open-hearted feminist curiosity in the practice of inquiry on how gender, global and mobility come to matter in the lived experiences of people on the move. An open-hearted approach (Penttinen 2013) means being open to different stories of lived experience and being ready to question the unquestioned assumptions that guide our inquiry. It means being open to different theoretical perspectives as well as different levels of analysis and seeing what can be learned from them, instead of only defending one's position or point of view. This book is an *invitation to a journey* with us *to imagine* the multiple and interconnected ways in which gender, global and mobilities intersect, instead of simply providing information and conclusive answers to how gender is configured in global mobility.

THE ETHICS OF OUR APPROACH: CRITICAL THINKING AND PRACTICE

Our method of making sense of gender and global mobilities stems from our background in ethnography, activism and academia. In this book we provide theoretical tools and a range of case studies to develop an understanding of how gender and mobility concretize in individual experiences, in specific geographical locations and at the intersections of gender, race, culture, politics and economy. Each chapter is informed with a particular theoretical perspective and introduces the main concepts specific to each theoretical insight. These theoretical perspectives are (1) migration and mobility studies, (2) queer studies, (3) feminist economics and global political economy, (4) feminist policy analysis and critical border studies and (5) feminist research on violence. In chapter 7 we shift the focus towards the future and invite the reader to imagine global mobility drawing on a basis in posthumanist ethics of worlding. We combine these theoretical perspectives with open-ended narratives, which leave room for the reader to analyse and read between the lines and figure out how processes of power and politics of representation are configured in the lives of people on the move and how they oppose, resist and transform these same practices.

Therefore, contrary to common academic practice, we are not arguing for any particular theoretical approach over or against another perspective. This is an ethical choice as we see how such internal debates within academia actually take the eye off the issue, that is, the people on the move and their real-life trajectories. We recognize how easy it is to get lost in the internal academic game and competition and lose sight of what the purposes were for inquiring about the politics of gender and mobility in the first place. Therefore, we ask academic researchers, teachers, students and activists alike to remind themselves of what the motivations and purposes were to ask questions on gender and global mobilities. What purposes does the knowledge production on gender and global mobilities serve? And perhaps even more importantly, who are we accountable for?

As a means to move towards creating ethically sustainable academic knowledge, we contend the necessity of *multidisciplinarity* and openness to engage in conversation across disciplinary boundaries. We argue for the importance of moving out of our comfort zones and familiar (disciplinary or cultural) backgrounds in order to create novel insights together and take responsibility for how our own belief systems and positions of privilege guide our perceptions. Academia in itself is already entangled with the processes of power, politics of representation, colonial powers, gender order and specific positions of privilege and otherness (Mohanty 2003, Ahmed 2004), which enable and restrict mobility.

The ethics of our approach is therefore informed by the following three key themes: (1) We ask the reader to recognize that understanding gender and global mobilities is really about real-life people on the move, whose lives are not easily categorized or do not fit into existing theories about migration. (2) We ask the reader to care about these lives of real people and recognize how we are all connected. (3) We ask the academics in different fields to open up to a multidisciplinary conversation and recognize the value in combining or collaging different perspectives on the same question in order to enhance academic research in this complex and continually changing world.

Therefore, for us, analysing gender and global mobilities is not only an intellectual exercise confined to the domain of academia but also a matter of recognizing the complexities and potentialities of real lived experience. Regardless of the abstract theorizing academics engage in, there are real persons on the move all the time. And they do so using creativity and variety of networks, despite the manifold difficulties imposed on them, often in ways that defy the theories that should explain their possibilities and constraints.

It seems that we are undeniably living in a world of extreme contradictions. While mobility is celebrated as a value and a fact in the contemporary world, access to mobility or potential for mobility (motility) is highly uneven for differentially positioned people across the globe. For so many, mobility is indeed an obligation, a risk that needs to be taken in a situation where staying is no longer an option due to the lack of livelihood or a devastating conflict that one needs to escape. Moreover, bodies are differentially mobile by their location in the axes of healthy/impaired or able-bodied/disabled. One may find it necessary to rely on other people with sight or hearing. For another, it may be impossible to move one's body at all without help from others. We emphasize that the academic research work is never separate from the complexity and messiness of the interconnectedness, hierarchies, struggles and opportunities that emerge in contemporary world. Owing to information technology and social media, the exit from the field and return to academic sphere is never clear cut. In the contemporary world, the fact that we are already entangled with the world and that our actions and inactions have consequences cannot be hidden under the pretence of distance. Everything we do counts.

In this book we bring forth the individual level through stories, anecdotes and fieldwork diary entries in order to bring the reader close to the lived experience of people on the move. As we bring attention to how people on the move manage, make choices or respond or react to constricting conditions imposed by outside realities, we show that these people are full human beings, with emotions, feelings, sexualities and desires. In other words, people on the move are not different from anyone else or stick figures. They are not the "other" or the "object" of research. This is first and foremost a question of ethics.

Most importantly, in bringing forth the lived experience of people on the move, we ask the reader to care about the people on the move. Writing in such a way that the reader can feel transforms the illusion of distance between self and other. As the reader is brought close to the individual lived experiences of the people on the move, she cannot presume the illusion of distance that academic inquiry provides. This is in line with new ethnography, feminist pedagogy and postmodern qualitative approach to research and writing.[1] These approaches can be seen as sharing similar principles, for example, empowerment of minority groups and experiences, and privileging multiple voices. Most importantly, these approaches challenge the hierarchic dualisms that guide our perception such as those between researcher and the field, professor and student, and researcher and activist.

Both postmodern qualitative approach to research and writing and feminist pedagogy as a practice of generating and enabling learning challenge traditional notions of what social scientific text looks like or what learning is in a classroom setting. For us, these starting points imply that scientific writing is never innocent (Richardson 1997), but it always involves multiple positionalities, which need to be rendered visible in line with feminist research ethics and practice (see, e.g., Ackerly and True 2010). Carolyn Shrewsbury (1997: 167) has framed feminist pedagogy as a project that seeks to empower students "to learn to think in new ways, especially ways that enhance the integrity and wholeness of the person and the person's connection with others," valuing the diversity of experience and facilitating the development of a voice of one's own (Mohanty 2003). Thus, learning is an active engagement with students and teachers as well as with the materials used in the classroom. Adhering to feminist pedagogy in teaching and learning about global mobilities entails that the hierarchies as well as privileges in academic research on gender and global mobilities can be openly discussed, and the classroom can be used as a space that creates new insight.

Therefore, multidisciplinarity as a practice is not something fancy, but rather a method of being curious and open-hearted to different points of view and different experiences, understanding and disentangling privileges, and being open to learn instead of conquer. It is a practice of appreciation for diversity of different disciplinary practices in forming research questions, selecting materials and writing. Important here is the recognition that the classroom is not separate space from the sphere of academic research or a secondary activity to research, but a space for collaborative learning.

The teaching tools in this book are based on student-based active learning pedagogy (Biggs 2003) informed by the values of feminist pedagogy (Chow et al. 2003). We follow the idea of research-led teaching, which means the practice of building curriculum on the basis of teacher's research projects as well as enhancing research through the practice of dialogue in the classroom. Research-led teaching as a space for transformative learning (hooks 1994) builds on respect for the diversity of students in the classroom and the recognition of students as active participants in collaborative learning, instead of knowledge consumers. In our own practice of teaching, we emphasize the role of students as academic experts in training and hope to inspire readers of this book to also take this book as a resource for enhancing one's own practice for critical thinking than simply as a source of information.

We the authors have a background in using feminist methodology and ethnography in studying gender in the context of political science and international relations since the turn of the millennium. Elina has done research on how globalization of the world economy produces gendered and ethnicized subjectivities in the context of global sex industry. The transition to market economy at the time of the Soviet Union's breakdown resulted in the loss of jobs and closed down whole industries in a very short time period in Russia. Unemployment affected especially women, and they started to look for other opportunities to make any income to support themselves and their families. At the same time, in the 1990s, the sex sector began to grow and normalize within consumer culture. Elina was curious about the ways in which these globalization processes concretized in actual spaces such as erotic bars, brothels and camping sites where Russian and Baltic women came to sell sexual services to local men in Finland. We will return to these findings in chapters 4 and 6. From the sphere of global sex industry Elina moved on to research the politics of gender mainstreaming in the context of international crisis management and peacekeeping, which was implemented mainly by the increase in the share of women within the operations. She interviewed female police officers in order to find out how they felt about the expectations placed on them on the basis of their gender, such as improving operational effectiveness, being able to reach the local population better and being able to keep their male colleagues from misconduct. This research took her also to Kosovo in 2008 at the beginning of the largest EU-led mission, the EULEX. Currently Elina's field has moved from geographical locations and physical spaces to the Internet. Her current research at the time of writing this book is on the experience of violence and healing process in the context of intimate partner violence (IPV). As part of her research she moderates online support groups for women and does phone interviews in order to ensure the security of targets of violence. Elina also works closely with local NGOs who offer support for targets of IPV and sexual abuse, also among migrant women. She participates as an academic expert in NGO-led national campaigns against IPV.

Anitta has worked with North African women in France in her research situated at the intersection of the feminization of migration debate and the temporally simultaneous yet not fully connected discursive emphasis on attracting skilled migration into Europe. She was interested in understanding how these debates might meet and which could be lived outcomes in the lives of women who are, on one hand, highly skilled and, on the other hand, often portrayed in the mainstream media in the early 2000s only in terms of family making or in successive headscarf debates in France. These insights feed into the following chapter where we examine the conceptual history of migration and mobility studies. In 2010, Anitta moved on to a long-term interest of hers and began to work more systematically on the issue of undocumented mobilities across and around the Mediterranean Sea. This research has taken her to an array of border areas, such as the borders between Greece and Turkey, Greece and the Former Yugoslav Republic of Macedonia (FYROM), Turkey and Syria, Morocco and Algeria, Morocco and Spain, and France and the United Kingdom. The research process has led her to examine issues such as knowledge formation, local and transnational solidarity practices, and technologies of control in concrete border locations and beyond them. We will return to these findings in chapter 5. In parallel with her academic work, Anitta takes part in different civil society and activist endeavours by serving as a specialist in migration and asylum issues and by contributing to reporting on human rights issues in Europe, North Africa and the Middle East. These engagements inform and feed back into her research on similar topics.

TOOLS FOR THE JOURNEY: CONCEPTUALIZING GENDER, GLOBAL AND MOBILITY

The questions of gender and global mobilities are being asked in social sciences, humanities and beyond. The academic fields that undertake the questions of gender and mobilities range from, for example, political and social sciences, feminist global political economy, feminist and queer migration and mobility studies, human geography, social anthropology, diaspora studies, regional studies to sexuality studies. Asking feminist questions has often meant at first focusing on where women are in the context of migration and mobility. This has denoted emphasizing that gender needs to be added as a variable in analyses of mobility. Further on, it has signified moving on to recognizing how gender and other potential intersectional axes are configured in the systems of power that shape gendered mobilities. We will return to these issues in further chapters. In this section we will move on to define how the concepts of gender, global and mobility are applied in this book.

Is gender enough?

When we want to understand how global mobility is gendered, is the concept of gender enough? To answer this question, we must first stop to consider what the word *gender* brings to mind. Is it women? Is it women, sex and gender minorities, and men and boys? Or is it more abstract in the form of poststructuralist theorizing, bringing to mind a range of femininities and masculinities that are enacted into being in multiple ways?

In this book we want to emphasize that thinking about gender alone is not enough in trying to understand how gender is configured in global mobility. Therefore, we introduce the concept of intersectionality to be better able to recognize how gender, race/ethnicity, class, dis/ability and sexuality converge in gendered experiences. The concept of gender alone may also serve as a means to silence or ignore the lived experiences of non-normative gender and racial identities and struggles that fall outside white, middle-class, able-bodied, heterosexual concerns.

The concept of intersectionality was introduced in the early 1990s in the context of feminist scholarship by black feminist and queer scholars for the purpose of recognizing the multiple intersecting differences such as class, race/ethnicity, dis/ability, sexuality, positioning in the life cycle, nationality and migratory status (Collins 1990, Crenshaw 1991, Puar 2012). Legal scholar and critical race theorist Kimberlé Crenshaw (1991) coined the term so as to pay attention to the ways in which the specifics of black women's experiences and struggles fell out of feminist projects as well as from racial politics. She highlighted that, in order to understand forms of discrimination black women were subjected to, it was necessary to embrace these intersecting struggles simultaneously – that is, what it means to be a woman in patriarchal and sexist social order and to be black in a racist society at the same time.

The concept of intersectionality has two-fold function. First, it is a concept that draws attention to how different forms of discrimination intersect in particular situations. As, for example, Crenshaw's illustrations point out, a black woman in the United States has to struggle with both sexism and racism in culture and society. Therefore, the concept of intersectionality is useful also for different levels of analysis, such as structural intersectionality and political intersectionality. The second function of the concept is a methodological one. Intersectionality as a methodology is more than pointing out a specific situatedness or positionality of a person in the social world according to axes of gender, race/ethnicity, class, dis/ability and sexuality at a given point in time. Thus intersectionality as a method is not about explaining a person's experience by placing her on a grid. Instead, intersectionality as an approach means developing understanding, as Leslie McCall (2005) argues, of the distinctions between intra-categorical, anti-categorical and inter-categorical intersectionality or, as Ange-Marie Hancock (2007) points out, of the discrepancies between unitary, multiple and intersectional approaches. In these lines of inquiry, attention is paid to the ways in which fluidity of categories can be recognized; hence, the assumed stability of categories of multiple inequalities is disputed (see Walby, Armstrong and Strid 2012). It is this idea of fluid intersectionality that we work from in this book.

Intersectionality refers to the points at which power relations meet. Taking the body as an example, feminist theorist Sara Ahmed (2012: 14) points out that "how we experience one category depends on how we inhabit others." Ahmed brings the notion of intersectionality to the level of individual experience. Different intersecting categories are also something that is concretely lived through. Here the body and embodiment of subjectivity constitute the domain by which gender and social subjectivity can be theorized. This means that the body itself is the site of politics. Poststructuralist feminist theorizing enables seeing the body as performative, producing and reiterating gendered and racialized scripts, yet capable of challenging, resisting or at least disturbing the smooth functioning of power enacted by given readings of the body (Ahmed 1998: 110–117, 2000; Puumala, Väyrynen, Kynsilehto and Pehkonen 2011). One example is the march by people stuck at the border between Greece and the FYROM in March 2016.[2] The borders across the so-called Western Balkan route had been successively closed over the winter of 2015–2016, first for others except Afghans, Iraqis and Syrians, and then for everyone. This closure left thousands of people who were not deemed eligible for crossing the border waiting in the makeshift campsite for several months. Tired of waiting, a group of some two thousand people – men, women, small children, elderly people in wheelchairs – decided to go past the fenced border post and enter Macedonia via fields and forests. They were eventually returned to Greece, but by taking this action they showed how border controls can be resisted, and they are not to be treated solely as docile victims waiting for merciful acts that may come one day. We will return to these questions in chapter 5, where we discuss corporeal forms of border control.

Last, the idea of intersectionality is useful in thinking about political projects and their overlapping and cross-cutting effects (see Crenshaw 1991, Walby et al. 2012). This could be done, in the context of global mobilities, through analysing the impacts of policies that regulate mobility and the discrepancy between expected outcomes and reality. We may ask, for example, how a policy on family reunion posits different family members. Who are considered as constituting a family? What is the impact of income requirements on the right to family life? Or what kinds of gendered presuppositions are implied in different immigration policies? How do contemporary visa requirements work together with demands for enhancing intercultural encounters and facilitated mobility in the contemporary world? What about policies regulating return, which often refer to different expulsion measures: what kinds of gendered consequences do they produce? How differently are men, women and sexual and gender minorities affected by these measures? We will return to these questions in chapter 5, where we focus on borders and institutional approaches to global mobilities, and in chapter 3, where we examine the implicit heteronormative assumptions in migration and mobility studies.

Does global mean worldwide?

When we talk about *global* mobility, what do we mean by it? Does the word refer to planet earth as a stage on which these mobilities are taking place? Or does it refer to the scale of phenomenon? In this book the global is also invoked in this way. We will provide a range of examples of mobility, which will allow the reader to sense how the experiences of mobility concretize in different parts of the globe. Yet the word *global* in this book is first and foremost used to refer to the global political and economic processes that produce and shape the world we live in. Therefore discussing global mobility means addressing the power relations that shape the global flows of people.

Feminist analysts have been adamant in disclosing the practices of power that is required to keep power relations in place (Spivak 1988, Enloe 1996, Mohanty 2003) and how global elites and institutions actively create and maintain these relations (see, e.g., Kofman and Youngs 1996). Feminist analysis of globalization of the world economy includes examining how these processes are inherently gendered, produce gendered outcomes and potentially transform gender orders. This includes recognizing how gender is configured in the neoliberalist ideology that drives and legitimates globalization processes such as deregulation, offshoring and demands of flexibility of labour. Feminist analysis means looking at how world politics and economic restructuring concretize at local and societal level in gender-specific ways.

It is possible to discern two significant historical moments that have impacted the globalization of the world economy. The first is the end of the Cold War and the collapse of the Soviet Union, and the second is the 9/11 attack and the following war on terrorism. The early 1990s was a time of optimism and victory of the Western world view as great adversary to liberal democracy had fallen apart and adopted the transition to market economy. The end of the Cold War was named as the end of history and the triumph of liberalism. At the same time, the advances in hard and soft technologies seemed to compress space and time. The opening of borders, air travel as well as the Internet, enabled many people with previously hampered access to international mobility to travel and communicate in new ways, changing significantly the relations between centres and peripheries, global and local. The dominating ideology of individualism concretized in the consumer culture and growth in leisure and pleasure industries, including tourism to exotic locations as well as online. Triumph of liberalism also meant the adoption of market ideology in the context of governments across Europe and also transforming citizenship towards consumer model. At the same time, however, a restrictive visa regime began to be imposed by the European states, in order to channel mobilities, for example, from the global South. These visa procedures made it effectively more difficult for citizens of the African continent, for example, to access the territory of the European states.

The second historical moment, 9/11 and the following war on terror, shifted global restructuring by combining globalization of the world economy with militarism. In this book we adopt the term *post-9/11 global restructuring* (Marchand and Runyan 2011) that refers to a set of processes in which neo-liberalist globalization is advanced through military means. The war on terror has been seen as having a civilizing function of remedying rogue states, and it has been legitimized by a discourse of human rights and women's rights (Elshtain 2003, Sjoberg 2006). In this way, military interventions since 9/11 adopt discourses that have been used of international humanitarian efforts. In the context of post-9/11 global restructuring we also witness a process that intensifies and directs global mobility. Military interventions, peacekeeping operations and civilian crisis management missions change fundamentally the local environment in which they are situated. The inflow of international troops impacts local economies and generates new jobs and new business. Yet it also increases trafficking in women and girls for the purpose of prostitution and sexual abuse, thereby producing human rights violations. Important here is to note how advancement of democracy by military means has long-lasting effects on local communities and how these processes induce and shape the global flow of people. We will return to these processes in chapter 6.

It is also in the context of the post-9/11 global restructuring and the 2008 financial crisis that we witness contradictory practices with regard to global mobilities. This is evident in the processes of downsizing, subcontracting, outsourcing and offshoring of production from the global North to low-cost and ultra-low-cost countries. On the one hand, there is a continued demand for compliant and flexible labour, also named as feminization of labour (Peterson 2012) and, on the other hand, the securitization of borders and further tightening of immigration policies, which indeed impacts concretely global labour migration. Paradoxically, it may be undocumented migrants who are able to best sustain their jobs in these times of intense change.

It is important to note how globalization produces contradictory outcomes. As one of us has argued elsewhere (Penttinen 2008), complex global flows of people, money and images generate landscapes of shadow globalization, in the form of acceleration of informal economy, organized crime and human trafficking for the purposes of prostitution and slave labour. In thinking about global mobility, it is important to remember that not everyone enjoys the same possibilities or opportunities to enjoy global consumer culture or pursue personal careers in an open globalized world. Globalization can also mean the destruction of local economies, stagnation, friction and formation of new peripheries (Faber and Nielsen 2015). These processes also shape the flow and direction of people and their mobile trajectories.

Migration or mobility?

What purpose does the concept of mobility serve? How is it different from the concept of migration? And whose mobility are we talking about? In this book we use the term *mobility* instead of *migration*, emphasizing that mobility is a broader concept that does not necessarily presuppose a form of permanency. Moreover, the concept of mobility embraces both physical and virtual mobilities that increasingly intersect with the advances in information technology and their availability to ever larger audiences. However, these concepts overlap and they are sometimes used interchangeably when referring to movements across borders. We draw on feminist critiques on mainstream migration and mobility studies that challenge common sense assumptions in these strands of scholarship, including the idea that mobility is necessarily empowering and immobility, its counterpart, is inevitably disempowering (Hanson 2010). As with social sciences more generally, there has also been a mobility turn within migration studies, which defies the implicit linear notions of migration studies. Mobility turn builds on the ontology of movement as a starting point, but it is not necessarily feminist research.

The main feminist critique of the concept of migration begins with the acknowledgement of how the concept of migration draws on a linear model of push and pull factors dictated by the greater economy. Thus, the movement of people is seen as something that happens in response to the turns of the economy and global production. Indeed, migration studies has been strongly influenced by neoclassical economics developed in 1966 by Everett Lee (Pessar 2003: 21) and rational actor theory.

According to the push and pull model, people migrate towards better opportunities of work and economic well-being for themselves and for their families. They are "pulled" towards certain areas of economic prosperity such as affluent developed countries. In turn, lack of resources pushes people to move from these areas and look for better opportunities. This push and pull model would explain, for example, the move from rural areas to cities as there are more opportunities for work and education in cities than in peripheries. As migration is seen as a response to the economy, the movement of people for the purposes of labour is also seen as operating according to the logic of supply and demand.

Feminist critique of push and pull theory of migration (Pessar 2003) maintains that this model is based on the idea of a "Western man" who makes rational choices to increase well-being for himself and his family. Pessar emphasizes how Lee's push and pull theory is ontologically gendered and explicitly so. The rational actor making choices on migration is a male subject. Pessar quotes Lee in saying that in this movement according to push and pull factors "children are carried along by their parents, willy-nilly, and wives accompany their husbands though it tears them away from the environment they love" (Pessar 2003: 21, original Lee 1966: 51). One could almost make the claim that early migration studies is actually one form of gender studies, as it explicitly focuses on the motivations and trajectories of male migrants. In this model women were not counted as migrants themselves but were seen as followers.

In migration research the process of adding women to research agenda and adding gender as a variable paved the way for further analysis of understanding how intersections of gender, race and class matter in enabling, maintaining and constricting movement in the continually changing landscape of the globalized world. Moreover, in these processes of gendered global mobilities, there are many strains and contradictions across gender, class and race divides. These processes are never stable or have fixed outcomes.

Crucial part of feminist approach to scientific inquiry is to emphasize that representations of the world are never just reflections or descriptions of the world but that they are also productive and thus also always political. Representations of gender influence how we understand gender norms and identities and can have concrete consequences that influence people's lives. Therefore, the way in which we seek to represent migration/mobility in academia is also constitutive of realities. Research is never isolated from the social, political and economic spheres. Thus, methodology is always tied to ethics.

Pessar (2003) emphasizes that ontological assumptions about migration as well as the methods we use in research influence what kind of information we get and consequently what we claim to be true and telling about migration. Pessar explains how the idea of migration as emancipation is maintained mostly through studies that use surveys as a method of research.

One common example is household surveys in areas from where large numbers of migrants have left. What is being surveyed is, for example, the impact of mass migration to the local economy and community relations. However, ethnographic research and in-depth interviews enable us to bring out more complexity into the story and allow individuals to share the contradictions and constraints of migration. These contradictions may be easily glossed over when answering a survey with preset questions. This is not to say that survey methods lie about the reality but that with ethnographic field research it is possible to gain more nuances. Ethnographic approaches permit to be more sensitive to how individual people on the move navigate the contemporary world and how, in turn, the global flow of people changes or perhaps even transforms cultural practices, institutions and values. Therefore, the study of migration according to a utilitarian model or study of mobility in complex globalized world would also imply different research questions, research design and research methods.

Feminist migration and mobility studies as well as feminist economics have criticized the push and pull models for being inherently gendered and rendering a too simplistic understanding of the structural and personal factors that guide people's choices and actions. Personal choices and strategies of survival are hardly always rational, independent or free from outside circumstances. People live in the objective reality consisting of social, cultural, political and natural worlds. The private realm of personal relationships and commitments, gender identity and sexual orientation, as well as personal hopes and desires, cannot be easily separated from the outside conditions. These different levels, whether personal, such as gender, sexual orientation and family relations, or cultural and class backgrounds, national politics and global political economy, all influence the ways in which individuals can make life choices such as whether to move to another area or country or to stay put.

Research addressing the question of global mobilities builds on the ontological assumption of movement as the starting point of research. The "mobility turn" or "new mobilities paradigm" (Sheller and Urry 2006, Urry 2007) departs from traditional analyses of push and pull factors of labour migration in order to open the analysis of movements from a wider, relational perspective. In this line of inquiry mobility is seen as characterizing the contemporary period in manifold ways. The constitutive character of mobility refers to the centrality of increased potential and capacities to move and to be connected with the rest of the world. The "mob" is seen as constantly in movement. On the contrary, migration is understood as a more permanent way of moving from one place to another (Urry 2007: 7–8). Mobilities are simultaneously addressed as enhancing possibilities of discovery and opting for different lifestyles, yet connected with tightened surveillance and attempts to control unwanted mobilities.

In this book we embrace feminist research ethics and maintain a sense of awareness of how we frame research questions and concepts in order to capture such a complex phenomenon as gender and global mobilities. Taking *movement*, instead of stability, as the ontological starting point for analysing gender and global mobility in contemporary world allows understanding this phenomenon without forcing it into simplified models. Yet it does not mean dismissing how national and global politics enable and constrict movement and how this takes place in gender-specific ways. However, an underlying theme in this book is to recognize the margins of freedom people enact in the context of objective reality in which they live and move, even in the utmost constricting conditions.

ORGANIZATION OF THE BOOK AND INDIVIDUAL CHAPTERS

The rest of the chapters each represent a specific form of theoretical insight into the question of gender and global mobility building on feminist research. The themes are (1) migration studies, (2) queer studies, (3) global political economy and feminist economics, (4) critical border studies and feminist policy analysis, (5) feminist research on violence and abuse and (6) posthumanist ethics of worlding.

We begin each chapter with an open-ended narrative that illustrates how the main theme and level of analysis is concretized at the level of individual experience and mobile trajectories. These narratives present experiences and actions that go against the common sense or stereotypical representations of gendered mobility. These narratives can be used as case studies for problem-based learning in the classroom. The narrative enables the readers to practise thinking about how to use theory to understand and make sense of individual experiences, how different policies and practices of migration affect people's lives and how they navigate their own lives. Starting with a personal narrative, as in this introductory chapter, serves the purpose of inciting the readers and students in the classroom to think about what would they do in similar situations and how their life experiences are the same as or different from the ones told in the stories and thus think about our shared experiences of being human in contemporary globalized world.

In each chapter we provide the main forms of insight into the given topic from the particular theoretical approach. As already mentioned, we do not argue for any particular approach in gender, mobility or global studies but show how different theoretical perspectives offer different forms of insight and operate at different levels of analysis and how all of these are useful and necessary when we want to make sense of gender and global mobility.

We wish to inspire readers to recognize the value of multidisciplinarity and continue discussion on how different theoretical perspectives work together in deepening our understanding.

The following chapters are organized as follows: opening narrative sets out the theme of the chapter, following key themes of how feminist research on such puzzles theorizes the issue. Each chapter is representative of how specific theoretical insight approaches the question of gender. Chapters 2, 5 and 6 open directly to the problematics of gender discrimination and seek to expose how intersectional analysis of gender allows us to recognize the complex ways in which policies and politics impact people on the move. Chapters 3 and 4 open with a theoretical discussion as queer theoretical and feminist global political economy perspectives seek to analyse the underlying gender order and implicit assumptions about gender and sexuality, which guide academic inquiry and organization of global political economy. Each chapter includes case studies as text boxes, which can be used as study assignment for problem-based learning. At the end of the chapter we provide possible essay questions, discussion points, study assignments and extra resources for classroom use, such as films. We include a wide range of references for further study and exploration.

In chapter 2, "Intersectional approaches to human mobility," we discuss the move from the analysis of gendered categories of migration towards intersectional approaches to human mobility. The chapter outlines how migration studies has conceptualized gender and migration and emphasizes how intersectional approaches can enhance these. We show how intersectional approach enables us to see the complexity of the situation for the gendered individual on the move than traditional analysis, which focuses on migration status and gender. Therefore, we emphasize the importance of feminist research methodology and feminist ethics in the research design and practice. Therefore, the categories of migration are critically addressed in order to show how they use and regenerate gender stereotypes. We discuss concrete trajectories of globally mobile individuals, hence emphasizing lived experiences of mobile trajectories. We combine these real lived experiences with representations of gendered and ethnicized mobilities in order to illustrate how representations of mobility come to matter and how they are embodied and enacted into being. The examples chosen for this chapter are selected so as to portray a wide range of categories from different parts of the world in order avoid reiterating and reinforcing stereotypical, even false, representations of the people on the move.

Chapter 3, "Globally mobile life," draws on queer mobility and diaspora studies in order to investigate experience of mobility that exceeds normative notions of gender, race and sexuality. The shared point of criticism in queer mobility studies is to disorient from the unquestioned heteronormative white middle-class notions about love, sexuality and family that guide inquiry in migration and mobility studies. We combine these discussions under three concepts: motherhood, sexuality and home. We show how implicit assumptions may limit our capacities to acknowledge the diversity of lived experience and recognize migrant workers, refugees and other mobile subjects as thinking-feeling beings with their own desires and hopes. Unquestioned assumptions about gender or sexuality may prevent us from developing profound understanding of how mobile subjects make sense of their own lived experience in changing circumstances and how indeed, due to migratory trajectories, people, their identities and values do not stay the same.

The relevance of feminist analysis of global political economy in understanding how gender is configured in global mobility is discussed in chapter 4, "Global political economy and global mobility." In this chapter we outline the basics of feminist economics, which is a practice of paying attention to the value of unpaid reproductive work as well as undervalued and underpaid care work for the operation of globalized world economy. We discuss how the public-private distinction resonates with gendered hierarchic dualisms and binary oppositions. These are relevant in understanding what is considered valuable in society. Global mobility constitutes in itself an economy of scale in the form of remittances. Therefore mobility is also used as "development mantra" as a major contributor to the development of economies in underdeveloped countries. We end with a discussion on gendered risk in the context of financial crisis and the sex sector.

Chapter 5, "Policing borders and boundaries," turns attention to the issue of policing borders and boundaries, which concretize in an array of bordering practices. The chapter works, from an intersectional perspective, through policies that both enable and restrict global mobilities, border control and detention. This chapter centres on the concept of *border*, understood both as concrete locations where global mobilities are regulated and halted and in the way of *bordering practices* that create hierarchies of global mobilities also outside designated border areas. We do this through examples from different migratory contexts, including the ongoing refugee "crises" in the Mediterranean. In doing so, we present institutional and security-focused approaches to global mobilities and ask how gender figures and feeds into these approaches. In the final section of the chapter we discuss the roles of international and intergovernmental organizations such as the UN Refugee Agency (UNHCR) and the International Organization for Migration (IOM).

Chapter 6, "Abuse, crime and mobility," addresses in detail the forms of exploitation and abuse that are present in the context of global mobilities. The analysis of abuse and crime in the context of global mobility draws on feminist research violence and feminist security studies. In this chapter we discuss how economic transitions, war and conflict enable criminal networks to thrive. We outline the UN definition of trafficking and discuss in detail what the constitutive elements of act, means and purpose mean in practice.

We discuss the process by which criminal networks recruit and groom their victims and how they exploit people in vulnerable positions. The mobilities of trafficked people are characterized by constriction, exploitation, enslavement and violence. With this analysis we seek to show how the being involved in trafficking represents a form of abuse of global mobility. We end the chapter by focusing on what it feels like to experience the violence and abuse in the context of trafficking and what it takes to heal from the emotional wounds induced by sexual abuse.

In the last chapter, "Re-imagining global mobilities," we turn the gaze towards the future by asking what might be the ultimate value of this book for understanding and researching global mobilities: What do these insights indicate in terms of future academic work in studying mobilities? What kinds of political implications and possible policy suggestions could we draw on the presented and discussed insights? In the chapter we come back to the questions of responsibility and ethics in practice of research. We include new materialist and posthumanist perspectives in order to imagine and re-evoke feminist solidarity in the complex entangled globalized world. We discuss this in the context of the entwinement of global economy and securitizing practices, that is, the economy-security complex and how it concretizes at borders and beyond. We propose a move towards sketching the possibility for embracing mobility by building on posthumanist ethics of worlding (Barad 2007) and ethics of homelessness (Khosravi 2010). Through a diffractive reading of Barad and Khosravi, coupled with feminist ethics of encounter and solidarity, we envision ways of relating to each other in sustainable ways.

DISCUSSION POINTS

1. How do the concepts of migration and mobility concretize in your own life? Or someone close to you?
2. Can you name different structural conditions that concretize in the possibilities to travel and move to another country for work?
3. How does gender, race and class configure in your own life choices and possibilities? Or someone close to you?
4. What motivates you to study gender and global mobility? What are you most curious about?

ESSAY QUESTIONS

1. If you were to study gender and global mobility in your own field, how would you design a research project? What level of analysis of gender and global mobility would be most familiar to you?

2. What makes research feminist? How would you make feminist research questions in your own field?
3. How does social media and the Internet change research relationships?

EXTRA MATERIALS

Biutiful (2010). Directed by Alejandro González Iñárritu. With Javier Bardem, Maricel Álvarez and Diarytatou Daff. Global distribution. © Copyright: Menage Atroz and Mod Producciones.

The Terminal (2004). Directed by Steven Spielberg. With Tom Hanks, Catherine Zeta-Jones and Stanley Tucci. Global distribution. © Copyright: DreamWorks LLC.

Fire at Sea (Fuocoammare) (2016). Documentary directed by Gianfranco Rosi. Distribution: 01 Distribution. © Copyright: 21 Uno Film.

Questions: How is the access to global mobility figured in the film? What can you say on the variety of lived situations of mobile lives via examples drawn from this film? How would you use intersectional analysis to make sense of the relations between different characters in the film?

NOTES

1. For postmodern qualitative writing and new ethnography see Ellis and Bochner 1992, Denzin and Lincoln 1998, Behar 1996, Dauphinee 2010, 2013, Doty 2001, 2010, Penttinen 2008, 2013, Kynsilehto 2011b, 2014. For feminist pedagogy see Shackelford 1992, Chow et al. 2003, Crabtree and Sapp 2003, Mohanty 2003, Feigenbaum 2007.

2. Teofilovski 2016.

Chapter 2

Intersectional approaches to human mobility

Born in French Algeria, Meriem had accompanied her migrant father to France and spent her childhood in a French boarding school. Her mother never felt at home in France; she had preferred to stay in Algeria, where the rest of the family joined her during school holidays. After beginning her university studies in journalism in Paris, Meriem decided to move back to Algeria, to finish her studies at the University of Algiers, and to embark on her journalistic career there. She envisaged her future in contributing to the newly independent country, by working and participating as a full citizen. As a woman this was not an easy task. It turned out to become even more difficult when she married a Frenchman, and thus began to be seen as a traitor to her freshly independent nation. Refusing to surrender, she continued her engagement in the feminist struggle in Algeria and wanted to raise her family there. After several threats targeting her personally in the midst of the civil war in the 1990s between the state and the Islamist opposition, however, she gave up her resistance and joined her family who had already earlier escaped to France. Despite the emotionally demanding new beginning in France, she found work that was already at the outset up to her skills and founded later her own enterprise to make again better use of her multiple skills. Her migratory trajectory combines different reasons and motivations for cross-border mobilities, some more chosen than others. At the same time, her story illustrates the changing character of categories deployed in migration research when observed from a life-story perspective.

(Kynsilehto 2011a, b)

In this chapter, we discuss the move from the analysis of gendered categories of migration towards intersectional approaches to human mobility in the context of migration and mobility studies. We present the main conceptual categories of migrants and emphasize how intersectional approaches can enable us to recognize the complexity of the lived experience of the people on the move. Thus, although categories such as labour migrants or refugees resonate with legal categories and policies, and they have been useful in organizing migration research, lived realities of people who traverse the globe cannot be reduced to single categories. In line with feminist methodology and ethics, we emphasize that categories of migration need to be examined critically in order to unravel how they use and regenerate gender stereotypes. The use of categories for research purposes matters. As Meriem's story seeks to illustrate, concrete trajectories of globally mobile individuals that bring forth lived experiences of mobile trajectories challenge representations of gendered and ethnicized mobilities.

In traditional migration research, which we introduced in the previous chapter, push and pull factors have been used to explain migration patterns. These factors represent the macro-level causal relationships that are conducive to human movement across international borders. People move because they are pushed due to economic decline, political instability or outright war. Then they are pulled towards areas of economic growth or towards safer locations. Following these patterns, mobile individuals are located into categories such as labour migrants that are further divided into different employment sectors in order to investigate a particular type of migration. Another organizing principle can be drawn between forced and voluntary migration, which means in practice a separation of migration for the purpose of economic well-being from migration for the purpose of fleeing political persecution or a war.

Recent migration research has shifted the focus towards investigating the variety of trajectories mobile persons engage in while crossing international borders. In these strands of research, the agency of mobile persons and their capabilities to make choices is increasingly taken into account alongside structural reasons. Hence, people on the move are seen as real persons who decide how to react and respond to the conditions that enable and constrict movement.

The shift in perspective from macro-level analysis to migration trajectories entails also a further reconsideration of categories traditionally used in migration research. The categories migration research has used originate from migration policies, which are built in order to govern, manage and control mobility (see chapter 5). Migration policies create, define and redefine legal categories that seek to channel mobilities and, in so doing, mould suitable and unsuitable categories of people to enter, stay and exit a given country. Migration policies therefore have concrete impacts on people's lives even though they don't necessarily correspond to lived realities, which is one reason for many people to find themselves without a legitimate migration status.

Traditional migration research has largely followed categories used in policy making. Meanwhile, critical migration scholars have sought to unpack these categorizations from the perspective of a variety of migration trajectories.

Feminist migration scholars have turned the focus towards recognizing where women are, what they do and how they are positioned within existing migration categories. Paying attention to women in particular has necessitated a simultaneous analysis of categories used in policy making, recognizing the complexity of lived realities and critique of limitations of traditional migration research for its failure to recognize diversity.

The intersectional approach to migration and mobility draws especially on postcolonial feminism, queer theory and critical disability studies and therefore endorses the view that the normative assumptions of migration categories need to be examined carefully. Intersectional analysis of mobility starts from the premise that people whose social locations differ may also be differentially mobile people. This means, for example, recognizing that women who have accumulated social capital by education and experience or by family relations may find it easier to move. Alternatively, women (or men) who have children or other people in need of care on a daily basis may find it extremely difficult to move, due to increasingly restrictive policies regulating family migration and difficulties in arranging long-distance care (see box 2.1).

In this chapter we argue that intersectionality as a conceptual tool enables us to understand multifaceted trajectories, and the manifold ways in which different axes of demarcation simultaneously enable and impede acts of

---

BOX 2.1

Critical disability studies draws attention to the implicit assumption of able-bodiedness that guides migration research. The main point is to demonstrate that the status as able-bodied is not a fixed identity but provisional at best. Thus, disability is something that can affect anyone. Our bodies are vulnerable to accident, attack and disease, and able-bodiedness is eventually lost through aging. Disability studies seeks to disentangle the category of dis/able by reminding of its variegated disaggregation: differences in its type (physical/intellectual), in impact (minor/full paralysis), in onset (disability at birth/gradual/sudden), in perceptibility ("hidden"/"visible"), in variability across time and space and in prevalence (variation by sex, ethnicity, age and environment) (Rohrer 2005, Shildrick 2012). Moreover, the objective is to challenge the negative connotations of the term *disabled* and challenge the norm of able-bodiedness in culture and society.

Study assignment: How is the norm of able-bodiedness configured in the space of your everyday environment?

mobility, better than traditional categories of migration or the distinction between forced and voluntary migration. The example from Meriem's migrant trajectory recounted earlier illustrates much of this variety: in this condensed account we already find categories of family migrant, student migrant, returnee, highly skilled migrant as well as those of voluntary and forced migration. None of these categories alone would suffice to understand her mobile trajectory (Kynsilehto 2011a). Moreover, from her story we can read multiple and shifting positionalities along the lines of gender, age, sexual orientation, nationality, class, positioning in the life cycle and the vulnerability of the body by the very fact that it may be hurt, mutilated, raped and killed.

We maintain that in order to understand gendered global mobilities, we need to take the twofold task of analysing categories and categorizations in conjunction with lived experience. Migration research, global media and migration policies create categorizations of mobile people that, through continuous circulation of imageries, become permanent representations, constituting even iconic representations of a given group. Most migration researchers focus on specific ethnic groups or migrants working in a particular sector of the labour market in a given country. These ways of categorizing mobility are the dominant way of organizing research, and they serve as a way to formulate research questions about specific ethnic groups or forms of mobility. Hence, categorizations can be seen as one way of organizing realities, a form of logic through which research endeavours are organized, and thereby one way of building our understanding of the world. In this chapter we have sought to portray the widest range possible of examples from different parts of the world in order avoid reiterating and reinforcing stereotypical, even false representations of the people on the move. Moreover, as the examples highlight, especially in ethnographic research, static categories rarely work as *the only* grid of intelligibility, for human lives always extend beyond the fixities.

This chapter is organized in three sections. We begin the intersectional analysis of mobility by focusing on feminist research on different employment sectors. We discuss how feminist scholarship unpacks common sense assumptions behind manpower, care and service sector and skilled migration. The second section moves on to feminist approaches to refugee studies. We discuss how the category of forced displacement due to a violent conflict or environmental reasons requires intersectional analysis. In the third part, we discuss global mobility for the family formation that encompasses marriage migration, international adoption and transnational commercial surrogacy. Finally, we reflect on a central but relatively neglected issue, that is, the meaning of gender in immobility for various reasons.

The cases selected in this chapter to illustrate gendered mobility are drawn from the media, reports produced by non-governmental and international organizations and research conducted in different parts of the world. They are intended to draw attention to the diversity of and within categories. They serve the purpose to think creatively about gender and global mobilities in order to recognize the impressive diversity that is already present, instead of reducing real individuals, groups and forms of mobility into simplified representations.

LABOUR MIGRATION

This section focuses the mobility of people from other countries to work in sectors where labour force is needed. We start by traditionally male-dominated fields unpacking the notion of manpower and then move on to conventionally feminine and feminized sectors of labour: care and service work. The third part discusses skilled migration as a more recent interest in migration studies. Here we use intersectional approach to show how research and perceptions of mobility require analysing gendered, ethnicized and classed underpinnings to understand, for example, how these positionalities translate into perceived or actual migration statuses in different contexts globally.

*Man*power and the gendered configuration of migration

Historically oriented migration research shows how migrant labour has often been recruited for the purposes of developing industries in the receiving country. The history of immigration into the United States, the UK, France and Germany illustrates this point (see, e.g., Castles 1984, Castles and Miller 2003, Noiriel 1988). Much of migrant labour was recruited to sectors that demanded physical strength, such as mining industry and construction. In these sectors foreign workforce quite literally meant *man*power. The movement of people was seen as at first fulfilling a temporary labour need that, in time, turned into more permanent forms of settlement often with the successive arrival of families. An insight that was gained in hindsight was that rather than recruiting manpower, there were people arriving instead.

Curiously enough, the idea of labour migrants as men moving from one country to another has persisted despite research evidence that has shown the phenomenon to be more complex than that. Two aspects contribute to the representation. First, there is the perception of the male body as possessing the qualities of physical strength and perseverance that are seen as more suitable for the much-demanded manpower than the qualities associated with the female body. Second, as we will discuss in more detail in chapter 4, masculine productive work has been valued higher than feminine reproductive labour. These two factors have contributed to the traditional assumption that the male labour migrant is representative of migrants in general and that it is the labour migration of men that matters as the most as an object of research.

Feminist scholars have pointed out that this gendered image, even in countries where the recruitment of foreign workforce was the most intense in masculine sectors, does not cover migrant populations as a whole. Instead, the enforcement of this analysis of migratory flows contributes to rendering women's participation invisible both in migration in general and in many sectors of labour in particular (Morokvaśic 1984, 2015). Yet the gendered configuration of labour migration is not only created by the demand for specific bodies and stereotypical gender representations. For example, when communities are formed in certain locations around a specific industry, such as the masculine mining industry in Bolivia (Bastia 2011), and the industry is later closed down, migration elsewhere becomes a "necessity with no choice" via any available channels and with any "lead migrant" for whom a possibility opens. Alternatively, when the main breadwinners in international migration are women, in particular via migration channels that facilitate the mobility and recruit specifically women to work in sectors such as public and domestic care work, gender relations are likely to be altered in these communities (e.g. Preibisch and Encalada Grez 2013).

Construction work continues to be a sector that recruits internationally in many different locations across the globe as there is need for qualified labour willing to engage in tasks that involve long working hours and physically demanding conditions. These jobs are sometimes qualified as 3D jobs (dirty, dangerous and demeaning), referring to the kinds of work that nationals are no longer willing to undertake. These may include, in addition to construction work, many different types of low-paid tasks related to construction sites, such as industrial cleaning, where also many women work. Many jobs in these sectors require manual skills and serve as entry jobs without a necessity to possess advanced language skills of the host country.

As entry jobs, work in the 3D employment does not necessarily correspond to migrants' actual professional skills. For example, Bangladeshi men in Hong Kong that Ullah (2013) worked with were highly educated and had been employed in professional occupations prior to moving to Hong Kong. However, in Hong Kong they would accept almost any job available. Hence, they were usually employed in contractual labour and paid per hour in loading and unloading stuff for the wholesale shops, construction sites and factories, cleaning houses and other kinds of domestic work or as agents for recruiting customers for hotels, tailor shops or "fake" watch shops.

Migrant workers are also recruited to locations where important global festivities and sports events take place, to prepare the site for the arrival of global tourists. While the contractual labour provides much-needed income for the employees, the working conditions may be exploitative. Increased media attention to these particular sites may lead to attempts to improve these exploitative conditions in which migrant workers are forced to work.

See box 2.2 for an example of the nexus between human rights organizations and the World Football Federation as regards the labour rights of construction workers who are involved in building stadiums for global soccer tournaments.

In Finland, Estonian firms that operate in the construction industry have been subject to much public debate. As elsewhere, the fears expressed in this debate range from the concern that cheaper foreign labour will take over the construction sector from the national firms, of Estonian firms not paying taxes, to the possibly doubtable quality of the work itself. Alongside these xenophobic discursive tendencies, labour rights and work safety issues have surfaced from the more concerned groups within the society. In parallel with the actual cross-border movements of construction workers between Finland and Estonia, the imagery of Estonians coming to work in Finland mainly, if not only, in the construction sites is so prevalent that diverse administrations reiterate this imaginary in their dealings with Estonians moving to Finland. For example,[1] an Estonian man was met with astonishment at the taxation office, as he mentioned that he was not coming to work in construction sites. "Really?" was the follow-up by the taxation officer, who had inquired about the employment that the tax card was for. This example illustrates the automatized response by authorities and public administration that reflects

---

BOX 2.2

Countries in the Persian Gulf recruit a large number of migrant workers to fulfil the labour shortages in employment sectors where there is not enough domestic labour force or where nationals are unwilling to work. The construction work for the 2022 FIFA World Cup in Qatar, for example, revealed several problems in the working conditions and the lack of labour rights such as equal pay of migrant workers. In November 2013, Amnesty International (2013) published a critical report that denounced these exploitative practices, and the UN special rapporteur for human rights of migrants, Francois Crépeau, notified the World Football Federation for the lack of respect for migrants' rights. The World Football Federation answered to these critiques by saying that they take these accusations seriously and call for all the companies involved in the construction work for world football tournaments to remember the commitments to labour rights.

Study assignment: Look for information on the nationality of workers and their working conditions in a recent sports event. Can you find correct information? What kinds of sources can you trust?

the generalized representation and ethnicized imaginaries produced by the media about Estonian men in Finland. Representational configurations often feed into a spectacle of the other and thereby construct unnecessary fears and concerns. These representational configurations neglect the dynamic character of mobility as they seek to freeze the world into static models and categorizations.

Gender in service and care work

Service work refers to a wide array of different jobs ranging from restaurants and hotels to all possible reception and sales work where the workers are in contact with customers. As service work involves a relationship with a customer, it entails bodily work and emotional labour. In contemporary world especially low-paying service work is increasingly done by globally mobile workforce. Ethnic restaurants have been probably the first visible examples of migrant work: for example, Chinese restaurants and Turkish kebab houses are nowadays frequent additions to the culinary scenes in even the most remote corners of the world. Many of these restaurants hire staff directly from the country of origin, and ethnic restaurants may also serve as entry jobs for migrants and refugees already residing in the country.

Sarah Dyer, Linda McDowell and Adina Batnitzky (2010) address how the emotional and embodied labour is performed by migrant workers through the case of hotels in west London. In their analysis of personnel in hotel and restaurant industries in London, they draw attention to nationalities involved and highlight especially the diversification of migration statuses among migrant workers. What their research shows is that gendered and racialized stereotypes are particularly salient in service work that includes contact with customers (Dyer et al. 2010: 637). These gendered and racialized stereotypes are something that workers need to negotiate as they enter into contact with the customers, and they also underpin the expectations of the recruiting personnel when they hire migrant workers. For example, service work at the front desk and housekeeping are both feminized jobs but require different forms of emotional labour. Whereas the front desk necessitates a welcoming attitude and keeping calm, housekeeping demands docility and deference. In turn, these expectations are something to which the workers have to adapt in order to secure their job. According to Dyer et al. (2010), employers preferred migrant workers in particular for the housekeeping work because the workers needed to remain docile and adapt to the working conditions as this would also guarantee the continuation of their residence permits in England. Thus, migrant workers were considered to be ideal for the demands of housekeeping work – more suitable than staff who had permanent residence in the country.

Service work is not only about the type of work that is performed in public spaces. In feminist migration research the role of domestic labour is recognized as an important area that serves as an entry-level job for already residing foreign nationals or necessitates recruitment form abroad. Indeed, domestic labour is also the kind of low-paid work that nationals are often not willing to do. Therefore, the study of domestic labour has focused on the fig- ure of a woman moving from a poorer country to a richer one for the purpose of care work. Emphasis on *global care chains* (GCCs), as initially suggested by Hochchild and Ehrenreich (Hochchild 2000, Ehrenreich and Hochchild 2003), and further developed by Yeates (2004) to comprise institutionalized sites of care as well, enables us to recognize the interlinked lives and loca- tions of those who become globally mobile in order to fulfil the need for care in another country and to the lives and locations of family members left behind. It is a framework to trace how the intersectionalities of gender, race, ethnicity and class are configured, embodied and enacted in the worker- employer relationship in conjunction with the globalized world economy that we will return to in chapter 4.

To analyse these links, research has been conducted with domestic work- ers and nannies by paying attention to the care drain that emerges as women leave their children in the care of others. In other words, when someone travels to fulfil a care need across the globe, there are always others who are left behind in the care of others. Taking a life-story perspective in a transna- tional research setting, Ruba Salih (2001) recounts the migrant trajectory of Samia, a Moroccan woman who had lived in Italy for a long time by the time she was first interviewed. Migrant domestic work had already been a dream to Samia's widowed mother, who had to decline an employment offer in London under pressure of caring in proximity for her children. Samia wished to try something different from her familial surroundings in Morocco and decided to try her chances in Italy. Despite her meagre contacts in the begin- ning, she was lucky in securing employment first as a domestic care worker for an elderly lady, then gaining new contracts as her network of contacts widened. She married a fellow Moroccan in Italy, had children and settled permanently. Later her mother engaged in transnational grandmothering by living intermittently in Casablanca and Reggio Emilia, which facilitated Samia's work in combining her duties as a caregiver, factory worker and part- time care assistant. This story illustrates multiple generational chains in the quest for becoming mobile across international borders. Moreover, it points out very concretely the paid and unpaid care arrangements entangled in the gendered mobile lives.

Institutionalized and more informal forms of care are not fully separate but entwined in many ways. Drawing on their extensive study with domestic workers and foreign nurses in Singapore, Huang, Yeoh and Toyota (2012) discuss the practices of organizing eldercare both at the institutional setting of nursing homes and in private homes. Their research findings show that, despite the different regulations concerning the migrant status of persons entering a professional environment, on one hand, and the domestic sphere, on the other, the categories of domestic workers and nursing professionals become blurred. In other words, trained foreign nurses are employed as domestic workers performing demanding care tasks when they fail to get their professional qualifications acknowledged in order to work in formal care institutions. Through information gained via interviews with employers, Huang et al. show how hierarchies of foreign workers play not only on gendered and national hierarchies but also along other intersecting dimensions, such as skin colour, language skills and cultural notions attached to certain nationalities.

These insights call for researchers to remain sensitive to a wide variety of intersectionalities that may enable us to complicate and look beyond given research paradigms and indeed iconic representations of migration. In the following chapter we return to this question by teasing out the heterosexual and heteronormative assumptions in the GCC literature. Queer studies perspectives have raised important critiques of the existing analyses and pointed out how most research on GCCs has taken the relation of a mother, often in heterosexual marriage, to her biological child as the privileged site of transnational, or global, care. Therefore, however compelling and often heartbreaking the image of the global nanny working abroad caring for other people's children is, this is not the whole truth about the way domestic service work is organized. The emphasis on women as mothers leaving their children in the care of others omits, for example, the experiences of both gay and straight men and single women even in such research settings where these groups and individuals figure among the research participants (Manalansan IV 2006, Yeates 2012).

Care work is a form of embodied and emotional labour, that is, *bodywork* by definition: embodied care workers provide for the corporeal needs of persons they care for. Due to its nature as bodywork dealing with leaking elderly bodies (Twigg 2004, also Twigg et al. 2011), eldercare has been perceived as a form of work that increasingly needs foreign labour force to provide it. In the domain of transnational care work, certain characteristics associated with particular ethnicities and nationalities make some embodied caregivers appear preferable over others. Think for a moment: Whom would you visualize when thinking of a caring person across a global scale? In the Singaporean context, for example, Philippine and Indonesian women are perceived as the ideal ones for performing elderly care, drawing on assumptions of sociable character and suitability for quick learning of new tasks connected with Philippine care workers and patience and servility attached to Indonesian women. This imagery is also promoted by local maid agencies. Other preferred caregivers would be Burmese women, who, despite the quality of slowness attached by the employers to this nationality group, are perceived as patient, willing to please and having an enhanced respect for the elderly. An available pool of domestic workers is thus organized, in the minds of the employers, along a hierarchical organization of nationalities (Huang et al. 2012). The hierarchical organization of nationalities may result in important differences in salaries. In Lebanon, according to a survey conducted by Jureidini (2010), Sri Lankan domestic workers, who constitute a majority of this pool of labour in the country, receive on average half the salary of Filipina domestic workers, while Ethiopian maids' salary falls in between the two.

Domestic work, despite its feminized underpinnings, is, however, not only performed by migrant women. Recently more and more research is done in the area of men performing domestic work, thus providing a complementary angle through which to examine how gendered and racialized division of labour manifests in the context of globalized care work (Sarti and Scrinzi 2010). Through an ethnographic approach, Lena Näre (2010) has examined the ways in which Sri Lankan men negotiate their masculinity when engaged in cleaning and caring work in Naples, Italy. She shows how intersectional categories work in different ways in relation to different everyday contexts: in the workplace, male domestic workers may be required to feminize their comportment to match the expectations of employers and embody docile, asexual and unthreatening Sri Lankan masculinity. However, in their own community and family they may enact traditional masculine role as providers and breadwinners for the family. Therefore, intersectional analysis is something that enables us to comprehend the relational character of social categories and how these social categories are in constant flux and matter of (re)negotiation even in the course of as little time as one day.

Gendering skills and privilege

Majority of critical social research has focused on the positions of the least privileged in the context of labour migration. Thus, the interest in the experiences of skilled or highly skilled migrants is relatively recent. Feminist research on skilled international mobility has revealed that, similar to research on labour migration more generally, again the mainstream research on highly skilled migration has mostly focused on male migrants' experiences and on sectors where men constitute a majority, such as information and communication technologies (ICTs), engineering or transnational banking (see, e.g., Beaverstock 2002, 2005). Thereby the use of conceptualization of "skill" and "being highly skilled" already reiterates gendered undertones (see Iredale 2005, Kofman and Raghuram 2006, Raghuram 2004, Raghuram and Kofman 2004).

Family migration is one domain that forms a crux of different forms of mobility, including mobility of the highly skilled. Building on her study on expatriate Indian women as professionals in the ICT sector in Belgium, Hannelore Roos (2013) questions the individualistically oriented approach underpinning migration policies. She shows how women arriving as accompanying spouses within family migration schemes are far from being classifiable as non-productive (see also Raghuram 2004, Yeoh and Willis 2005 and chapter 4), and in practice the move abroad may also benefit their own work careers. In other words, the categorization of the spouse as someone who moves with the skilled migrant prevents from recognizing how the mobility of a family or a couple can be a beneficial career move for both of them and beneficial for the receiving country as well. In some occasions, it is indeed family formation that facilitates the woman's mobility up the social ladder in the eyes of her childhood family and community as she is able to build a career in another country. This being said, women move individually and as heads of households across the globe to engage professionally in demanding skilled occupational fields such as in the health and educational sectors, but skilled women also migrate within other migration categories. Their manifold contributions have however often remained hidden from public debate, as the dominating representation of migrant women is the image of women as welfare recipients rather than providers of social welfare (Kofman and Raghuram 2006).

The severe shortage of health professionals and their uneven distribution at the global scale has been recognized since a long time already. According to this recognition, there are less medical doctors and nurses than needed, especially in the global North, where the population is ageing rapidly and will thus need more care services in the future. Several countries, such as the UK, for example, have already faced the situation in which there are not enough native-born persons to fill up these labour shortages, so international recruitment has become a necessity. Thus, an important number of health care professionals have moved from one country or continent to another in order to work abroad.

Targeted recruitment of health professionals is not only a recent phenomenon, however: UK recruitment offices for nurses and midwives were established in several African countries as early as in 1948. The recruitment process slowed down since the Immigration Act of 1971 established work permits, and it had been practically stopped by mid-1980s, before starting anew with a great intensity at the turn of the new millennium. South African, Nigerian, Zimbabwean, Ghanaian and Malawian nurses have been recruited in important numbers, some of whom have sought better pay and other career opportunities; others have moved to travel and explore another culture

(Likupe 2006). While for some working in the UK has provided a positive experience, many have reported suffering from racism and deskilling: the earlier work experience gained abroad did not pay off, or the promotions have gone by (Henry 2007). In some contexts, such as for the Zimbabwean community interviewed by JoAnn McGregor (2007), migration to the UK has been equated with working in the lowest sectors of the care industry regardless actual education statuses or earlier work experience, captured in the demeaning saying that going to Britain will mean "joining the BBC": not the British Broadcasting Corporation but "British Bottom Cleaners."

Jennifer Nash (2008) argues that privileged positions need to be studied intersectionally, similar to the underprivileged. As one of us has shown by engaging with migratory trajectories of four highly educated North African women in France (Kynsilehto 2011a), the notions of skill and success may be shown in a new light when examined through a life-story perspective. These trajectories illustrate different ways of migrants making their skills valued in various migratory moves, both voluntary and forced ones, and the ways in which using one's professional skills is made difficult. The example of Meriem that was presented in the beginning of this chapter is one of these trajectories, and it is one that recounts successful ways of integrating and reintegrating the labour market without significant career breaks.

Consider, then, another trajectory: that of Zineb. She is also Algerian, teacher by formation, and had worked in France before she was compelled to leave Algeria during the civil war in the 1990s, due to her women's rights activism. Upon arrival after her forced departure, she was first able to guarantee a couple of one-year work contracts at a French university in the northern parts of the country. After her work contract was no longer renewed she joined her husband in Marseille, in the south of France, to have her family stay all in one place. After several attempts to enter work-life as a teacher at the primary or secondary level of education, she gave up: her younger colleagues treated her as a real beginner and gave her assignments below her skills and level of experience. She was not ready to accept this positioning, so she decided to resign and rethink her career options in some other field, to reskill. This step was far from easy, as she had grown disillusioned with a system that pushed her away despite her own motivation to contribute, in a context where the decision to move to France had not been a matter of choice but rather one of life and death.

FORCED DISPLACEMENT

Refugee studies is an important body of scholarship where feminist scholars contribute by analysing gender within forced migration and further on with intersectional approaches that provide again more nuanced readings of the need for asylum and lives as refugees. We will now move to another way of categorizing mobilities: to the distinction between refugees and migrants or forced and voluntary forms of migration. As the earlier part of the chapter has illustrated, this distinction is not clear-cut when examined at the level of individual lives. It doesn't necessarily correlate with legal categorizations used for the mobile people in question either, as states seek to redefine and narrow down the criteria necessary for qualifying for international protection.

Gendering refugees

In this part of the chapter we turn our focus on the pertinent, and also often heartbreaking, images of individuals and groups for whom mobility is clearly not a matter of choice. When people are compelled to move because the environment is no longer safe for them stay, the politics of who qualifies as a refugee becomes a matter of life and death. This discussion will continue in the chapters 5 and 6. It is here that we introduce how refugees are categorized and show how circulating images and imageries also come to matter in the process.

Violent conflicts, complex humanitarian emergencies and environmental degradation are recognized as the main reasons that force people to leave their places of birth. At the same time, it must be recognized that local contexts for seemingly abrupt violent conflicts are also always entangled in the long history of complex webs of colonial and postcolonial power relations. "Common" histories narrated by distinctive groups emphasize different hierarchies of power, and these clashing narratives and changing affiliations within different power relations contribute to different violent conflicts and humanitarian emergencies that make "staying put" impossible for sometimes very large groups of people. One need only think of the current conflicts in Syria and the brutal violence performed by the ISIS, or the Islamic State, in Iraq and Syria.

Environmental reasons for forced displacement include floods, drought, earthquakes, hurricanes, tsunamis and storms that create various forms of complex humanitarian emergencies and intensify longer-term environmental degradation. One example of such complex environmental emergencies is the tsunami that hit the coasts of the Indian Ocean on 26 December 2004. The tsunami killed approximately 230,000 people in fourteen countries and destroyed coastal communities, particularly in Indonesia, Sri Lanka, India and Thailand. As it happened at a peak festive season, thousands of tourists from the global North were among the dead and otherwise affected by the tsunami, and some managed to film the tragedy with their own equipment. However, the disaster and its aftermath produced uneven consequences for different affected groups. Immediately after the tsunami, several cases of child trafficking were reported. While the number of tourists from the global

North who were killed in the tsunami is known by individuals, the number of local poor people from the affected communities who were killed in the same disaster will never be known: they were "swallowed by the sea or hastily buried in mass graves" (Keys, Masterman-Smith and Cottle 2006: 195), qualified as a health hazard. To fully understand and analyse complex humanitarian emergencies, an intersectional lens that accounts for multiple bases of identity is indispensable (Hyndman and de Alwis 2003).

Currently, the rising sea levels already threaten the existence of whole islands in the Pacific Ocean, which are estimated to sink in the fairly near future.[2] This phenomenon also calls for new ways of thinking about migration policies and boundaries of nation states, because environmental disasters do not respect state borders and, as in the case of sinking island states, the territorial grounding of state sovereignty will no longer hold. Where should citizens of those countries go?

When a person stays in the country of origin in her or his search for a safer haven, he or she is referred to as *internally displaced person* (IDP). When a person crosses an international border, she or he becomes a *refugee*. Worldwide, the majority of refugees reside in the global South, even if political discourses in Europe, Australia or North America create an illusion of masses of people coming to seek asylum in the global North. In this discourse, the asylum seeker becomes a scapegoat for many social ills, such as taking over jobs while "burdening" social security systems in place in the countries of destination. In the meantime, it has become increasingly difficult to access to asylum in global North (see, e.g., the discussion on border surveillance in chapter 5). Moreover, countries that are closest to current conflict zones and thus receiving the majority of refugees, such as Jordan, Lebanon and Turkey for refugees from Syria, or Kenya for refugees from Somalia, are increasingly reluctant to host large numbers of refugees in the long term.

Globally, approximately half of the refugee population is estimated to be women. This means that women's experiences of being a refugee should count at least as much as men's experiences. However, what is specific about women is that they often flee with their dependents – persons whose survival needs to be guaranteed by a refugee woman. When women are counted with their dependents together, the figure easily raises up to 80 per cent. Women are also specifically targeted by gender-based violence and gendered forms of persecution, which constitute gender-specific reasons for fleeing their homes. Examples of gender-specific reasons for women to be forced to flee are female genital cutting (FGM), widow burning and sexual violence against women in conflicts as a strategy of war (Boyd 1999, Freedman 2007). Domestic violence and protecting one's girl children from FGM are also forms of gender-based violence that constitute reasons to flee, and, as such, they render return impossible, as it is the home that is the main site of violence.

In addition, women are the target for gender-based violence during various states of displacement and in refugee camps.

Gender-based violence that targets men and boys includes sexual abuse and humiliation: men and boys may be raped or forced to rape their mothers, children or other women or men in front of other protractors. Young boys as well as young girls may be kidnapped to serve as sexual slaves for combatants or forced to perform sexually humiliating acts, including rape, when recruited as child soldiers. Gender-based violence has been recognized by the UN as an integral element to wars and conflicts as a result of feminist lobbying (UNSCR 1325). This means that gender-based violence is recognized as a strategy of war instead of a spillover of violence to the private sphere (Skjelsbaek 2006). Therefore gender-based violence needs to be considered a central dimension when thinking about the need for international protection, that is, asylum.

The Balkan wars in the 1990s following the breakdown of Yugoslavia were a crucial moment that brought attention to gender-specific violence, torture and rape as a strategy of war in feminist research and activism. Violent ethnic cleansing that included killing men and young boys characterized the Bosnian war (1992–1995). The events escalated in the horrendous Srebrenica massacre in July 1995, where more than 8,000 persons died. Another strategy used for the ethnic cleansing was rape, sexualized torture and forced impregnation of women. These practices highlighted how women's bodies constitute the battlefield on which the war is fought. As the woman's body represents the continuity and purity of the nation, rape and forced impregnation of women were used as a strategy to destroy and instil humiliation the rival ethnic group. Due to the Balkan wars, a million people fled to other countries and an even larger number of people were internally displaced.

What is relevant here is to recognize how ethnographic case studies can illustrate how gender is configured in the refugee communities in the receiving country. Drawing on her ethnographic study with Bosnian Muslims (Bosniaks) in the Netherlands, the UK and Bosnia, Nadje Al-Ali (2002) explained how gender relations within refugee families changed after the war. Whereas many of her interlocutors in exile, both men and women, expressed a loss of identity and self-esteem as a result of violent rupture from the community left behind, it had been relatively easier for women to find employment outside the home and to integrate in the local society. On the other hand, for many men the rupture indicated a renegotiation of traditional roles and an even stronger commitment to ethnic, national, political and religious identities. In addition, they had become closer to their immediate families (Al-Ali 2002: 255). Stef Jansen (2008) names the refugee men's quest for reconstructing their identity in diaspora as "misplaced masculinity." Based on Jansen's study with Bosnian refugee men in Australia and the Netherlands, these men did not construct their identity in relation to the present-day Bosnia-Herzegovina engaging in ethnopolitical and religious struggles of the current phase of the nation-building.

Instead, their reminiscence was directed at the multi-ethnic collectivity that existed before the violent rupture, during the time of socialist Yugoslavia.

Since the mid-1980s, feminist scholars have worked towards gender analysis of refugee experiences in order to break the stereotypical image of the refugee woman as victim. The objective of feminist research has been to recognize how refugee women are *victimized* by the complex gendered power relations operating economically, socially and politically, instead of being *victims per se* (Hadjukowski-Ahmed, Khanlou and Moussa 2008: 6). They have shown that emphasizing refugee women's and girls' vulnerability to gender-based violence may, however, also become counterproductive. Vulnerability may be represented as a property of refugee women and not as a result of power relations that locate women in a vulnerable position. Understanding vulnerability as a property is apparent in the UN discourses that emphasize the "vulnerability of women and girls" (e.g. Hadjukowski-Ahmed et al. 2008). In these discourses, the image of refugee women is that of a passive victim of violence to evoke pity and justify rescue operations. This image of the victim renders invisible the multiple ways in which refugee women actively make choices and strive for their own and often of their relatives' and communities' survival.

Feminist scholars have emphasized that the very notion of refugee is embedded in gendered scripts. Jennifer Hyndman (2010: 453) summarizes: "The persistence of a stable category, 'refugee,' enables refugee-serving agencies to meet their mandates, but can also serve to infantilize and/or feminize refugees in relation to the new host society where they find themselves." The argument is that groups and individuals who are caught in protracted refugee situations (PRS) are pathologized in the global North as dangerous and deviant (Hyndman and Giles 2011). This imagery follows a gendered script. According to Hyndman and Giles, the prevailing iconography represents as "good" refugees those who stay in one place, close to the area they have fled and take whatever assistance is given to them. The norm for the refugee is to remain passive and feminized. On the contrary, those refugees who actively seek more liveable spaces further away from the very first area of asylum are represented as a threat and thus masculinized.

Next we present three different contexts and ways of reading gendered displacement. The first one is from a widely circulated image in the global media since mid-1980: the image of a young Afghan girl who has given a face to forced displacement (see box 2.3). The second example draws on the approach that emphasizes refugee women's agency, depicting Guatemalan refugee women's organization *Mama Maquin* (see box 2.4). Our third example discusses gender specificities in the space refugee camp, designed for temporary dwelling for a limited number of people, but which may host people for a much longer time and much larger numbers of residents than initially intended (see box 2.5). Here gendered displacement due to the ongoing war in

BOX 2.3

IMAGING GENDERED DISPLACEMENT

A world famous example of instrumentalizing the plight of refugees is the image of Sharbat Gula, a thirteen-year-old Afghan girl living as a refugee in Pakistan at the time photographer Steve McCurry took her picture. This picture has embodied anonymous, voiceless displacement since it appeared on the cover of *National Geographic* in June 1985. In turn, Steve McCurry became very famous after the publication of Gula's image whereas she remained in poverty. Her image travelled across the world as a beautiful, aestheticized example of dehistorization and the denial of refugee experiences (cf. Malkki 1996). In the picture, Sharbat Gula stares at the viewer, with a look in her eyes that is simultaneously angry, brave and ready to run away. The picture incites imagining wilderness, fighting rebels in the mountains and courageous girl children struggling for their survival, yet it leaves Gula's story unheard. It thus serves as an example of erasing even the need to hear refugees' own views on their situation and calls into question the ways in which young persons' images can be used for commercial purposes when they reside in "elsewheres" as regards the global North.

BOX 2.4

REFUGEE WOMEN GET ORGANIZED

Refugee women have also formed alliances and organized collectively for peace and return to the country of origin. The first widely known case of refugee women's self-organization is Guatemalan women who were staying in 120 camps operated by the UN Refugee agency (UNHCR) in Mexico and spontaneous settlements at the Mexican-Guatemalan border. These women established their own organization, *Mama Maquin*. The organization ensured women's participation in the relief operations and conducted awareness-raising workshops. Mama Maquin also played a central role in the peace process in the 1990s. In the repatriation negotiations they successfully lobbied for the principle of equal ownership of private and communal property that was later enshrined in the Guatemalan law and jurisprudence. Upon the return of the refugees in the villages, the organization contributed to rebuilding the villages and establishing normality in the war-torn society (Hadjukowski-Ahmed, Khanlou and Moussa 2008).

BOX 2.5

**GENDERING REFUGEES BEFORE THE CAMP,
IN THE CAMP AND BEYOND THE CAMP**

The civil war in Syria began in the spring of 2011 as one of the popular uprisings in North Africa and Middle East that were glossed as the Arab Spring. Millions of people have been displaced within the country and across international borders. Most refugees live in camps and urban areas in the neighbouring countries Jordan, Iraq, Lebanon and Turkey. As has been the case in violent conflicts elsewhere, sexual violence and humiliation are used as a way of terrorizing population, both in open areas and as a method of torture in detention (Anani 2013, EMHRN 2013). Sexual violence also constitutes one reason to seek refuge elsewhere. Once escaped into crowded refugee camps in the neighbouring countries, women and girls often continue to be subjected to sexual violence and humiliation, including rape (see Freedman 2007: 36–42). One way of getting by religious moral codes that strictly forbid rape has been to pronounce a short-term marriage, counted in days or even hours, which enables calling these de facto rapes "marital sex." Civil society actors also report on cases of young girls having been sold to be married as a means for refugee families to survive the extreme poverty and lack of available income-earning opportunities in the country of exile. These acts, which can be simultaneously characterized by survival and trafficking in human beings, show one of the ugly sides of protracted conflicts and their impact on people who are forced to flee.

Syria serves as the context. These three examples represent different feminist approaches to examine gender in the context of forced displacement.

UNDOCUMENTED MOBILITY

In this part of the chapter we focus on the specific problematics of categorizing and representing undocumented or "irregular" migration. This category comprises both labour migrants and refugees. "Being undocumented" refers to staying in a country without a valid administrative title for residence. As such, it often denotes situations where a person stays after the expiry of a visa or a residence permit, or the grounds for permitted residence may

change. It may be a phase before one is able to lodge an asylum claim or refer
to staying in the country after receiving a negative decision on one's asylum
claim. Intersectional analysis pays attention to different dimensions of human
life and thus helps to understand how irregularity is a matter of migration
status or lack of it and how this is shaped by gendered, ethnicized and classed
configurations that render the world not only unequal but unjust.

Undocumented or irregular forms of mobility are subject to heated debates
across the globe, which bring together various images and imageries of the
people on the move. On the one hand, states reaffirm their individual and
collective desire to control the populations present in theirs and other states'
territories in the name of national security (see chapter 5). On the other hand,
more humanitarian discourses express concern with regard to the diverse
human rights violations that occur in a situation in which mobile individuals
are not visible in any official registers. Moreover, campaigns against human
trafficking tend to overlook the crucial role extremely restrictive migration
policies play in leaving large numbers of people without a legal access to
mobility that in turn increases migrant women's vulnerability to different
forms of exploitation and abuse (Andrijasevic 2010). When undocumented
mobility is represented as a form of a threat, as people *en masse* seeking to
break through borders, individual itineraries and multiple potential forms of
agency are lost in the crowd.

As has been shown through many examples thus far, migration statuses are
manifold and complex. Undocumented or irregular status is something that a
person may end up with in the midst of changing migration statuses, such as
when the residence permit is tied to a specific employer (e.g. Pande 2013), or
as a result of changing legislation conditioning regular stay that the person may
not be aware of. Sometimes undocumented mobility is a phase, albeit perhaps
a long one, in the journey towards a documented status (Khosravi 2010).

Cristiana Giordano (2008) explores the trajectories of undocumented
migrants with foreign sex workers in Italy. She presents the story of a Nigerian woman, Joy, to illustrate how one person is able to live through the
challenging conditions of undocumented migration and gain official status.
Joy's story is indicative of many disparities across global scales: her family's
difficult economic situation back in Nigeria constitutes the reason for her to
leave school, and the practical impossibility of obtaining a visa to any European country pushes her towards illegal entry using a fake passport. Upon her
arrival in Italy she is told she owes an enormous debt to her traffickers and her
Madam, and the only way to pay this debt is through selling sexual services.
In time, she is able to break free from the hold of traffickers and finds a way
out with the help of a rehabilitation programme in Italy. Joy's story is, Giordano argues, an emblematic example of the many women she encountered
during her ethnographic fieldwork. Joy's example refers to women who come

to Italy, work for some time in the sex industry, denounce their traffickers and pass through a rehabilitation programme and are able to integrate into Italian society as legal residents (see also Andrijasevic 2010). Giordano argues that current politico-legal constellation favours and produces specific of political subjectivities, meanwhile creating states of liminality when the subject loses the authority vis-à-vis her own story. The hardships and mismatches in Joy's narrative enabled Giordano to see how the politico-legal constellations are configured in individual women's lives.

However, it is important not to be caught up in romantic ideas of finding a possibility of integration into a society via undocumented migration. Irregularity signifies very real violations of basic rights. As already mentioned, some categories of workers, for example, domestic workers in Jordan and Egypt, are explicitly excluded from laws that regulate labour. It is therefore important not to forget the structural conditions that render certain categories of globally mobile workers particularly vulnerable. These structural conditions produce and maintain institutionalized exploitative relations. Amrita Pande (2013) has argued that it is indeed the system of required sponsorship for obtaining a residence permit such as the *kafala* system in Lebanon – that is also applied to refugees from Syria who reside in the country – that allows for the abusive relationship between the employer and the domestic employee to emerge and be maintained. The stereotypical image of an abusive Arab Madam exploiting her domestic workers illustrates such relationships. However, when a structural problem is privatized into a systemic exploitation of some women over other women in the household, it serves to shift attention from the legal structures that have enabled the exploitative arrangements of labour in the first place. In this case, if the worker was to escape her sponsor, she would become an "irregular" migrant. Thus the legal structure is such that it sustains the dependency of the workers and, in so doing, it permits the exploitative conditions to endure. Unless the domestic worker accepts these conditions, she will lose the status as a regular migrant and thus becomes "undocumented."

Still, even if the migrant woman has initially entered under a documented migrant status and engages in regular domestic work, the reality of the situation in the receiving country can become so difficult that sex work may become a better option. This may be the case even if the shift to sex work would deprive her from the status as a regular migrant: irregular status might provide an escape from an abusive situation. Consider the experiences of a group of women who had initially entered Dubai through a regular labour scheme to work in domestic and care work (Mahdavi 2013). During their migratory trajectory, they had entered the sex industry either for additional income or to work in this sector exclusively. One of the women, Meskit, had paid a large sum of money to an intermediary and entered the United Arab Emirates irregularly to work as a servant. She had left Ethiopia for the sake of survival, both hers and her family's, due to heavy debts they had accumulated after Meskit's father had died. The family Meskit was first working for abused her in many ways: confiscated her passport, left her without food, locked her up in the house and refused to pay her salary and the male family members tried to abuse her sexually. She escaped the unbearable living conditions and found an Emirati man whom she thought would be good for her. Shortly after they had a baby, however, the man refused to continue their relationship and sent Meskit away with their baby. In order to feed her child she needed to find new employment and found one at a restaurant. However, as the restaurant refused to pay her salary, she found herself yet again with nothing. She was unable to leave the UAE regularly because she had entered and resided there irregularly and leaving would result in heavy fines (see also Pande 2013). To make ends meet, she joined a group of women working in a bar and providing sexual services. Meskit's story illustrates a trajectory where the conditions drive the mobile individual to resort to any strategies of survival available, yet leading her from one exploitative situation to another. Her exploitation was possible exactly because of her undocumented status.

Undocumented status is not always something that is chosen deliberately or out of desperation, but it may be imposed upon a person due to the way migration categories are implemented in practice. An undocumented status can be acquired at birth, such as in case of a child who is born to a mother whose residence has not been regularized. In this way border control extends to the birth clinic. Tyler argues that it is indeed the *pregnant body* of a potential migrant mother that has become a target of intensified control fuelled with the fear of "health" or "baby tourism" in British citizenship policies (on the case of Ireland, Fanning and Mutwarasibo 2007: 447).

Baby tourism here denotes the idea of women entering into a country in the global North usually within humanitarian migration channels, who then give birth to gain a passport for the baby. Potentially, via such an arrangement the mother could gain a passport herself as well. Tyler uses the example of a baby "Mary" who was born to a West African teenage mother while detained in Britain and explains:

> Mary, like thousands of other children born in Britain each year, is in the extraordinary position of *having entered Britain illegally at birth*. With the cut of the umbilical cord and her first breath she became subject to the full force of Britain's border controls, including indefinite detention within a rapidly expanding, privately owned, "for profit" immigration prison estate.
>
> (Tyler 2010: 69, emphasis in the original)

Tyler argues that the mother and her children are then kept in intense precarity, at the brink of being deported at any time. Contrary to received ideas about welfare mothers abusing the system, she shows how families of failed asylum seekers live in poverty with strict minimum, below the minimum living standards defined for families to live in the UK.

As all the previous examples have shown, undocumented immigration status often results from practices enabled by the state. People are deliberately left into a liminal state, where access to various rights is restricted.

GLOBAL MOBILITY FOR THE PURPOSE OF FAMILY FORMATION

In this part of the chapter we turn to global mobility for the purpose of family formation that constitutes a significant form of global mobility. We begin by discussing transnational marriages through kin networks and transnational marriage agencies where the focus on the spousal relations connected with cultural, gendered and ethnicized expectations. Then we move on to transnational adoption and commercial surrogacy, which emphasizes parent-child relations and highlight economic inequality between different locations across the globe.

Migration for the purpose of family formation comprises of both reuniting spouses and families as well as finding a partner from the country of origin. Research shows that it is not unusual for children with migrant parents[3] to seek a partner in the country of one's or one's parents' origin as a means to maintain a continuing relation to this country and region, even neighbourhood.

The preference for a partner who comes from the country of parents' or grandparents' origin may be generated by the perceptions of peer migrants as already estranged from the cultural norms of the country of origin. Young migrant women living in Europe, for example, might be regarded as having loose mores and a Westernized lifestyle that is not deemed acceptable for a suitable candidate for marriage and potential mother. Young migrant men who already live in many European societies might be, following media portrayals, regarded as potential criminals or school dropouts, which make them seem less promising candidates for the demands of responsible husband and father. Thus, finding a spouse in the country of "origin" creates a new form of mobility, which follows the previous migratory trajectories of parents or grandparents.

The quest for finding a suitable partner as a means to mobility has been increasingly facilitated by the Internet. What has been referred to derogatorily as "mail-order brides" (see, e.g., Tolentino 1996, So 2006) has been increasingly reconfigured into a global marriage market giving access to a wider choice of potential partners across the globe. These changes have also developed into forms of "commodified cross-border marriages" (Wang 2007) that have replaced, to an extent at least, traditional arranged marriages. Challenging the conception that transnational marriages are always about women's betterment of their social position, of "marrying up," feminist research has shown how the reasons women give for choosing a partner in a particular location are much more diverse (e.g. Toyota and Thang 2012, see chapter 3). Another way of looking at these marriage patterns is to see how the individuals who live in such transnational marriages actually develop creative strategies to match the demands imposed by their social groups with their own personal needs and desires (Casier et al. 2013). Even though choice for a partner from the same cultural background is often represented as an indication of lack in societal integration it can also be a form of resistance for women. They may be seen repelling against the prevalent ideals of femininity of the dominant culture (Espiritu 2001).

In addition to transnational marriages, international adoption is considered as a form of migration for the purpose of family formation. Countries regulate this form of international mobility in different ways. For example, Russia passed a law in 2012 to deny the possibility for American citizens to adopt Russian children. Other countries, such as China, have added a requirement that adopting parent(s) have to at least an A-level diploma or a degree from professional education and require that age difference between the parent(s) and the child cannot exceed forty-five years.[4] South Africa provides a significant market for international adoption, largely due to racialized poverty in South Africa where also deception has been used to lure mothers to give their children away for adoption.

Global hierarchies cross-cut and enable forms of exploitation in the context of international adoption. New hierarchies are further created in the receiving country. The internationally adopted children need to negotiate their sense of belonging in their new country of citizenship as well as make sense of their autobiographical and family-related past in relation to these different geopolitical and class-divided landscapes.

Currently, transnational commercial surrogacy has become an alternative to international adoption for willing-to-be parents in affluent countries to start a family. Many countries in the global North forbid domestic commercial surrogacy, or the domestic commercial surrogacy is expensive that it is out of reach for most families. Yet countries such as India offer the possibility for transnational commercial surrogacy, to such degree that Pande (2010) has argued that the preparations resemble an assembly line, designed for the purpose of not only producing babies but also manufacturing perfect mother-workers. As a part of these preparations, women who offer the service of surrogacy for transnational adoption stay in efficiently organized yet isolated space of surrogacy hostel.

Commercial surrogacy has indeed become a survival strategy for some poor rural women who are in desperate need for income for their own families. Being a mother is a requirement to be recruited as a surrogate. The production of qualified candidates for commercial surrogacy comprises the ideals of motherhood and employees. Surrogates are expected to cultivate their motherly instincts vis-à-vis the foetus as well as respect the terms of the contract. Instead of emphasizing the victimhood of the surrogates only, Pande (2010) explains how the women she worked with creatively resisted the control they were subjected to in the surrogacy hostel, where they were obliged to stay during the pregnancy. These strategies of resistance related to the ways in which women used discursive strategies to frame their conditions on their own terms, as well as to the emotional ties women were formed with each other across caste and religion divisions in the highly isolated space of the hostel. Such relationships might not have been formed in other situations.

GENDERING IMMOBILITY

Last we discuss a relatively neglected side of mobility, that of immobility. Studies on transnationalism and the "mobility turn" in social sciences have emphasized immobility as an integral dimension of mobilities. This category in mobility studies includes populations who "stay put," while others move abroad. It is argued that in order to understand the impact of mobility on societies, groups and individuals who are affected by mobilities need to be included in the migration and mobility studies. What happens to them after a significant number of people have migrated? How are these effects gendered?

As the opening narrative of this chapter showed, Meriem's migrant trajectory begins with childhood memories of accompanying her migrant father to France, where she attended school until the first years of her university education. In the meantime, her mother had preferred to stay in Algeria, at her home environment among her friends and kin. For both Meriem and her mother the living conditions changed fundamentally as Algeria gained independence from France. This reorganization further impacted the ways in which mobilities were configured within the state territory and across newly defined international borders.

Caroline Archambault (2010) argues that the label of "wives left behind" (cf. McEvoy et al. 2012) is built on the understanding of lack of agency of those "staying put." Basing on her study with rural families in Ugweno, Tanzania, she proposes that staying can indeed be an empowering strategy that actually offers women more economic autonomy and social well-being than joining the global flow. Staying in the rural areas signifies sustained ties with one's family and friends, and it is nourished by the sense of belonging, of being linked to the soil. It also serves as a practical way for the family to be able to keep connected to the village, as someone needs to take care of the farm when others are absent earning cash that has become difficult to gain by leaning on agriculture only.

The gendered division of labour and household tasks are further discussed in chapter 4 in relation to economic impact of migration. Feminist researchers analysing detention centres (Mountz 2011) and camp conditions (Hyndman and Giles 2011) have pointed out how states use immobility to prevent access to protection. We will discuss these structures and practices of control in chapter 5.

CONCLUDING WORDS

This chapter has focused on categories used in migrations studies and migration policies in conjunction with various experiences and imageries of the people on the move. The categories in migration studies reflect the division between forced and voluntary migration as well as regular and irregular migration. In the discussion we have shown how various trajectories of people hardly ever fit in a single category: a person can be in several categories at the same time and move in and out of categories due to life circumstances and changing immigration policies.

In this chapter we have laid out a number of situations in which mobile persons make decisions concerning their futures in constricting and continually changing circumstances. As we already remarked in the introduction, these examples challenge the rational actor theory that informs migration research focusing on push and pull factors. We do not imply that people make their decisions irrationally but, rather, that they do so in the context of multiple rationalities, such as migration policies, family relations and cultural factors. These factors matter in the way people design and decide which directions to take for one's life. Moreover, these processes are conditioned by complex power relations and global hierarchies that are inherently gendered.

To take up again Meriem's story this chapter started with, her trajectory shows how gender matters in relation to nation-building. Whereas the participation of women in postcolonial independence struggles was widely heralded, full participation was not equally welcomed at the time of newly gained independence. In order to make the decision to leave Meriem had to take into account her own goal to contribute to the nation that she considered herself part of and the very real danger this presented if she continued to participate. Her situation made her family constantly worry over her fate. Meriem's story illustrates the concrete dilemmas that people need to take into account when considering the available options and whether to move or not to move.

As the chapter has shown, the categories used in migration research need to be understood as overlapping and fluid in order to recognize the complexity of mobile trajectories. Furthermore, the use of categories both in research and in policy making can be enhanced by intersectional analysis, which brings awareness to how a person is affected by multiple and intersecting systems of power. Moreover, intersectional approach calls for recognizing how people on the move are able to make choices when carving out their mobile trajectories in the context of constricting conditions. In the following chapter, we will continue this discussion from the perspective of queer migration and diaspora studies that challenges the implicit heteronormative assumptions that guide mobility studies. In this chapter our goal has been to critically discuss the ways in which categories are used in migration research and migration policies, because these have also real-life consequences for the people on the move. The selected films can be used as a resource for further discussions on the possibilities for agency and subjectivity of people on the move.

DISCUSSION POINTS

1. How are gender, ethnicity and family relations figured in the depictions of "migration crises" and/or "refugee crises"?
2. Where are the largest groups of refugees coming from at present? Where are they staying?
3. Who are performing cleaning services in the surroundings familiar to you?

ESSAY QUESTIONS

1. What is the purpose of the distinction between voluntary and forced migration? How can it be problematized?
2. Explain feminist contributions to the analysis of skilled migration.
3. How is the norm of able-bodiedness present in the categories traditionally used in migration studies?

STUDY ASSIGNMENTS

1. Search for legislation on migration sponsorships in your country. Is this a possible way to get a regular migration status? Which social rights are included in this sponsorship scheme?

2. Read the box 2.3 on Sharbat Gula and search for her image. What are the iconic images for refugees today? How do social media reproduce and reiterate iconic images?
3. Look for examples of refugee women's organizations and their stance related to the conflict(s) they had to flee. What is the focus of their work? What are their claims?
4. Familiarize yourself with refugee camp infrastructure. Identify potential risk areas. What would you suggest to reduce risks?

EXTRA MATERIALS

Dirty Pretty Things (2002) is a story of a Nigerian migrant working at a hotel in London who is asked to participate in criminal exploitation of other undocumented migrants in order to gain a residence permit in the UK. Director Stephen Frears. Cast: Chiwetel Ejiofor, Audrey Tautou, Sophie Okonedo.

How is access to a migration status negotiated in the film?

Terraferma (2011) recounts the story of an Italian fisherman and his family who help a group of undocumented migrants stranded on an overburdened raft. Directed by Emanuele Crialese. Cast: Filippo Pucillo, Donatella Finoc-chiaro and Mimmo Cuticchio. Distribution: Bellissima Films. © Copyright: Cattleya.

Analyse the film from the perspective of mobility and immobility.

NOTES

1. This example draws from discussions with international colleagues at the University of Tampere.
2. See, for example, Siddle 2013.
3. Generational transmission of the positionality as a migrant is much criticized in migration research.
4. See international adoption agencies for more information, for example http://www.holtinternational.org/welcome/countryCriteria.php?country=China (last accessed 21 October 2014).

Chapter 3

Globally mobile life

Preceding the enlargement of the European Union in 2004 and in its immediate aftermath a fear of "the Polish plumber" was triggered in France. The threat that was foreseen concerned large masses of workers who would invade the country and take over construction work and other manual jobs from the French nationals. The figure of "the Polish plumber" as the symbol of a sudden increase in Eastern migration appeared in political speeches and it was widely circulated in different media. The fear proved to be wrong, as there were no large masses coming to take over jobs. Meanwhile, the heated debate capitalizing on this fear overlooked altogether how crucial migrant workers from Poland had been since the 1850s and especially in the post–World War II for the reconstruction in France. In fact, many of the migrant workers from those periods have been naturalized as French citizens since. These aspects, migrants' manifold contributions to the economies and societies of settlement, tend to be forgotten in the fear-mongering discourses. Marketing professionals in Poland, however, were quick to deploy the fear-provoking imagery by turning it around. Images of the muscled and oiled, beautifully tanned and sexually appealing male body dressed in blue overalls were used to advertise vacation options in Poland for the French, subverting the fear factor, and to yield laughter and erotic appeal for the discovery of the country and possibilities Poland had to offer.

Currently Polish migrants constitute the largest migrant nationality group in the UK. Politicians and the media have used the images of the Polish to symbolize how migrants take over jobs and abuse the social security system, instilling fear of the other in the population. Since the British voted in favour of the UK exiting the European Union, Brexit, outright violence against Polish migrants in the UK has increased, leading to the death of a Polish man in the street of Harlow, Essex.[1] We emphasize here that the representations of ethnic others need to be taken seriously, as these representations can be used to stimulate hatred and violence.

In this chapter our focus is on how implicit heteronormative, white, middle-class assumptions about gender and sexuality guide perception in mobility and migration studies. Our objective is to challenge these assumptions from the perspective of queer mobility studies and to draw attention to the manifold lived experiences that mobile subjects embody. We draw on queer mobility, diaspora and critical disability studies as a way of bringing attention to how hegemonic norms about sexuality, love and family direct inquiry and may prevent from recognizing the diversity of lived experience of people on the move. As Luibhéid (2008) argues, migration studies have implicitly built on the idea that all migrants are heterosexual or on their way of becoming so. This is not so much an argument to recognize that there are migrants who do not identify as heterosexual, but rather a criticism of how implicit assumptions operate within theoretical models of migration.

Throughout this book the underlying theme is to look for and recognize the discrepancies between theory, practice and multitude of lived experience. Queering migration studies means paying attention to how the power/knowledge regimes that are configured according to the binary logic of normal–deviant, able-bodied–disabled, heterosexual–queer, Western–liberal and other–primitive contribute to how individuals are differentially situated in the society. The practice of critical thinking that we embrace here has to do with the queering migrations studies that begins with the assumptions of utilitarian model of migration, seeing people on the move as rational actors responding to the demands of the global economy and that reiterates hegemonic norms about motherhood, love and what is a sense of home in opposition to elsewhere.

Mai and King (2009) emphasize that it is about time that we account for people on the move, regardless of their migratory status or trajectory, as full human beings having desires, hopes and dreams. For example, migrant labour workers may be acting on their desires for sense of adventure in the faraway country (Ahmad 2009) or to escape abusive and hostile family situations and not experience the longing or nostalgia for the home country. Queer migration studies (Mai and King 2009, Manalansan IV 2006, Luibhéid 2008) emphasize that mobility itself is a process that deeply transforms the sense of identity, sexuality and the family of both migrants and the people left behind. They build on a poststructuralist theory of gender that emphasizes that identities, sexualities or any intersectional positionalities are never fixed or stable, but in continuous movement and becoming in relation with the others' mobile trajectories. In this way, the queer approach to mobility is a form of disorientation from the normative ontological and epistemological notions that guide inquiry (Ahmed 2006, Gopinath 2005, Halberstam 2012). The queer approach to mobility studies thus means paying attention to how the hegemonic norms, such as heteronormativity and homonormativity, are configured in individual experiences. It is necessary to recognize the implicit Western, white, middle-class notions that inform these analyses.

Queer mobility studies is therefore not only about recognizing what is specific about the mobility of individuals belonging to gender and sexual minorities, as we acknowledge that the binary opposition between heterosexuality and LGBTQI – lesbian, gay, bisexual, transgender, queer or questioning and intersex – is already embedded in regimes of power and knowledge. In other words, it is not only the sexual minorities and gender non-conformative persons who have to respond and negotiate heteronormativity in the society, but everyone has to do so. What is at stake is capability of being recognized as a subject in society that then enables one to claim individual rights and agency (Butler 1990).

Similarly, the opening narrative of the Polish plumber exemplifies how the combination of masculinity and sexuality was framed as a threat to the stability and purity of the host country. These men were framed as both stealing jobs from local men and seducing local women. In hindsight, it is easy to see the ridiculousness of these nationalist claims as neither of the fears did actually manifest in the French context. Moreover, the image of the Polish plumber became appropriated by Polish tourism industry to attract people to experience all that Poland can offer, including tall, blond and chiselled men. Queering migration studies means exactly this. Puar argues that it is an approach that "underscores contingency and complicity with dominant formations" (Puar 2005: 122). It is a practice of paying attention to change and contingency that emerges in relation to others as well as to dominant formations such as heteronormative scripts and structures that frame individual experiences.

In this chapter, we inquire about the unquestioned assumptions in migration and mobility studies through three distinct yet overlapping themes which are (1) motherhood, (2) sexuality and (3) home/homelessness. Our approach to these themes is in alignment with how Puar (2005) describes queer assemblage as a method in diaspora studies that recognizes the "spatial, temporal, and corporeal convergences, implosions, and rearrangements" of bodies and seeing "how affect in conjunction with representational economies, within which bodies . . . interpenetrate, swirl together, and transmit affects to each other" (Puar 2005: 122). Whereas Puar draws from affect theory to explore how individual sense of self is touched and formed in relation to others, we emphasize here queer feminist approach to gendered subjectivity in the context of mobility. This is demonstrated by different case studies throughout the chapter.

There are two underlying themes in this chapter in particular that inform our approach in the book more generally. One is to be attentive to how unquestioned assumptions and hegemonic norms (Sherry 2004, Luibhéid 2008,

Manalansan IV 2006) such as heteronormativity influence the way we formulate our research questions and limit our ability to recognize the fullness of life experience. Thus research based on hidden norms can perhaps unintentionally dismiss the subjectivity and capability of mobile subjects, when they are viewed, for example, as mere rational actors or statistics. Unquestioned assumptions about gender or sexuality may prevent us from developing a profound understanding of how mobile subjects make sense of their own lived experience in changing circumstances and how indeed, due to migratory trajectories, people, their gender and sexual identities and values do not stay the same. The second theme, in this as in the previous chapter, is to investigate the range of lived experiences that defy outside circumstances, creating new meaning and sense of self in the continuous unfolding of lived experience.

QUEER MIGRATION STUDIES

Mobility studies that are informed by and build on queer theory have looked at how gender and sexualities come to matter and are reconfigured through the experience of mobility. In other words, queer theory builds on poststructuralist and critical cultural theory traditions. *Queer* as a prefix refers to subversive and critical mode of inquiry, which builds on especially feminist poststructuralist theory on gender. Luibhéid (2008), for example, calls queer migration study an unruly scholarship that brings to light the unquestioned Western, capitalist, neoliberalist and heteronormative assumptions that are implicit in migration studies and opens space to recognize how sexuality is in fact central to how migration flows are managed and how migration policy is formed. This will be discussed further in following chapters. In this chapter we emphasize the implicit norms in migration research and call for attention to how mobility allows desires and affection and a sense of connectedness to manifest in non-normative ways.

Poststructuralist feminist theorizing informs queer studies approach to gender and sexuality. Important here is Butler's theory of gender performativity, according to which gender identity is not a property of a person but a doing (Butler 1990). Therefore, gender is not a biological fact or a person that is fixed. Gender, according to Butler, emerges out of productive power/knowledge regimes, which Butler names as the heterosexual matrix. This refers to normative heterosexuality as the organizing principle of society, based on binary construction of gender. Butler draws on Foucault's theory of bio-power in developing her theory on gender as a performativity. Performativity does not mean performance in a way that everyone would be totally free to perform their gender and sexuality. Instead, performativity operates as a system of power/knowledge that produces individual subjectivity through the constitutions of hierarchic binaries between subject and other, normal and abnormal, sane and insane, and heterosexual and queer. These binaries act on bodies and are enacted into being. The boundary between subject and other, normal and abnormal is always historically specific and subject to change. Here it is important to note how the construction of queer liberal identity can also be constructed against the migrant others (Murray 2013), and it thus uses the similar logic of constructing subjectivity by being positioned against the category of the other (Puar 2002).

Critical disability studies converge with these commitments by emphasizing how the idea of the normal associated with the able-body is a historically specific construct, especially related to the demands of industrial revolution and the development of statistics as a mode of inquiry. We have already discussed the problematics of the use of statistics to explain migration in the introductory chapter. In the previous chapter, we argued, in line with critical disability theorists, that it is indeed the status as able-bodied that is a provisional, not a fixed, identity (Rohrer 2005, Shildrick 2012). Here, it is important to note how the arguments of disability have been used to exclude women, black and migrant populations from society. Disability is viewed negatively as something to overcome or as a term that is not applicable (Davis 2013). For example, women have been seen traditionally as disabled by their gender. Pregnancy and childbirth hinder women's capacity to work full time. Or they have been seen as too emotional or weak and thus not suitable for leadership positions. The counter-argument would be to prove that women are not in reality disabled by their gender but able to contribute to the workforce similar to men. Or the counter-argument for migrant populations would be that they are not disabled by their cultural background, as they can assimilate and adopt the values of the host country. Both queer and disability studies aim to challenge the implicit negative connotations of the other and recognize how these are the result of how hierarchic dualisms operate in culture and society.

Yet queer is more than just theory about gender and sexuality. Queer is a mode of inquiry, strategy and form of activism. The word *queer* has formerly referred in a derogatory sense to non-normative desires and sexual practices but also to non-normative identities such as homosexual, lesbian, bisexual, transgender and intersex. Currently these are referred to with the abbreviation LGBTQI. Former queer activism has been a form of appropriation, in which this offensive term was given new meaning and used as a source of empowerment, as the famous slogan "We're here, we're queer, get used to it" exemplified.[2]

Important contribution of queer studies has been the analysis of power/ knowledge regimes that contribute normative heterosexuality and normative homosexuality. These are named as heteronormativity and homonormativity and these concepts do not imply hetero-queer binary logic. Luibhéid (2008: 171) explains that the concept of heteronormativity "is valuable for its ability to articulate how normalizing regimes produce heterogeneous, marginalized subjects and positionalities in relations to a valorized standard of reproductive sexuality between biologically born male-female couples who belong to the dominant racial-ethnic group and the middle class." Halberstam (2012) emphasizes that heteronormativity is also produced culturally through the normative scripts of heterosexual love, namely the idea of dating leading to marriage, settling down and having children and living happily ever after (see, e.g., Halberstam 2012). The concept of heteronormativity, however, enables us to see how the conceptualization of what is according to the norm, and what is deviant from it, is deeply embedded in society and culture in complex ways. Heteronormativity in the society becomes apparent in the way in which individual rights are organized, which we will return to in chapter 5. In this chapter we emphasize how heteronormativity is apparent in cultural scripts of gender and sexuality that are negotiated and differentially expressed by people on the move.

Homonormativity, on the other hand, refers to the representational ideals of the homosexuals. This normative homosexuality is characterized by middle-class consumer subjectivity, a sense of fashion style and trendiness, liberalist values and individualism. TV shows that aired in early 2000s such as *Queer Eye for the Straight Guy* and the character of Stanford in *Sex and the City* as Carrie's homosexual friend have since been characterized as the epitomes of homonormativity, as they represent the correct, acceptable homosexuality and neoliberalist ideals of success and consumer subjectivity (see also Gopinath 2005, White 2013). This representation of gays as financially well off and happy is in stark contrast to former representations in which homosexuals were presented in films as lonely, depressed and suicidal (Karkulehto 2011). Yet queer migration studies takes this idea a step further by highlighting the kinds of experiences and positions that have been rendered invisible and unspeakable in both migration and queer studies and emphasizes the relevance of recognizing how migration constructs sexual identities (Luibhéid 2008). More importantly, it shows how the binary opposition between normal and deviant is operationalized in these positionalities.

The goal of queer migration, diaspora and disability studies is to ask how individual people live up to these norms, negotiate or transform them. How is the heteronormative and homonormative white middle-class able-bodied gender order challenged and re-created through a variety of lived expressions and embodiments? Queer as a methodology can be summarized as an approach that highlights contradictions, paradoxes, openings and fractures in representations of gender and sexuality. Queer methodology highlights mechanisms, strategies and systems, which create and enable hierarchical relations between centres and margins, subjects and others, normal and deviant, and us and them. Academic scholarship is not outside these regimes of knowledge and power.

Before proceeding to our main themes of this chapter, we emphasize that queer approach is ontologically post-structural. In practice this means that while the focus of inquiry has been on how normative heterosexuality or homosexuality frame and limit experiences, there is still an inherent optimism and sensitivity to the continuous change and transformations. Indeed, dominant formations are recognized as ontologically contingent, historically specific and subject to change. It is integral to queer studies to be on the look-out for transformations in gender orders. It is also for this reason why studying global mobilities from the queer perspective is also useful for migration scholarship more generally.

The rest of this chapter is organized under three different yet overlapping themes, which are *motherhood, sexuality* and *sense of home/homelessness*. These themes are used as prisms that enable us to discern the fluidity of identity, sexuality and the sense of belonging in the experiences of people on the move. These are chosen here for the purpose of highlighting how migration and mobility studies has framed these issues in normative ways and avoided non-normative expressions.

MOTHERHOOD

What does it mean to be a mother? Immediately, a range of images may come to mind: some stereotypical images from soap and detergent advertisements or more iconic ones such as the Madonna. Asking a question about motherhood already implies a set of values, about motherhood as such. What does it mean to be a good mother? What happens to children when their mother fails to be a caregiver? In the context of global mobility, the phenomenon named as transnational mothering immediately brings to light similar questions or assumptions about what the relationship between mother and child is supposed to be.

Transnational motherhood refers to set of circumstances in which women move to a country other than the one where their children live. Often this is analysed as women from less affluent countries travelling to work as domestic workers and nannies in more affluent countries. These women often are mothers themselves. This phenomenon is also referred to as the "care chain" or the "care drain" (Hochchild 2000). As discussed in the previous chapter, this refers to the global chain of care that is created when a woman moves to the house of employer to care for the employers' children, or to institutionalized sites of care (Yeates 2004), and leaves her own children in the care of others.

Transnational mothering has also been named as one of the most important "global injuries" of our time. This title perhaps refers more to the drain aspect of the care chain, highlighting the deprivation of the close proximity of the mother to her biological children. The labelling of transnational motherhood as a global injury is not done in order to induce guilt in the women who leave for work elsewhere, but instead to draw attention on the emotional costs to family members, especially children of female labour migrants in the care sector. Indeed, it is assumed that transnational mothering leads to an emotional (irreparable) injury. Why is this assumption made, what makes such a statement possible?

The mother-child relationship indeed is considered to be a special one. It is a sacred relationship almost. Mothers' love towards the child is seen as unconditional, as an essence of true love. A mother will love a child, even at times when the child is behaving badly or when the mother is angry with the child. We all long for this unconditional love and to be embraced in motherly love. Women who might not love their children in such a way risk being labelled as selfish or deviant. Motherhood is about self-sacrifice for the purpose of the well-being of one's own children. Motherhood refers to the care, nurturing and upbringing of children. It is associated with the kind of empathy and care upon which entire peace-movements can be created (Sylvester 1994, see also Ruddick 1996).

There is somehow something very universal and timeless about motherhood, so much so that it is relatively easy to get carried away with the heartbreaking image of the mother leaving her children behind. Thus, the seemingly neutral term can be seen as representing the ideals and values of what being a good mother is supposed to be and how the relationship between biological mothers and children is supposed to be formed. This image of loss indeed implies great suffering, and we can be easily captivated by it. But can transnational mothering be anything else?

Motherhood, maternal instincts and mothering are certainly contested terrain and central to feminist theorizing (see, e.g., Ruddick 1996, MacMahon 1995). The shared understanding in contemporary feminist theorizing is that motherhood is historically and socially constructed. One of the most basic, unquestioned assumptions about motherhood is the idea that mothers and children live in close proximity, in other words, in the same household. It is in this setting of physical closeness in which mothering can take place. In the case of transnational mothers, this physical proximity is obviously challenged. Can a woman still claim to be a mother, even if she lives abroad and leaves her children in the care of others, perhaps even for years at a time? Or can she still be a good mother and feel that she has succeeded in the ideals of mothering even from a distance? Does being a mother immediately mean that she has already failed?

In all cultures we have ideals of motherhood, which stem, for example, from religious imagery such as the Madonna figure, seen as a self-effacing mother (Hondagneu-Sotelo and Avila 2003, Guevarra 2006). Similarly, in all cultures we have the mythical figures of evil women, who seduce and take advantage of men and who neglect or harm their children for selfish ends. Variety of representations of Madonna and Whore figures still circulate in visual arts and literature as well as in popular culture.

Yet we can also find in secular scientific literature traces of the unquestioned assumptions that close proximity between mother and child is a necessary condition for successful motherhood. As Hondagneu-Sotelo and Avila (2003) discuss, since the 1990s there has emerged an abundance of literature in psychology that discusses the importance of the role of the mother in early development of the child. It is this close, consistent and loving relationship in early childhood that ensures the physical, emotional and psychological well-being of the child. Attachment theory emphasizes the relevance of a loving and attentive caregiver for the development of the child well-being without explicitly stating that this has to always be the biological parent to the child. However, it is the cultural construct of motherhood especially in the global North in which the idea of the primary caregiver is implicitly assumed to be the biological parent who gave birth to the child.

In the case of transnational mothering, women are still mothers, but not physically present in the lives of their children. In other words, even though they are no longer the primary caregivers to their own children, their role as a mother is not erased. In this case, they will not be able to care for the children according to the demands of religious ideals of self-sacrificing motherhood or according to secular scientific ideals of mother-child relationship. Still, they have to make sense of who they are as mothers and what being a mother means, in a context of changing cultural demands say from the Philippines or Mexico to the United States, Saudi Arabia or Europe as well as changing circumstances and phases of life. Children once left behind do not remain children forever, but instead become teenagers and adults. Even if the mothers and children are reunited after years of separation, it does not mean that the relationship is easy or necessarily nurturing. Indeed, Hondagneu-Sotelo and Avila (2003) explain in the context of domestic workers in Southern California who were able to bring their children to the United States that the move posed many challenges for the children who were in their teenage years. Even though they were reunited with their mothers, they had to face a completely new situation, new country, culture and society as well as new stepfathers or mother's boyfriends at the precarious time of their own adolescence.

Motherhood is also associated with emotional labour. Mothers are expected to be emotionally there for the children, comfort them and console them when they are hurt. Women are expected to be the ones who make sure that children eat right, do their homework and learn good manners. Even if women are working mothers, the emotional role or emotional labour of motherhood is hardly diminished. Mothers are expected to want to be with their children first and struggle internally if they have to place the children in the care of others, even if it would only be for the period of the working day. In turn, women who do not struggle with the contradicting demands of working life and motherhood may be seen as cold and selfish, perhaps even heartless.

Children are also seen as needing especially the care of the biological mother in order to grow up healthy and whole. The care of someone else is somehow second best. There is something special in the relationship between biological mother and child that cannot be replaced. In a way, the discourse on "care drain" emanating from feminist mobility studies also implicates and reinforces this ideal. This is apparent in the oft-quoted argument that the costs of transnational mothering are yet to be calculated. These are seen as emotional costs for the children left behind as well as costs for the society, implying that these children will be experiencing emotional trauma or that they are more likely to become social delinquents if their biological mothers are absent. Yet also included in the idea of costs are the emotional costs to the children cared by the migrant nannies, as they are not taken care of by their biological mothers either, even though, or especially because, they live in the same household.

It is perhaps for these reasons that paid domestic work abroad is often framed as the hard choice women are forced to make. Women do it because they have to, because they are hard-pressed by the outside conditions, economic insecurity and lack of work opportunities that would enable them to stay and care for their own children. The motivation to travel for domestic work elsewhere is seen therefore as stemming from economic necessity, from hardship. This maintains the ideology of motherhood as a sacrifice, as a practice of self-effacement. She has had to sacrifice even the role of a good caring mother for the well-being of her children and the social recognition that comes from it. She has sacrificed the emotional reward that comes from caring for the children, and she continues to sacrifice her time, which most often is highly controlled in situations of live-in maids where boundaries between working hours and emotional ties are less than clear.

.The racialized and ethnicized underpinnings of motherhood are also highlighted through the example of domestic work. As we discussed in the previous chapter, care work globally is seen as the most racialized and gendered of occupations. It is in this line of work that women from lower-class backgrounds work for middle- and upper-class women and move to other countries to perform this work. Paid domestic work is also unregulated and often below minimum wage, especially in the case of live-in domestic workers even in high-income families (Hondagneu-Sotelo and Avila 2003, Mahdavi 2013, Pande 2013). Live-in domestic workers hardly can control the hours they are working or their contracts. Especially if they are undocumented migrants, their position is even more vulnerable, as we have seen in chapter 2. Still, the income that, for example, Latina women make in California goes far in their country of origin, and they are able to provide for their children's schooling and create better opportunities for their children to build their own lives (Hondagneu-Sotelo and Avila 2003). Does the financial reward compensate for the lack of proximity?

Transnational mothers who work in paid domestic labour in the global North need to negotiate their own sense of self, self-worth and dignity with regard to both an under-appreciated line of work and what it means to be a mother, when one leaves children behind for considerable stretches of time and works during this time caring for other people's children (see, e.g., Parreñas 2005a, b). Yet this does not necessarily entail that women feel guilty about leaving their children behind or would prefer having their own children with them in the host country (Moukarbel 2009). As already mentioned, bringing children to a different culture in which they are more likely experience a loss of social status than gain is something that the mothers consider before bringing their children along.

Yet it also has to be recognized that working hard and providing for the family from a distance may actually enable women to experience a new level of respect and appreciation from their family and local community. Being able to provide and send remittances gives a sense of self-worth as well as recognition in the local community back home. Transnational care arrangements can also change gender relations. For example, a Mexican woman employed in Canada through a seasonal work scheme explained this in relation to her sister who had stayed in Mexico: through remittances, "she becomes the woman and I become the man" (Preibisch and Encalada Grez 2013: 792).

Therefore, being a caring mother does not necessarily have to involve close proximity with the children. Motherhood can also be a way of caring from distance. Certainly, the fact that children can have more and better options to build their own lives than the biological mother could ever have can be emotionally rewarding for a mother. This does not mean that women need to take on the masculine role of the father as a provider. Can there be feminine ways of being the breadwinner and provider from a distance?

Keeping in touch and being part of everyday lives of children for migrant workers has changed considerably due to information technology. E-mail, video calls and text messaging allow migrant women to maintain contact with children and the rest of the family members more easily than ever before. Information technology can be thus seen creating new possibilities for communication, closeness and touch. Yet this also entails new challenges for family relations. Madianou (2012) explains how before e-mail, letters were sent home regularly in order to assure that "all is well." Letters took time to be written, time in the mail and time to respond to. In the contemporary context in which instant communication is possible through instant messaging, Skype calls and social media, both the joys and troubles of the children and of the mother are brought into awareness perhaps on daily basis.

With these new technologies, mothers can be in touch with children in order to be there for emotional support, albeit from a distance (Madianou and Miller 2011). Mothers can give motherly advice on pertinent issues as they arise as well as know how their children are doing in school or how they are feeling each day. It is possible to share a mealtime together via Skype and thus have a sense of family being together at least for the duration of the call. Yet video calls do not always make up for real physical contact with loved ones and can also create feelings of intense sadness and distance after the call ends. Or a mother can experience even more frustration if children are really in trouble or lose interest in schoolwork, as there is so little one can do from a distance to actively solve life's smaller or bigger problems. Children might not be too keen on continually updating their long-distance mother about their whereabouts, activities or feelings even though the new technologies allow it. Excessive texting and calling can also feel smothering to the child.

Hondagneu-Sotelo and Avila (2003) also speculate on whether the idea of collective motherhood in Latin American cultures is something that enables Latina women to leave their children behind and engage in care work elsewhere and not be as guilt ridden as their Western counterparts might be from such arrangements. In the context of collective motherhood, the close proximity of biological mother and child is not seen as necessary for the well-being of the children. The care of grandmother or aunt can satisfy the emotional, physical and psychological needs just as well as the biological mother could. Care for children does not have to mean immediate and intimate care either; in other words, remittances can be a form of loving care that contain a deep sense of guardianship for the children.

However, "being a mother" is also the "job" which live-in domestic workers are hired to do, although perhaps more indirectly. Live-in domestic workers can be in an ambivalent position with respect to their own limits and free time as they are both at work, but also part of the family (Moukarbel 2009). Indeed, as live-in nannies, they are expected to invest emotionally in the care of the small infants but not become too emotionally involved in order to prevent the children from attaching to the nanny more than their own mother. Live-in domestic workers are aware of this ambivalence and the impossible demands of both emotional closeness and distance at the same time. Hondagneu-Sotelo and Avila (2003) discuss how women make sense of the fact that both they and their employers have left their children in the care of others. In other words, the employer and the nanny are not that different after all. Then which one is the good mother, and who is the bad mother? Are they both good mothers or have they both failed? It is at this point that the idea of collective motherhood may even enable a moral superiority for the Latina domestic worker over Western white middle- and upper-class women. After all, the live-in nanny has left her children in the care of close family members. Paid caretakers would be an exception. Western white middle-class women, on the other hand, seemed selfish and self-interested and not having the inclination to give motherly care to their children even if they had the financial security to do so, without having to work, and lived in close proximity with the children. The Latina domestic workers were also often judgmental of their employers' self-absorbed lifestyles, such as obsession with workout regimes and beauty treatments, which was seen as time that would have been better invested in caring for the employer/biological mothers' own children.

It is in these cases that sometimes the relationship between employer and domestic worker can open to dialogue and perhaps change the practices of motherhood. Some nannies in Hondagneu-Sotelo and Avila's study explained how they took the initiative with their employers and advised them on childcare and the children's emotional needs. They tried to make their employers aware that children need and appreciate the closeness and time the mother/employer can give to her own children and that material affluence apparent in American upper-middle-class homes cannot compensate for intimacy, affection and love. In some cases, these conversations were fruitful and the employers were able to see how they could be more involved in their children's lives. The relationship between employer and domestic live-in nanny could turn into a rewarding relationship, which enabled emotional growth of the employer and perhaps recognition for the live-in nanny as a person in her own right.

Yet this was not always the case. The downside for domestic workers who performed their role as a caring mother too well could also trigger the intense feelings of jealousy and resentment in the biological mother. It may be hard to watch if a baby responds with joy and giggles to the care of the paid helper but hardly ever does so with the birth mother herself. Perhaps it is at that moment that the employer may begin to feel that it is her who has failed at being a good mother even though she lives in the same household as her children.

SEXUALITY

The narrative of transnational motherhood can also be read as a story of loneliness and loss of intimate relationships. Women leave their families behind and trade the loving relationships for long working hours and loss of privacy working as live-in maids. They can be seen as making the ultimate sacrifice for the well-being of others and destined to live lonely and isolated lives. But is this true? What if women (too) travel abroad for domestic work in order to experience a new country and culture, to have an adventure and sense of independence or perhaps to escape the confines of an abusive relationship?

It is important to note that the story of self-sacrifice and long working hours can also work well for the migrant women with family members and others who may question the women's motives. Moukarbel (2009) writes how this story enables them to hide motivations such as the ones listed earlier, which are indeed considered suspect if a woman is also a mother and wife. This narrative of self-sacrifice can also be a means of protecting oneself, especially if the spouse has been abusive. The story of loneliness and endless working hours is so widely accepted as truth about the migrant women's experience that it will stop any further questions. She will not have to answer to or explain any further about where she has been or with whom she was. The story of controlled life ensures the safety of the woman during her visits back home, and it allows one to keep the "affairs of the heart" a secret. As such, it may be told in order to protect one's privacy and honour. It is indeed the story of sacrifice that also protects the woman's freedom, her own life and her possibility of having sexual relationships in the host country.

In a way, one can see how the story of sacrifice and long working hours, loneliness and loss of privacy has a life of its own. It is a narrative that is reiterated by migrants and a lens through which migration is studied. As labour migrants work such long hours and leave their families behind for years, they may even be seen as needing less intimate relationships or sexual relationships than the people who do not migrate. Can a live-in domestic worker or a labour migrant have romantic and sexual desires, let alone affairs? And what if, as Moukarbel (2009) suggests, the new love affair is the reason for staying in the host country and not the financial gains from the work the women do?

Sexuality of the lone migrant population can be easily ignored because the prevailing idea is that people migrate in order to gain financial benefits for the family. The story of personal sacrifice for the well-being of the family is also used to explain male migration, but in a different way. As explained in the earlier section, women found meaning in being good mothers by providing for the family from a distance; for men being able to provide for the family can also be about being a responsible father and, most importantly, a self-sufficient and successful man in relation to other men. As such, leaving home is a rational and indeed responsible thing to do and takes place in the context of possibilities and constraints that the global political economy creates. Submitting to the demands of long working hours and precarious work abroad is seen as a choice that men make for their families and perhaps for their own selves as a way of asserting being independent and strong. Yet these migrating men are regarded as not having romantic sentiments, longing for long-term intimate relationships, missing their children or, at worst, even experiencing a full range of emotions.

Indeed, Ahmad (2009) argues that the conjunction of (Muslim) male migration and sexuality is seen as suspect or even dangerous. In political discourses male migrant sexuality is represented as a threat to the society of the host country. If migrants are more than lone asexual migrants, that is, migrating or reuniting families, there is the danger of high rates of immigrant reproduction, which would potentially alter the racial demography of local societies and neighbourhoods. According to Ahmad, the utilitarian model that sees migrants as rational individuals travelling for work opportunities produces them as a population who either are or should be ready to give up relationships and (sexual and romantic) desires for the opportunity of working in the host country. Thus, being able to migrate to the global North should be enough. Having relationships, sexuality and romance in the same way as people in the host country would already be pushing it. The negative caricatures of lone male migrants resonate with nationalist discourses that demand purity of the nation and the social body. These discourses have been used in the past to control intimate relationships and procreation of people with disabilities, gender non-conformative persons and others (Davis 2013).

Ahmad (2009: 310) writes in the context of British nation on the stereotypes of Muslim migrant men:

> [T]he increasingly dominant representation of Muslim men as political and economic threat to the security of the nation has precipitated new misconceptions. Islamicised masculinities are now homogenized and singled out with increasing frequency for demonisation through the perpetuation of a now familiar taxonomy of clichés and caricatured stereotypes: pathological "honor-killing" patriarchs; zealots prone to hatred of Western sexual decadence; fundamentalist religious sociopaths bent on murderous terrorism.

Ahmad argues that in the context of global economy and contradicting migration policies, Pakistani male migrants are constructed as disposable labour and not as full human beings. He draws on Butler's theorization of gender to analyse how lone male migrants are constituted as objects, without desires or even feelings. Ahmad (2009) writes how leaving Pakistan as a male labour migrant may mean giving up the possibility for intimate love relationships in the context of contemporary intensified neoliberalist globalization. Men work long hours in menial jobs. The desire for freedom and affluence that arises at the moment of seeing returning migrants may be hard to realize in contemporary world. This contrasts with the past, for example, the 1970s and 1980s, when migrant men were still able to bring their families to join them, create local supportive migrant communities and live a fulfilling and rewarding life in the host country. The times in the past when mosques were built by collective effort are remembered with fondness. However, the possibility of living a fulfilling and balanced life has been severely diminished. There is a loss of intimate love relationships as well as spirituality, when everyday life is filled with work. Yet Ahmad insists that it is still the uncertainty and possible risk which brings a sense of allure to mobility.

There can be a sense of uneasiness in addressing lone male migrants in these terms, as having both the desire to migrate and the desire for the risks and uncertainties involved. As such, lone (Muslim) male migrants, or anyone else, would have to be regarded as full human beings, who live in the moment and embrace life as it unfolds. Travelling to new places is a sensuous experience. And it can be so even if one is a lone male migrant. The men in Ahmad's study recollected memories of flirtation and sexual adventure in the midst of the precariousness of irregular migration from Pakistan to the West. In Ahmad's study, embarking on a risky travel was a way to assert one's masculinity and status. Certainly desire for such an adventure goes against the grain of the utilitarian model of migration, given, for example, that the level of income in Pakistan for some of the men in Ahmad's study was also relatively high in the home country.

The earlier description of lone male migrants asserting masculinity through risky travel is perhaps a less common way to exemplify the sensuous and erotic element of travel. Sensuousness of travel is usually associated with tourism and the sensations it brings, new places and new encounters. It is even possible to fall in love with a place one has travelled to, so much so that one does not want to leave. This experience of falling in love with the place often also involves falling in love with a person, and so it may be hard to discern which love relationship came first or inspires the tourist to stay (Toyota and Thang 2012).

Queering migration studies means questioning the racial and gendered binary oppositions that inform the distinction between tourists and labour migrants. Whereas migration study has neglected recognizing labour migrants as full human thinking-feeling beings, tourists from the global North can be seen possessing these qualities, often by exploiting the places they travel to and then returning refreshed and rejuvenated to their home countries. Queering the labour migrant/tourist binary means looking at how love and desire between people and the place inform people's choices and perhaps also in ways that are not beneficial to their well-being.

This entangled love of a place and a man has been the object of Frohlick's (2009) study, in which she explored the romantic relationships involving white Western women and black Caribbean men. These relationships turned out to be something utterly different than most literature on women's romance tourism would entail. She explains that, contrary to common perceptions of romance tourism, white (female) Western tourists do not always have the upper hand in commercial sexual (love) relationships. Nor does a Western passport automatically entail freedom to come and go, especially when one is in love.

Frohlick's (2009) study showed that falling in love with the place and with the man led some women into situations in which their mobility and emotional well-being was severely diminished. After an intense, all-consuming romance, the love relationship with the local man turned into a source of hurt, emotional and physical abuse. These white Western women chose to stay in the in the Caribbean even after the relationship had already gone sour and the black lover had turned into a moody guy disinterested in "investing" in the relationship. The reason for this, according to Frohlick's study, was that the women wanted to hold onto romantic scripts of love leading to marriage and loyalty to their partners, even though their partners did not share the same beliefs. The women found themselves in a situation in which they believed they were experiencing true love and devoted themselves to the relationship while their partner was already seeing other tourists and having sexual relationships with them. This example shows the impact of heteronormative grand narratives that informed these women's choices even though the reality did not match a romantic love story or even that of a healthy relationship.

Staying in the destination after the tourist visa had expired also meant that the white Western women were at the same level as the locals by trying to make a living in the precariousness of the tourist industry, often for minimum wage and with the uncertainty that comes with it. The women found themselves living in a situation in which they could only make enough money to pay the rent and food, also covering their boyfriends' expenses and knowing full well that it was hardly a rational thing to do or an empowered way to be.

For this reason, Frohlick argues that romance tourism is not only about freedom to explore one's sexuality or even being calculative in relationships with lower-class men in tourist destinations. In her study, the women talked about being obsessed with their black Caribbean partner and being guilty of "loving too much" – a term familiar from Western self-help books they read. They would stick to the relationships despite their partners' recurrent sexual affairs and even despite physical and emotional abuse. Love relationships in these circumstances turned into something other than a source or joy, intimacy and shared commitment.

What is at stake here in addressing the above examples of Pakistani men and white women is that that they highlight how perceptions about love, sexuality and desire induce mobility in non-normative ways. Mai and King (2009) argue that addressing migration in this way is difficult, for our common sense assumptions about love and sexuality reflect the heteronormative white middle-class ideals according to which romantic love is about a sense of freedom and also leisure (cf. Cabezas 2006). Romantic love is developed through dating and time spent together on romantic getaways, during dinners in fancy restaurants or having fun outdoors or in amusement parks. We see these scripts in romantic comedies and popular culture directed towards female audiences (Halberstam 2012). From this romance during leisure, the relationship is supposed to develop into serious commitment and raising a family together. It is important here to recognize how heteronormativity operates as a system of power that produces subjectivity. Having that long-term relationship means being recognized as a subject within a society that values long-term relationships as a sign of success and well-being. Conversely, failing in living up to these standards may induce of sense of shame and exclusion. In this way, sticking to an abusive relationship may have more to do with trying to live up to the norms of society than individual challenges to leave an abusive situation.

The examples of Pakistani men experiencing illicit travel as sensual adventure (Ahmad 2009), Sri Lankan maids finding their passion and love affairs in Lebanon (Moukarbel 2009) and the failed romances in the Caribbean (Frohlick 2009) show the ambivalence of norms and institutions in relation to the range of lived experiences and mobile trajectories. Moreover, these examples show how mobility itself changes and transforms sexual desires, identities and perhaps even gender relations. This is important because using the familiar utilitarian model and implicit heteronormative assumptions about love and sexuality in the context of mobility draws migrants as stick figures, devoid of feelings, or, at worst, as dangerous and dehumanized others.

Current queer migration studies, according to Luibhéid (2008), is also critical of emancipatory and assimilationist notions that inform the study of sexual migration. Sexual migration refers to the mobility of LGBTQI persons from conservative cultures to more tolerant societies, which enables a sense of freedom and the possibility of reinventing oneself (see box 3.1). The catchy phrase "out of the closet and out in the world" characterizes what sexual migration ideally is supposed to be and do. This phrase also represents the homonormative assumptions informed by Western neoliberalist culture. It is up to the individual to take a chance and move to another society in which there is space to live freely as a homosexual. Yet these assumptions withhold a valorized binary between the global North as liberal and progressive and the global South as backwards and repressed. Mobility to the global North means not only freedom but also assimilation into the culture and different set of challenges. Yet sexual freedom may come at a price of dealing with everyday racism implicit in the United States and Europe. Last, we turn to the concept of home that enables us to challenge common sense assumptions about mobility.

BOX 3.1

The case of Venezuelan *transformistas* in Europe can be used as an example of sexual migration. Vogel (2009) explains how the term *transformista* refers to a homosexual man *marico*, who travels to Europe, engages in sex work and, through a series of plastic surgeries, is able to transform into a beautiful and feminine *transformista*. This new status is about engaging in a lifestyle of freedom and luxury, but also a possibility of evaluating one's social status. A marginalized position as a homosexual man is literally left behind, as she lives her life in Europe and is also able to provide for her mother back home in Venezuela. This is something appreciated by the whole of society. Engaging in precarious yet lucrative transgender sex work in Europe is a means to an end in this process of transformation, which enables them to cover the costs of surgery and acquire luxury items and designer fashion that are integral to the identity as a *transformista*.

Discussion points: How does recognition of sexual migration challenge gender stereotypes reiterated in migration studies?

HOME

"Home is where the heart is" is a well-known phrase. It reminds us that you can feel at home anywhere you move, any place you decide to settle. Perhaps we associate being at home with being with loved ones, and thus material surroundings or a specific environment do not matter so much. It is indeed a feeling of the heart, how we find some places familiar and others unfamiliar, and indeed how we can transform unfamiliar places into familiar ones, so that they begin to feel like home.

Sara Ahmed (2006) discusses mobility as a form of orientation towards the world. Perhaps we become aware of our orientation at the moment when we are "disoriented" or when we are out of place. By focusing on the experiences of people on the move and reflecting on our own moments of mobility we can become aware of our perceptions and beliefs about what home is and what being at home means. Moving to a new country can feel both exciting and thrilling. There are numerous things to figure out once one has arrived: how to move around in a new city, where to buy groceries and perhaps how much effort one is willing to put into finding foodstuffs that resemble something like "back home" in order to prepare similar dishes. There is also the process of unpacking and arranging furniture and thus making the new dwelling feel like home. Transforming a space into a home is a way of orienting to that specific space, Ahmed explains. Placing photographs of family members transforms an unfamiliar room into a familiar one; the moment when the family sits down for dinner creates a feeling of being at home in the new country or place.

Home is also seen as the place for relaxing and self-actualization (Wise 2000). It is at home that one can really be truly oneself and unwind out of the view from outsiders. It is a space that is shared with loved ones, with people who are family members and the family obligations that follow. Feeling at home thus relates to physical space, the objects and people in it, as well as the sense of time and feeling of being safe in one's own world and distanced from the rest of the world.

In migration and mobility studies, the concept of home, sense and being at home are objects of study (Waitt and Gorman-Murray 2011a, b, King and Christou 2011). How do people on the move experience and conceptualize what and where home is? Important in this research is letting go of an idea that home and elsewhere would follow a linear logic. Perhaps the country of origin never quite feels like home upon return. Reverse culture shock may feel even more shocking than the original one as a person recognizes how once familiar customs and practices feel strange, unfamiliar or ill-fitting. Mobility can transform the orientation towards space also more fundamentally; that is, being on the move may feel more akin to being at home, and staying put may feel strange and uncomfortable, as we will discuss further later. In such a situation, mobility would be where the heart is, not the destination where one is settled in or the place left behind.

The trouble in understanding home and family in migration and mobility studies has been its underlying heteronormative nuclear family and middle-class connotations (Waitt and Gorman-Murray 2011a, b). This has also real consequences for migrants, as discussed in chapters 2 and 5. The heteronormative middle-class ideals about home and family also imply that home and family involves people who care and support each other. Indeed, the example of home being the moment in time when a family sits down for dinner implies that it is in the place called home that an ideal loving family lives.

However, homes are not always about safety and support. Homes are also places of abuse, intimate violence and emotional neglect (McKey 2005). And yet, the story of the happy family may also be reiterated similarly to the narrative of self-sacrifice or loneliness, perhaps not to protect one's honour but to protect from the shame that the disclosure of violence and neglect in the sphere of the home could entail.

Queer migration studies (Carrillo 2004, Manalansan IV 2006, Ascencio and Acosta 2009) challenge the idea of home as source of well-being and self-actualization by describing how it is indeed the hostility towards homosexuality that motivates gay men to move towards more tolerant cities and countries. As defined in the above section, sexual migration usually refers to migration from countries in which homosexuality is marginalized and life-threatening towards more tolerant countries. Sense of home in the context of sexual migration refers to a future point in time and space in which one will find the freedom and support of an openly gay community. However, moving to the global North in order to gain sexual freedom may not result in freedom and self-actualization in all the ways one has been hoping for (Collins 2009, Mirhady 2011). Moving to a more tolerant community is more a form of a bargain in which sexual freedom is gained at the price of racial oppression and financial freedom, which is especially evident in the case of Mexican migrants to the United States. As such, mobility enables an alteration in life situation and self-expression rather than utter freedom for self-expression and self-actualization.

Yet also the idea of home as a space to be escaped and overcome, or place of nurture and nostalgia, ties the notion of home to a specific place and time. Home is something that is left behind or created in a new way in the new place. This places home as a specific point on a grid in space and time. But what if mobility itself creates the sense of being at home (in the world)? What if being at home is not about finding and creating a home in specific place, but about being part of the world with the acknowledgement that it is always changing?

Studying the experience of Nordic female police officers who engaged in international civilian crisis management (CCM) missions,[3] one of us (Penttinen 2012) found that engaging in international crisis management turned out to be a transformative experience for some of the police officers who had worked on several missions in different "hot spots" of the world. What mission experience transformed was the sense of home and belonging as part of a global neighbourhood. This meant that the police officers began to value the relationships with the local people as being as meaningful as their own neighbours and family friends in the country of origin. Civilian security experts live in rental houses in the local area instead of military compounds, which allows them to get to know neighbours if one is moved to do so. Especially for the female officers, making and maintaining these contacts was imperative, and they wanted to differentiate themselves from the often racist and sexist attitudes of their international male colleagues. As one of the police officers stated: "They say we are so different (Nordics in relation to Africans), but the way I see it is that we are so much the same" (quoted in Penttinen 2012). Everyone wants to live in peace and experience well-being. And no one who is held at gun point really wants to die.

Home was not, in the case of female police officers on international missions, a place of refuge from the outside world, but indeed the outside world itself was experienced as home with all the uncertainty and change that comes with it. Being at home emerged from the real and authentic connections with other people based on a sense of shared humanity. The female police officers shared the motivation to "do everything that I can while I am there," which emerged as a way of being present and open to recognize what situation demanded for and people in question needed in each specific case.

The experience of the police officers in finding a sense of belonging as part of a global neighbourhood in which the concerns of the distant others are as relevant as one's own family resonates with how anthropologist Shahram Khosravi (2010) writes about ethics of homelessness, which we will return to in the concluding chapter. Yet Khosravi's conceptualization of homelessness also resonates with the concerns of queer migration studies by destabilizing binary oppositions between home and elsewhere and by directing attention to see how mobility can enable connectedness and communication.

Khosravi argues that only when we let go of the concept of home as a place that is ours can we move beyond the hierarchic binary between self and other, friend and stranger. As long as we conceptualize home as a place where we can invite someone in or make a stranger feel welcome, we will always reinforce the ontology of separation and difference that denies any real possibility of authentic communication and connection. The ethics of homelessness enables us to overcome this ontological separation. Khosravi summarizes the ethics of homelessness as follows: "Homelessness as a paradigm, as a way of being in the world, as a lifestyle, as ethical and aesthetic normativity opens the door to accepting the other as she *is*, not as how we want her to be. Only when *home* has vanished and humanity is no longer territorialized, only then, there will be a chance for humanity" (Khosravi 2010: 95–96).

CONCLUDING WORDS

In this chapter, we have drawn attention to how implicit heteronormative white middle-class notions of motherhood, sexuality and home prevent us from seeing the fullness of life experiences of people on the move in mainstream migration and mobility studies. Queer migration studies maintain that there is unpredictability and transformative potentiality in the diversity of lived experience, which also defies the limitations of heteronormative and homonormative ideals.

The basic message that this chapter conveys is that it is relevant in the context of migration studies to see how migrants are like everyone else, thinking-feeling human beings with individual aspirations upon which they make subjective decisions. In this way queer studies can be helpful as practice in questioning the unquestioned assumptions and norms that guide academic inquiry. As Mai and King (2009: 296) express: "It needs to be recognized beyond their common function as mobile workers within the global capitalist economy, and beyond their victimhood fate as refugees fleeing war and persecution, migrants and other 'people on the move' are sexual beings expressing, wanting to express, or denied the means to express, their sexual identities."

Love relationships and ideas of love and sexuality may very well be the reasons and motivations for movement and return alongside economic interests or political structures. Ahmad (2009: 311) emphasizes that "love, sexuality and romance lie at the heart of migration processes, even where it is largely absent in discourse itself."

The unquestioned assumptions or hegemonic norms lead us into making value-laden statements about the lives of others in the context of global mobilities. Perhaps the idea that mothers should live in close proximity with children leads us to see transnational motherhood as always emotionally draining for the mothers and necessarily harmful for the children left behind. Or we see lone male migrants as asexual and not having emotions or a need for close relationships as they work hard and long hours for the well-being of a family, as any respectable man or father should do. Or we see sexual migrants as overcoming the obstacles imposed on them in their home country by moving to the liberal and tolerant Western societies and by embodying and enacting homonormative values of individualism and success.

In this regard, Ahmad (2009) writes how these conclusions are understandable as most migration studies make these assumptions in a way "backwards." Because labour migrants work long hours of, for example, sixteen-hour working days in hard conditions, they are seen as asexual and not longing for or needing relationships as do people who have steady jobs and families – people who stay put. This in a way proves that labour migrants are rational actors travelling for work in order to secure financial well-being for the family and that they do not have the same sexuality and desires as the rest of "us."

Yet we argue that drawing attention to implicit heteronormativity and homonormativity is also an ethical question. Seeing how people on the move are full subjects with hopes, desires and dreams, and who actively make sense of themselves and the world, calls for responsibility in the representation of people studied, as well as awareness of the privileges in the academic study of global mobilities. Distancing migrants as somehow different (solely economically rational actors, devoid of feelings and desires) maintains an illusion of difference between "us" and "them." It is crucial to recognize diversity, plurality and change without the hierarchic framework that associates difference with deviance, abnormality or as disability.

I was entering Algeria together with a North African friend, not an Algerian national. My passage was very smooth: the border officer briefly looked at the personal identity page of my passport. Then he peeked into the visa page. I was allowed to enter. I stopped after the control booth to wait for my new friend, acquainted during the flight we had just exited. She was stopped for a much longer time, during which she had been asked several questions, including her relation to me as a European woman. She had replied saying that we were not actually travelling together but had met during the flight and realized that both of us were going to the same hotel, so we had decided to share a taxi to get there. The officer had grinned at her, not convinced, and asked again what would probably be her reason for entering Algeria. She had kept her calm, replied gently that she was attending an academic event. Eventually, she was allowed to enter the country. When she joined me she was shaking. – "Just go," she said. "I cannot believe I had to bear those questions." This story is one illustration of the mundane uneven practices gendered subjects may encounter at the border control, even if both possess a valid passport and a visa that has been accorded for the same purpose. Reading my white European habitus together with the passport issued from a Nordic country, the border guard allowed me to enter with a warm welcome and wished a pleasurable stay. For my friend with equivalent Arab habitus, my presence turned into a problem and a potential reason for suspecting her for loose mores, even prostitution, just by being together with me.

(Anitta's research diary, May 2009)

This extract, written on a trip for academic conferencing purposes, seeks to illustrate how, even when occupying similar professional positionalities, we are always embedded in the same structures we seek to unpack and analyse. It is easy to see how labour migrants and refugees are pushed and pulled by outside forces and not to recognize how the academic scholars themselves are also on the move entangled in the same currents, travelling the world doing fieldwork, attending conferences and perhaps experiencing adventure and sensuous travel while doing so. In the following chapter we take a closer look at the migration and mobility from the perspective of feminist analysis of global political economy. We will continue the discussion on the operation of hierarchic dualisms and binary oppositions in determining what is valuable in the context of labour migration.

DISCUSSION POINTS

1. Discuss in class how heteronormative scripts are narrated in popular culture, for example, in the storylines of romantic comedies. How are gender, race, class, ethnicity and able-bodiedness configured in popular culture?
2. Discuss how homonormativity is configured in the media. How are gender, race, class, ethnicity and able-bodiedness configured in the representations of gays in popular culture?
3. Discuss the relevance of media representation of migrant sexualities. Is there space for representation of migrant populations as full human beings in storylines?

ESSAY QUESTIONS

1. What are the implications of queer migration studies for understanding global mobility in contemporary times?
2. How would you apply queer and critical disability studies approach in studying migration and mobility?
3. How are the concepts of heteronormativity and homonormativity useful in studying global migration?
4. Explain how the notion of home can be problematized.

STUDY ASSIGNMENT

How are gender norms and normative notions of gender configured in our everyday spaces? Use the concept of heteronormativity as a lens to observe the physical environment in your daily life. Where can you find it? How is it present? If possible, document the presence of heteronormativity with digital camera. Create a collage either digitally or with printed images on cardboard. Create the collage intuitively, and let the process itself guide you. You can fill the collage with colours, texts, prints and glitter glue to make it an art work. Take time to view all the ready collages. How do the collages enable us to view the configuration of heteronormativity in critical ways? How does combining and collaging images of heteronormativity generate new insight into the concept?

This assignment can be done as a small-group project in a classroom.

EXTRA MATERIALS

TV show *Devious Maids*, starring Ana Ortiz, Dania Ramirez, Roselyn Sanchez. This show features the tensions between employers and four Latina household maids in upper-middle-class American homes. In this show the family life is seen from the perspective of the maids who serve their employers and whom the employers often depend on. The maids form a peer community and discuss their life challenges and strategies with their employers as well as seek to solve the murder of their friend.

Discuss in class how the TV show *Devious Maids* challenges the norms of motherhood, sexuality and home and how does the show follow these norms.

Last Chance, by Paul Emile d'Entremont (2012). This award-winning documentary follows the path of five LGBT refugees to Canada, who flee homophobic violence in their home countries. The documentary presents their struggles to integrate into Canadian society. National Film Board of Canada. https://www.nfb.ca/film/last-chance/

Discuss the challenges for sexual migrants to integrate in the host society. What do they leave behind? What kinds of new prejudices may they experience?

NOTES

1. The *Guardian* reported that six teenage boys attacked an eastern European immigrant on the street when they heard him speaking in Polish. The man died during the brutal attack. "Six teenage boys arrested over death of a Polish man in Essex," *Guardian*, 30 August 2016, https://www.theguardian.com/uk-news/2016/aug/30/five-teenage-boys-arrested-after-man-dies-following-attack-in-essex (last accessed 27 October 2016).

2. The queer activism in the early 1990s, which originated in the United States with the movement Queer Nation, included taking over the heteronormative public spaces which gays were excluded from or not welcomed in, such as bars and clubs or even shopping malls, and clearing space for the possibility of showing affection in public. http://queernationny.org/history, accessed 14 October 2014. See also De Genova (2010) on the uses of this slogan in migration activism by people without a fixed migration status.

3. CCM is a practice of state building and stability in post-conflict situations. Similar to military peacekeeping, civilian UN- and EU-led crisis management missions are organized by bringing international security experts on one- or two-year rotations. International civilian missions run for a number of years, but experts change. It is also common for security experts, such as police officers, border guards and civil servants, to rotate from one mission to another. Civilian and military crisis management has increased since 9/11, so much so that it is also referred to as peace-industry and security experts as peace expatriates (Penttinen 2015).

Chapter 4

Global political economy
and global mobility

"I have always been the kind of person who does not care what others think or what is considered the right thing to do. And I have always wanted to do things my way." Says Maria,[1] a return migrant, a wife and mother of three, in explaining her motivations in supporting her husband in taking a job abroad. This move would mean that she would have to take on a role of stay-at-home mom and take a break from her studies. Such a choice would indeed be something that goes against the norm in Finland where two working parents and university education are highly valued. In Finland children have subjective right to day-care, meaning that the community is obliged to organize a place in day-care at the time when parental leave ends, that is, at the time the child is ten months old. She continues to tell her story:

"At that time when the opportunity came to leave for France, I thought what a great experience it would be for the whole family. Of course, I knew it meant that I stay at home and do my part in taking care of the kids and the house. But it was an easy choice for me. At that point, I was still studying for a master's degree in languages, French and Swedish, but I already knew that I did not want to pursue a career in that field. I am more of a practical person, being a language teacher or an interpreter was not for me. And I had always known that if and when we have kids, I want to be there for them. So we decided to take the chance, to leave for France where he started work with a local contract. In France our life was filled with routines, boys to school in the morning, two-hour lunch break at home, back to school in the afternoon and then to the swimming practice. It would have been simply impossible for me to have had a job at the same. And just guess how many times my phone rang and the working parents in the neighbourhood would ask for my help with picking up their kids or look after them!

"There was one time, when we actually sat down together with my husband and calculated the monetary value of my contribution to this whole enterprise, which is our family. It was quite a considerable sum. If I had not been there, of course the kids would have had to be in day care when they were little. But it was more than that. If I had not been there, he could not have had the kind of job he has now at all, travelling so much and all the responsibilities. He would have had to have completely different kind of work, more regular kind of thing. He would not have been able to take the opportunity in France either. If I had not been there, we would not have been able to have the life we had.

"And I would not have had the time for myself, to really figure what it is that I want to do in life."

How would you measure the value of something that is immaterial, unseen and often invisible? Or something that does not have a clear beginning or ending, such as taking care of children, maintaining daily routines and creating a safe and loving environment for them to grow. Can the role of the mother in contributing to her son's success in junior swimming championships and helping out neighbours be calculated as having monetary value for the economy at large? Feminist economics and feminist political economy scholars examine exactly these kinds of questions. They aim to show how gender is configured in economic theory, policies and processes on a global scale. This entails discussing the implicit hierarchic dualisms between public and private, valuable and insignificant, and skilled and unskilled, as discussed in chapter 2 in relation to migration research. The purpose is to recognize how these assumptions inform what we see as relevant for national and global economy and how these concretize in the context of mobility.

In this chapter we focus on gender and global mobility from the perspective of feminist study of global political economy and feminist economics. As in the previous chapter, where we used the term *heteronormativity* as a means to explore unquestioned assumptions in migration theory, feminist economics questions the implicit gender norms and normative notions of gender that inform neoclassical economics. Moreover, it shows how these assumptions are configured, for example, in the gender-segregated labour market, thus framing the possibilities and opportunities that are available for differently gendered, able-bodied and racialized subjects. Last, feminist economics aims to show how possibilities of resistance to neoliberalist globalization of the world economy demonstrate how changes in the economy transform gender orders. In other words, in times of economic crisis the cultural norms and gender roles are also changing.

Our argument throughout this chapter on mobility in the context of global political economy is that it is imperative to recognize how gender is embedded in the ways in which what is considered of value and valuable in the world economy and how the conceptualization of value as that which is generated in public sphere produces gendered and racialized outcomes. In this chapter we expand the feminist criticism of categories used in migration research and policy-making in relation to feminist criticism of globalized world economy. It is here that feminist economics and feminist approach to global political economy enable us to broaden our perspective on global mobility. It takes on a broader level of analysis by analysing the power-knowledge regimes at the level of global economy. In practice, this means integrating the level of the intimate, private and often invisible to the analysis of global processes. The objective is to show how these are interlinked and also how these can be transformed.

These processes and power relations, which are at the heart of feminist economics, are also apparent in Maria's story in which gender orders were both re-created and contested. As the narrative shows, it is the invisible and unpaid work of the female spouse that enables the whole family to have the chance to live in France. Maria's role at home is just as important for the well-being and (financial) security of the family as the job that generates measurable income to support the whole family. For the husband it is a boost in his career. As for the children, they learn a new language and culture, which will be a resource for them for the rest of their lives. For her, it was also about a new experience and adventure. Her language skills were crucial in making this endeavour work for everyone and eased her husband's fears about living and working in a new environment (see box 4.1). It is Maria who encourages the whole family to move and believes it to be a great experience for the whole family. Although the main purpose of the move was Maria's husband's work, the noneconomic reasons were essential for Maria and her family to take the opportunity to relocate the whole family to another country. As we will discuss further later in this chapter, feminist economics shows how family relations matter in the choices and mobile trajectories people take. Similar to how mobility studies challenges the push and pull models of conceptualizing migration, feminist economics focuses on challenging the rational actor model that informs neoclassical economics.

This chapter is divided into two sections. In the first section we focus on feminist criticism of neoclassical economics and outline the implicit gendered assumptions that inform the conceptualization of formal and informal economies. In the second section we focus on how global mobility constitutes an economy of scale due to the value of remittances for economic growth and development and how globalized world economy produces gendered and ethnicized subjectivities. With these two sections we aim to give an overview of how feminist economics and political economy scholarship theorize how gender is embedded in globalized world economy and how this is reconfigured in global mobility.

BOX 4.1

The European Union (EU) is one economic area that has sought to construct a common labour market open to all citizens and long-term residents, with the same rights as the nationals. This is one reason why Maria didn't need to worry about the entry and stay requirements for her and the children when the family decided to move to France. These choices are not open on a global scale for everyone, but they are, instead, reserved for citizens within the EU, who are relatively free to decide where to settle. In addition to a privileged citizenship position and the right kind of passport, Maria's husband received an income that was enough to provide for the whole family so that Maria didn't need to look for paid employment, but she was able to devote herself to the well-being of the family, which made also their mobility possible.

Study assignment: Find out what kinds of possibilities there are currently available for highly skilled migrants from non-EU countries to bring their families with them. What are the possibilities for the spouse to study or look for work? How can they organize childcare or schooling for the children?

Find out differences between the EU countries with respect to social services available for labour migrants and their families.

FEMINISTS THEORIZE THE ECONOMY

In this section we will outline the implicit gendered assumptions within neoclassical economics in accordance with feminist economics (Bakker and Silvey 2008, Marchand and Runyan 2011, Peterson 2003). The main points of criticism include discerning how the concept of economic unit is inherently gendered, how public-private distinction informs what is considered valuable and productive in terms of economy at large and finally how participating in productive labour is considered a sign of progress within patriarchal societies and in the global South. In the previous chapter we introduced the concept of heteronormativity as a way to view implicit assumptions that inform migration and mobility studies. In the context of feminist economics and political economy, the concepts of gender order, gender norms and gender stereotypes are used in a similar way to highlight implicit gendered notions within seemingly gender-blind theories.

Homo economicus: Who is he?

The starting point for feminist criticism of neoclassical theory of economics is to focus on what is considered the singular unit of analysis, that is, the homo economicus, or in contemporary language, the rational actor. Feminist analysis emphasizes that it is necessary to recognize the history of this concept referring to a literally masculine subject, as with traditional migration research we discussed in chapter 2. The singular subject of the economics is assumed to be a male subject to whom women and children are dependents. In other words, traditionally it has referred to male head of household. The rational choices he makes in his self-interest are therefore choices that he also makes for his wife and children. In the contemporary global North, not all family formations follow this logic. Why is this relevant? It is relevant because it assumes necessarily masculine characteristics to the rational subject and defines what is recognized as valuable for the economy accordingly. In other words, rational actor theory presumes and reproduces gender norms and normative notions of gender.

Yet do people really make their own choices in a vacuum, based solely on calculated benefits for themselves? Feminists maintain that the ways in which people make choices concerning their economic well-being take place always in a web of relations. Moreover, people are influenced by those relations throughout their lives and not only in early childhood. Feminist theory maintains that the social relationships matter in the process of growing up into becoming an adult who makes his or her own choices. In other words, we all have family and friends who matter in the way we make choices. Furthermore, our choices are not necessarily always rational ones from a macroeconomic perspective, nor do they need to be.

Feminists point out how the rational actor theory presumes that people have grown up as soon as they are born[2] or that people do not change due to life experience. In other words, the rational actor theory does not recognize how family relations influence what decisions are made and which choices are available. Feminist economists indeed argue that it is naïve to think that people make choices based on solely their own individual interests regardless of the other people in their lives or regardless of the values they hold or experiences they have had.

As the opening narrative demonstrates, family relations matter in the process of making choices. The perspective of neoclassical economic theory, which places the economic man as a singular economic unit, would not have recognized the relevance of Maria's enthusiasm to take the opportunity to move and her language skills that were essential for her husband to feel safe about bringing the whole family to France. It was her rational choice to move, not his. More importantly, if it was not for her contribution at home, they would not have been able to move. In other words, if he had been a single head of household, they would have most likely stayed in Finland.

Feminist economists bring into the criticism of rational actor theory the fact that as people change, and the choices to be made depend on a person's life cycles, their values and priorities also do not stay the same. At its simplest, this means recognizing the fact that as children grow up into youth and adults who contribute to the society, the needs of a family change accordingly. Childrearing also is productive work for the economy at large in the long run, even though a caretaker's contribution would not have been calculated. Thus, the single economic unit of the household, or the rational actor, is a much more complex matter than neoclassical economic theory has assumed. It is exactly this complexity that feminist economics seeks to recognize and calculate its value for the economy at large.

The mainstream assumption as to what is the economy is that which has direct monetary value and which takes place in the public sphere of the market. Therefore, a distinction is made between productive work and reproductive work, the latter of which is considered as taking place in the private sphere of the home. Thus, next we turn to feminist criticism of public-private distinction and productive and reproductive labour.

Public-private distinction

The public-private distinction in the context of the economy refers most importantly to the way in which work and labour is defined and valued. Productive work is the work that takes place in the formal economy; it is the work done in factories, in the service industry, in retail. It is the kind of work that is calculated and recognized as contributing to the economic growth and circulation. The catch here is that the idea of productive labour is paired with its binary opposite, unpaid reproductive labour done within the private sphere.

We all know what reproductive labour is. It is the kind of work that never gets done. Reproductive work is the daily chores that need to be done over and over again. Once you have done the dishes in the morning, there will be more dishes to wash after lunchtime and dinner. The dishes will also have to be done the day after and the day after that. During the childrearing years, days are filled with the routine tasks of changing diapers, feeding and cleaning. The toys are scattered on the floor and need to be picked up time and again; the beds have to be made every morning. It is all the tasks that family life consists of. One does not need to be a gender specialist or feminist to recognize that this repetitive work is often seen as feminine or "woman's work."

Reproductive work is also something very personal. We all have had some relationship to a caregiver in our early years, and very often this person who took care of us was a woman. This is not to say that men do not do care work in the household but to recognize the fact that for the most part in our recent history care work has been done by women. This leads to also a kind of common sense assumption or intuitive feeling that care work is inherently feminine. In other words, men who engage in domestic and care work, such as male nurses, kindergarten teachers or nannies, may be seen as engaging in feminine work or even breaking gender stereotypes (Gittings 2016, Hussein, Ismail and Manthorpe 2016, Isaksen 2002, Näre 2010, Scrinzi 2010). This goes also for women who engage in masculine areas of work such as the military or business elites or in hard physical labour in car factories or paper mills.

The point here is to see that binary oppositions are always hierarchic and value-laden; masculine is the sphere that is prioritized and valued, whereas feminine sphere is less so—it is something soft and secondary. Women may seek to enter the masculine sphere for the prestige and perhaps look down upon those women who "remain" doing housework. There are numerous tensions here in different cultural contexts. In a postfeminist era, it may very well be seen that middle-class motherhood is esteemed as a way of exercising one's freedom. Or women in the Nordic countries who are expected to do it all, and thus handle work and family, may be disrespected if they buy cleaning services, especially if these services are provided by women who have migrated from less-affluent countries.

In other words, the masculine/productive labour is valued higher than feminine/reproductive labour, and the binary oppositions turn out not to be only discursive constructs or representational economies but have concrete consequences that are lived, reiterated and also transformed in the everyday lives. The question regarding reproductive labour is not only how it is culturally valued but that this cultural evaluation of work has direct monetary consequences; that is, work regarded as feminine is seen as less valuable or less important to the economy than productive/masculine work.

In this sense the project of feminist economics is indeed twofold. First, it aims to show how the operation of the public sphere, "the economy," depends on the reproductive (undervalued and underpaid) work that is done in the households. Second, the reproductive work is the kind of work that has direct monetary value, and this value can and should be measured. The work done in the households contributes to the economy in so far as it releases men/women into the workforce; hence, it is part of social production. There is someone who is taking care of the house and the children, while other members of the family contribute to the economic growth by the input of their labour outside the home. It is indeed because there are people (women) who take care of the work in the private sphere that the market economy can thrive. In the contemporary world where women are part of the labour force, the reproductive work still needs to get done. Either it is done on top of the workday, or it can be done by paid domestic workers. No matter who actually does it, it still needs to get done, and it is still mostly done by individuals gendered as women.

Participation in the formal economy as progress

In the previous sections we have outlined how the conceptualizations of reproductive and productive work build on gender order in which the masculine head of household is seen as the economic actor and female spouse and children as dependents. This serves as a theoretical model and does not imply to be a representation of reality. However, it does reveal the implicit valorization and prioritization of the public sphere over the private sphere (see box 4.1). In other words, working in the public sector is seen as more valuable than reproductive work in the household. Women's participation in the labour force is also seen as a sign of progress, as they also become active in the labour market and no longer remain as *passive* dependents.

Labour migration is therefore seen also from the point of view of the global North transformative force, which changes gender orders also in the sending country. De Haas and van Rooij (2010) argue that these ideas are reiterated in migration studies by using the concept of social remittances. This means that people migrating from patriarchal rural communities such as from Mexico or Morocco are touched and transformed by their experience of liberal societies in the global North. Upon their return, they bring back these values to their countries of origin, and these experiences will empower women to take part in the labour force. Otherwise, simply because men leave, women have to take on a more *active* role and engage in productive work, especially if the remittances begin to fade. This is a sign of progress and transformation of gender norms in traditional rural communities impacted by international migration.

However, what is crucial here is that these ideas of progress do not challenge the hierarchic, gendered and indeed racialized dualisms at work here. For example, can a woman who begins her day before others in the family wake up to prepare food, fetch water, collect firewood and take care of livestock and other duties be called passive or unproductive? Or, is the transformation of gender roles and gender norms in rural areas really the result of international migration to Western societies, or would it have happened anyway? De Haas and van Rooij (2010) emphasize that migration scholars have been too quick to associate transformation of gender norms in traditional societies with international migrations. Indeed, more than a representation of reality it reflects the practice of emphasizing countries in the global North as progressive and advanced, as opposed to the global South seen as backwards. On the basis of their research in Morocco, De Haas and van Rooij found that women especially in their midlife were not too pleased with being the head of household while their husbands were away (also Ennaji and Sadiqi 2008). For them, bearing all the responsibilities of one household, doing the housework alone and making all the financial decisions were not a sign of progress but a burden. They might have also encouraged their daughters to migrate on their own, or at least join their migrating husband, in order to not have to bear such a heavy workload. Therefore, the learning that takes place due to

---

BOX 4.2

Feminist economics and political economy scholarship have a long tradition in showing how macro-level processes in global market economy concretize at individual level, changing local communities and creating gender-specific opportunities and challenges. Their objective is to highlight the implicit gender assumptions within "common sense" assumptions behind neoliberalist globalization, economic growth and development. The focus of attention is on global governance, including international governmental organizations (IGOs) (Griffin 2010). However, there is also a sense of loneliness and isolation that can be read from the feminist scholarship on global political economy (Peterson 2003, Marchand and Runyan 2011). Marchand and Runyan (2011) discuss how the questions of economics and economic theory are often thought of as boring or even difficult to understand, as feminists have been more interested in cultural globalization. This attitude boils down to deep core beliefs that may have been acquired back in high school about math and statistics being difficult to understand or something that is for boys. Economics is a male-dominated sphere within the globalization scholarship, and thus it is hard to find a home or be taken seriously as a woman. Global political economy scholarship also operates at a level of abstract ideas and conceptualization of the global market without the level of the personal, which is central to feminist politics. It is understandable that feminist scholarship has gravitated towards softer and intimate aspects of globalization and thus ignored the "hard" stuff of the economy and global governance. This is problematic, for the operation of global political economy has a great, and often undesirable, impact on individual lives.

Discussion points: Is the presumption that natural sciences and math are difficult for girls to understand still alive in higher education? How does it manifest in practice? How has it changed?

international migration might not be the appropriation or absorption of values in the way narratives of progress might entail.

Global production for the purpose of the retail market is also seen as transforming gender roles in developing countries in which export processing zones are established. Indeed, global production does increase the possibilities for women to enter the workforce, but does this challenge or transform gender norms? Elias (2005) shows how the implicit assumption that men are heads of households concretizes in the kinds of jobs women are hired to do in the garment industry in Malaysia and Bangladesh and with what kinds of contracts. As long as women are seen as dependents of male family members, and not as the breadwinners of the household, women can be paid less for their work. After all, women's income is only additional income to the household and not the main one. Because of this ideology of patriarchal household arrangements, women may be regarded as only temporary workers as less permanent and less professional than men. Women will soon get married and leave their jobs in order to raise the family anyway. Therefore, even if women would be single heads of households or the only income-generating partner in the family unit and plan to work permanently, they can be discriminated against because of the implicit gender norms that inform hiring practices.

What is crucial here is, as Elias (2005) points out, that even though in practice women are treated as expandable labour and paid less, the very possibility of being able to engage in paid labour, no matter how meagre the pay is, is still seen as an equalizing move. In other words, it is difficult to demand for better working conditions or better pay if having a job in the garment industry under these conditions is already seen as a means for progress and move towards women's liberation from the binds of patriarchal societies and values.

GLOBAL MOBILITY: AN ECONOMY OF SCALE

Global mobility is an economy of scale. In this section we discuss how labour migration fares in the context of globalized world economy and how gender comes to matter in discourses that see the remittances as a sustainable means for the development of the sending country (Elson 2010, Kunz 2008). In this process, gender stereotypes come alive in the way in which the labour migrants are seen as the new export products and remittances as the "silver bullet" of development, which is more effective than development aid (Petrozziello 2011). The construction of labour migrants as export products depends on the images and imageries of gender, ethnicity and sexuality discussed in previous chapters, especially because remittances are private money generated by migrant workers, and the flow of remittances is dependent on individual interests in sending money. Moreover, gendered assumptions also inform the framing of productive and unproductive use of remittances, reiterating the hierarchic dualisms described earlier.

States, supranational entities, international and intergovernmental organizations, but also institutions such as recruitment agencies, play a role in mediating and regulating human mobility. In some countries, such as in the Philippines, there is a firmly established relation between the state and recruitment agencies (Guevarra 2006). Through this relation the exportation of migrant labour is channelled in ways that traverse educational institutions where migrant workers-to-be are formed, diplomatic missions abroad that market the exportable labour to receiving states and the host state structures where the migrant labour is to be accommodated. Remittances that migrants send to their countries of origin are central to these processes.

The World Bank has estimated that the value of remittances sent to low- and middle-income countries will be \$442 billion in 2016.[3] This marks a slow growth of 0.8 per cent since 2015, with the growth in remittances to Latin America and the Caribbean backed up by the growth in U.S. economy. However, remittances to developing areas declined after a time of steady growth until 2013. The main recipients of remittances, according to World Bank,[4] are India, Mexico, China, the Philippines, Nigeria and Egypt. Remittances are sent also to countries that the World Bank no longer considers as developing countries, such as Russia and Latvia. Yet the impact of remittances on the economic development of these countries is also considered significant. The numbers that World Bank presents are based on reported transactions of money, and therefore the real value of remittances can be estimated to be considerably higher, as there are many informal and unofficial forms of sending money back home. Moreover, activity in the informal and illicit economy contributes to remittances; these include remittances from unfree labour arrangements in global production and informal economy such as sex trafficking (Osezua 2011, LeBaron 2015). The scale of remittances can also be higher than gross domestic product, for example, in Central American countries and higher than development aid and foreign direct investment together (Petrozziello 2011: 54).

What is crucial here is that remittances keep flowing even in times of financial crisis, war or natural disasters. For example, Bach (2011) explains that during the years of financial crisis in 2008–2009, there was only a relative decline in remittances, and therefore remittances are still reiterated as the "New Development Mantra." Indeed, there is a lot of good that comes from remittances. They are seen as improving living standards, girls' literacy,[5] reducing poverty and increasing employment. Remittances contribute directly to the gross domestic product (GDP) and are used as investments in small businesses, improve infrastructure and increase consumption and services, contributing thus to economic and social development.

Even though individual migrants have to live and adjust to changing conditions, such as the economic crisis and its impact on job security and pay in the receiving countries, the sheer volume of remittances to developing countries balances out the individuals' challenges. Therefore remittances are considered *counter-cyclical* and a form of income that developing countries have come to depend on.

But do remittances lead to social development and empowerment of women in developing countries as World Bank leads us to believe? Bach argues that remittances are "a double-edged sword." Although it is clear that there are many benefits to recipient countries from the remittances (see, e.g., Taylor 1999), these can be also "used as an excuse to avoid investment in infrastructure, education, or social programmes thereby exacerbating rather than decreasing domestic inequalities" (Bach 2011: 133). Moreover, as Petrozziello (2011) argues, there is a difference between calculating productive and unproductive use of remittances. In other words, remittance that is used to start small businesses or used in the sphere of formal economy is seen as productive and contributing to the development of the country. Alternatively, remittance that is used for education and food is seen as unproductive, although it goes to the social development of the family.

Moreover, countries such as the Philippines pursue active policy in enabling and facilitating emigration and have designed special programs to educate nurses specifically for them to move elsewhere and, in turn, to send remittances for their families and thereby to fuel the national economy. Income from remittances is "a vital source of servicing debt and importing oil" and is the "second largest source of foreign currency earnings for developing countries behind FDI"[6] (Bach 2011: 132). Therefore, migrant workers can also be seen as the new "export" of developing countries tied to export lead growth in the context of neoliberalist global restructuring, in which these countries have been required to enter into free trade agreements under the Washington consensus. Emigration can be seen as serving the national interests of developing countries. Pajaron (2016) explains how Overseas Filipino Workers (OFWs) are called "new heroes," as they may be the sole providers of income for their families.

Gendered export products, such as the Filipina (female) nurse, according to Bach (2011), extend the nations' patriarchal policy outside its borders. Indeed, exporting women for the purpose of domestic and care work means that women are expected to do the reproductive work elsewhere and also act selflessly by sending remittances to the sending country to contribute to overall development. The work done elsewhere thus is based on gender stereotypes of self-sacrificing woman with the expectation that the women who migrate do not exceed the expectations based on them as women. Recently, along with reports on the various kinds of abusive situations exported labour may end up experiencing in the receiving countries, states such as Indonesia have also sought to limit their citizens from migrating to those countries that have not proven their ability to protect imported migrant labour (Elias 2013).

In the context of development policy female migrants are also seen as more altruistic and male migrants as more self-interested in the ways in which they remit and for what purposes (Pajaron 2016). This is true in so far as female migrants do remit money for the purpose of children's education and well-being, whereas male migrants invest in small businesses and start-ups in recipient countries. It is also evident that although female labour migrants make less money from their work, they send a greater share of their income in remittances and for wider group of recipients (Petrozziello 2011) than male migrants do, even if men tend to receive relatively better income.

However, the sectors that employ mostly women are relatively more stable in times of economic downturns, such as the "unskilled" work in the sphere of social reproduction and skilled work in the medical sector as nurses and doctors, than the male-dominated sectors such as construction work. Therefore, even though it seems counter-intuitive, undocumented (female) migrants might have relatively more continuity for their income than documented migrants might in the formal sectors. This factor challenges the gendered assumptions between productive and unproductive work and how these are seen to contribute to overall economic development is supposed but reveals also individualist logic of neoliberalist ideology and the built-in insecurity and uncertainty (see also Griffin 2010).

Migrant labour takes place in the contradictory context of demand for labour migrants for the purposes of global production, industry and care work and anti-immigration laws. At the same time as remittances are seen as the New Development Mantra that benefits the economic growth of the sending countries, it is necessary to pay attention how globalized world economy and global restructuring after 9/11 affects the migratory flows (see also Kunz 2008). Therefore, more important than the effect of cyclical downturns in the global market for the scale of remittances is the tightened control of migration and anti-immigration policies, which have especially reduced mobility from the global South to the global North, for example across the border between the United States and Mexico. Moreover, as often is the case, the impact of economic cycles to the poorest of the poor are easily forgotten (Bach 2011). Therefore, even though the scale of North-South of remittances have largely been unaffected by recent economic downturns, this has not been the case of South-South remittances and the alleviation of poverty through remittances from migrant labour in these regions is yet to be realized.

Gender stereotypes for profit

Feminist analysis of the global political economy emphasizes the need to analyse how globalized world economy also produces and reiterates gendered and racialized subjectivities. This means focusing on how formal and informal economies provide gender-specific forms of labour. It is no secret that the majority of female labour migrants travel the globe for the purposes of intimate labour in both formal and informal economies.[7] Intimate labour refers here to live-in domestic work, care work and sex work. Agathangelou (2004) groups these different forms of intimate labour as representing desire industries. In the rest of this chapter we will refer to the sex industry. Yet, what is relevant in Agathangelou's conceptualization that is telling of the way these industries operate is that perceptions and indeed desires about the other come to manifest in the relationship between the employer and the employed as well as service provider and client. These desires build on deeply embedded cultural beliefs and expectations of gender and ethnicity, which constitute gender norms and hierarchical gender order. Moreover, national policies that promote both care work and sex tourism as means of development and economic growth reiterate these stereotypes.

Penttinen (2008) has argued that globalization of the world economy operates as a system of power that produces gendered and ethnicized subjectivities. These positions become opportunities and indeed positions that are embodied and enacted into being by individuals whose gender, ethnic, cultural and racial background fits the gendered and ethnicized subjectivity in demand. In turn, the demand and desire for erotized and exoticized others concretize in the global flows of people in the intimate and pleasure industries. The global sex industry creates, maintains and makes a profit from gendered and ethnicized stereotypes, such as the "naturally feminine" Russian women who believe in traditional values, or "naturally subservient" Asian women who are ready to please a range of sexual kinks the clients wish to explore (Penttinen 2008).

This is relevant because the globalization of the world economy based on neoliberalist ideology and individualist logic erases the gendered and racialized power structures inherent in globalized world economy that channel what kinds of jobs and opportunities are available and for whom. Participating in the formal economy is seen as based on freedom and exercise of free choice, even though the opportunities available for individuals are far from equal and do not in any way reflect a levelled playing field in the way economic theory assumes.

The global sex industry is already an economy of scale and major factor also in global mobility. Sex business and commercial sexual services provide a means to make a living, which is especially available for women, in the context of economic challenges, such as economic restructuring (Truong 1990, Sassen 2000) and transition to market economies. Moreover, the normalization and mainstreaming of commercial sex into consumer culture implicitly reinforces gendered and racialized stereotypes. In other words, even though commercial sex is normalized into consumer culture, this has not resulted in a trend that men and women in the global North embrace sex work as the optimal way to make a living or a legitimate career option. Indeed, intimate and pleasure industries depend upon the exotic erotic others as service providers.

As one of us has argued (Penttinen 2008), global sex industry can be conceptualized as a form of corporeal globalization in which the effects of transition to market economies and post-9/11 restructuring (Penttinen 2015) are lived, embodied and enacted on gendered and ethnicized bodies. In other words, certain gendered and ethnicized bodies are seen as more suitable for intimate labour and sex industry than others. In turn, the position of the client of the pleasure industry is also a gendered and ethnicized position, most often occupied by a male-bodied individual from the global North.

In the context of globalization of the world economy based on neoliberalist ideology, both of these gendered and ethnicized subject positions of the sex worker and client can be seen as reflecting individual choice and freedom. Bringing sex industry as part of neoliberalist consumer culture in practice produces such normalization. In other words, taking part in the sex industry may therefore be seen as an optimal choice for someone who is gendered as a woman and from Russia; after all, there is a specific demand in global sex industry for the "Eastern girls" to be embodied and enacted into being. Taking a job in this intimate labour of the sex industry could even be seen as a rational choice and representing entrepreneurial spirit. This would also imply the normalization of gender and ethnicity in taking the risks that intimate labour necessarily involves for the service provider. Thus, this reveals the gendered and racialized biases in neoliberalist ideology, according to which specific bodies are more suitable for providing sexual services (care and domestic work) than others and bearing the risks involved. More importantly, the value of the sex sector needs to be calculated for the economy at large in order to recognize the real economic value.

The sex industry comprises licit forms of sex business such as pornography, sex shops and sexualized work such as hostesses and striptease performers and illicit forms of sex business such as selling commercial sexual services (in countries and states where it is prohibited), forced prostitution and trafficking in women, girls and boys for the purposes of sexual exploitation. The licit and illicit spheres are inextricably linked, and therefore the value of sex work in them should not be calculated separately. This means that erotic bars, which operate legally, offer a space in which sex workers can solicit customers. The porn industry also includes both licit and illicit forms of production, including also unfree labour arrangements and child porn. Often the organizers of both prostitution and porn operate in both licit and illicit activities. The sex industry also generates tourism and travel. In other words, formal businesses such as airlines, hotels, taxi companies, print media and online media benefit indirectly from both licit and illicit sex sectors.

What feminist economists want to bring awareness to is the ways in which risk and vulnerability is divided across gender, race and class hierarchies. Therefore, the objective is to recognize how the distribution of profits and risks are gendered in both desire and sex industries. In other words, sex bar owners, porn production, pimps, taxi drivers, hotel owners or customers bear fewer risks for their involvement in the sex trade than the women, girls or adolescent boys who provide sexual services. The abusive practices in the sex sector are discussed further in chapter 6. However, gendered risk goes for other forms of intimate labour as well such as live-in domestic work, where maids and nannies may have to face sexual harassment or abuse and be expected to provide flexibility and emotional investment for little financial remuneration.

In this way, the feminist economics is not something farfetched and difficult to understand. Feminist economics is grounded in an inquiry of very mundane everyday practices of the economy and trying to highlight the value of informal economy for the formal productive economy. The goal in feminist global political economy scholarship is to emphasize the gender-specific outcomes of globalization of production, neoliberalist market economy and consumer culture. The common sense assumptions of what we consider the formal economy to be and what kinds of work are considered valued and valuable concretize in gender-specific ways on what kinds of opportunities are available and for whom.

CONCLUDING WORDS

Feminist global political economy scholarship involves a practice of rewriting globalized world economy in such a way that it captures the gendered and racialized assumptions that are configured in how we understand what economy is. For example, Eisenstein (2004, 2007) names global economy as "capitalist racist patriarchy." Chang and Ling (2011: 31) use the term *techno-muscular capitalism* (TMC), referring to how "global restructuring valorises all those norms and practices associated with Western capitalist masculinity," which are universalized as global and which in turn create a "regime of labour intimacy" (RLI) as its binary opposite. RLI refers to the unpaid and underpaid work, usually done by women, which is seen not simply as response or side effect of global capitalism, but as its inherent constituent. Peterson (2003) theorizes, or rather "rewrites," the global political economy by creating a framework of three different and overlapping economies – the reproductive,

productive and virtual (RPV) – and investigates how they constitute the contemporary global financial market capitalism.

Gender comes to matter in the feminist analysis of globalization by highlighting how the processes of globalized world economy produce and reiterate hierarchic gender systems, creating also gender-specific effects, as in outcomes, consequences and opportunities, which differ along gender lines. In this chapter we have outlined how feminist economics and global political economy scholarship highlights the embedded gendered processes of globalized world economy and how gender is represented, produced and visualized in global politics (see, e.g., Marchand and Runyan 2011, Peterson 2003, Eisenstein 2007). Crucial to feminist economics and global political economy scholarship has been to recognize how the world economy operates as a system of power that produces gendered subjectivities, and how these are embodied, lived and resisted at individual and societal levels (see, e.g., Chang and Ling 2011, Penttinen 2008).

What is imperative for feminist economics is to imagine and create new economic frameworks, which would enable more people to thrive and increase general well-being by increasing possibilities for income and also better income for low wage and intimate and underpaid work. It is central in this line of scholarship to recognize feminist activism across the globe and actively inquire about alternative, more sustainable ways of imagining social systems and economy. Therefore, it is important to recognize how feminist theorizing of the global economy and global restructuring is not only about feeling powerless in the face of globalization as a force from above (Marchand and Runyan 2011). Instead feminist economics is a practice of paying attention to the ways in which people carve out their lives or navigate the waters of neoliberalist global restructuring, not only by responding or reacting to it but by actively creating new ways social organizing (Mohanty 2003, Piper 2015).

Therefore, feminist economists and global political economy scholars request that feminists who are interested in other aspects and practices of globalization join in and investigate the relevance of the economy in the way society and culture are organized. Globalization produces gendered effects because the underlying ideology is inherently gendered. What feminist global political economy scholarship seeks to accomplish is to go from the level of globalized world economy to the embodiment of gendered subjectivity and back, in order to develop deep understanding of how gender is embedded in the economies of scale. Sometimes the things that generate the greatest value in the economy are those things that go uncalculated and/or are undervalued and that is the everyday care without which the daily life even of business executives or political elites would not be able to function.

DISCUSSION POINTS

1. How would you theorize from feminist perspective the gendered consequences of economic crisis of the financial market? What is the gendered impact of outsourcing and offshoring of production?
2. What kinds of career opportunities are currently available in your area? Would you be interested in moving abroad for work? What factors do you have to take into consideration before applying for a job abroad? How are your family and close relationships influenced by your choices?
3. How would you calculate the value of unpaid care work?
4. Why some states export labour? What kinds of gendered consequences this practice may have?

ESSAY QUESTIONS

1. How is the public-private distinction relevant in understanding contemporary labour market?
2. How does the global sex industry capitalize on sexist and racist gender stereotypes?
3. How do feminist perspectives enable us to challenge and resist existing power relations of the globalized world economy?
4. Explain and analyse the concept of global care chains.

EXTRA MATERIALS

The Hundred Foot Journey by Lasse Halltsröm, starring Helen Mirren, Om Puri and Manisha Dayal. The film portrays the journey of migrant family from India settling in the south of France and starting an Indian restaurant. The story follows the lead character's pursuit for recognition as a top chef in France while remaining true to his mother's recipes and knowledge of spices. http://www.imdb.com/title/tt2980648/.

Discuss the representation of gender roles in the film and how these challenge gender norms and reiterate them?

UPROOTED: Refugees in the Global Economy (2001) produced by National Network for Immigrant and Refugee Rights, with Sasha Khokha, Ulla Nilsen, Jon Fromer and Francisco Herrera. This documentary shows how the global economy has forced people to leave their home countries. It presents three stories of migrants from Bolivia, Haiti and the Philippines who had to leave due to devastating economic restructuring and the challenges they face in the United States.

How is the distinction between voluntary and forced migration complicated by taking into account the perspective of global political economy?

NOTES

1. Narrative is based on personal communication with a female spouse of the returning migrant family. Maria is a used as pseudonym to protect the identity of the person, 28 December 2013, Finland.

2. For feminist critique of the idea of sovereign man in International Relations theory, see Sylvester (1994) and Steans (1998).

3. http://blogs.worldbank.org/peoplemove/trends-remittances-2016-new-normal-slow-growth, accessed 15 November 2016.

4. http://www.worldbank.org/en/news/feature/2013/10/02/Migrants-from-developing-countries-to-send-home-414-billion-in-earnings-in-2013.

5. According to UN-INSTRAW (2006), women send remittances home especially for the purpose of the girls' education.

6. FDI is the abbreviation for foreign direct investment.

7. See also UN-INSTRAW 2006 report.

Chapter 5

Policing borders and boundaries

In September 2013, a young Eastern European Roma woman called "Tanja" alleged that several guards at the Yarl's Wood detention centre for women and children have been sexually abusing detainees. Tanja was detained because her country of origin was unclear to the UK authorities, and they were in the process of determining where to deport her. She claimed that guards forced detainees to have sex with them in exchange for help with getting out of detention. Brave enough to report on the case, she was to become disappointed as the result of the investigation concluded that the interaction between Tanja and the guard was consented sex, not sexual abuse.

The response by the Ministry failed to acknowledge the hierarchies in place in the detention institution. It did not address the ways in which the guards always occupy a power position over the detainees. The detainees are placed in containment, whereas guards are there to control the detainees' behaviour and foresee that they do not escape the premises. The response simply stated that there are cameras to record any inappropriate behaviour by the guards, and that there is also a formal procedure in place for lodging complaints, which referred to a secure box where complaints can be deposed. It dismissed the power relations between the guards and detainees completely. It did not address the possibility that guards may use cover up for each other's inappropriate behaviour. The allegation was that the family room was used by guards as the place where they took detainees to abuse them sexually. This room was the only place where there were no cameras. It was ordinarily used by detainees to take pictures to be sent back for their families. The report did not mention what the implication for the guards would be if the allegation of the misuse of the family room was actually true.

The Ministry should have known that the sexual abuse of detainees can remain hidden from camera view in the premises of the detention centre. After Tanja's report, several other women detainees reported either on

sexual acts they had been subjected to, or on what they had witnessed been
done to their fellow detainees.

(Compiled from different media stories and
analyses of the case, September 2013)

The above narrative on allegations of sexual abuse at the Yarl's Wood detention centre raises important questions about gender and global mobilities.
Immigration detention is an institutionalized extreme form of restricted mobility, indeed a phase of immobility during a migrant trajectory that may last for
a long time (Conlon 2011, Mountz 2011). Its use is legitimized by concerns
over societal security, as irregular migration is associated with international
crime in wider political discourses. When detained, migrant bodies are confined to spaces where all their moves are monitored closely; they can be easily
counted and caught when need be. Detention serves the purpose of containing
unwanted individuals in order to sort out those who are deported and others
whose asylum claims can be processed, though getting one's asylum claim to
be processed doesn't directly open a way out of detention. The safety of the
detained individuals is not a topic that is raised in national politics, except by
the international, national and local human rights organizations and groups
that shed light on these practices.[1] Tanja's case constitutes an important opening for an investigation into practices in detention.

The case of Yarl's Wood highlights also another dimension of detention in the
present moment. As with many detention facilities across the globe, the operation of this centre is outsourced to a private security company. It is a concrete
example of how state sovereignty is outsourced to a private contractor (Tyler
2010, Conlon and Hiemstra 2016). This is important because public and private
sectors are regulated differently. In particular, the consequences for one set of
employees (civil servants) or the other (private-sector employees) are different.
What unites the two, however, is that sexual abuse of inmates is not permissible.

The opening story provides several nodes for thinking about the complexities of how global mobilities are sought to be regulated and controlled. The
central concept for this chapter is *border*, understood as both a concrete space
where global mobilities are regulated and halted and *bordering practices* that
create hierarchies of global mobilities also outside physical border areas.
As will be shown through selected examples, both the border and bordering practices come together at the points where actual bodies cross borders.
The case of Yarl's Wood exemplifies this in the case of what Tanja had to
experience, confined in a closed centre in the liminal space between being
fully inside the sovereign territory and fully outside the country. Bordering
practices are enacted in the way in which her case was handled. National and
supranational *policies* delineate the conditions under which an entry or exit

may take place. Policies effectively sort out those who can and those who cannot be allowed to enter, or sometimes exit, a given country. This chapter asks how gender figures and feeds into these practices and, as we have outlined throughout this book, how representations of global mobilities and their lived outcomes intersect in these approaches.

Feminist migration scholars have argued that migration policies are gendered and produce gendered outcomes (Boyd 1999, Kofman 1999, 2004, Piper 2006, Freedman 2007). These analyses are best done by combining textual analyses of policies with respect to their outcomes in the lived realities of people whose lives these policies target and seek to regulate.

In this chapter, we focus on different forms of regulation of mobility in a variety of locations across the globe. These forms of regulation include border control measures, visa policies and policies that regulate longer-term stay of foreigners. This chapter combines feminist security studies approach with policy outcome approach in order to analyse the securitization of human mobility. These are of interest for feminist scholarship because border control practices take the human body as an object that is subjected to manifold intimate forms of technologized scrutiny that are legitimated by the fight against transnational crime and terrorism. We will discuss in detail how the use of the seemingly neutral control relies on gendered and ethnicized presuppositions in the practice of racial profiling. One highly important field in which gender profiling converges with ethnicity and racial profiling is trafficking for the purpose of sexual exploitation. This will be discussed in the following chapter.

From border control, we proceed to the different practices of channelling global mobilities in the form of migration policies. In this second part of the chapter, we emphasize in line with other feminist scholars that migration polices produce gendered outcomes. One example of this is the preference for highly skilled migrants that draws on gendered notions of skill and conceptions of who is considered highly skilled (Kofman 1999, 2000, 2007, Iredale 2005, Kynsilehto 2011a). Furthermore, the explicit preference for highly skilled migrants posits the aspect of enhanced economic productivity as the ultimate goal that impacts, for example, whether the migrant workers in the category in question may bring their family members with them. In this part we also discuss student migration within skilled migration schemes. The category of student migrant encompasses and intersects with a variety of other migration statuses, such as those of family migrant and labour migrant. However, as we argued in chapter 2, categorical understandings of migration rarely take into account more than one reason for moving.

After discussing skilled migration we move on to gender analysis of the relationship between a person and a territory. This analysis includes visa allocation practices and the transmission of nationality to one's offspring. Formal and informal visa allocation practices are a way of regulating and channelling global mobilities. Informed by the notion of intersectionality, we examine these attempts especially by focusing on what these practices seek to exclude. What is relevant in transmitting nationality are the ways in which parental blood ties are considered along maternal or paternal, or possibly both, lineages in state policies.

In the final part of the chapter, we examine the role of international organizations in gendering global mobilities. Informed by the intersectional approach, we first look at the category and understandings of "vulnerable groups" in forced migration. Here we focus on the United Nations High Commissioner for Refugees (UNHCR), and particularly the gender guidelines the UN Refugee Agency has issued. These categorizations and guidelines rely on particular understandings of gender and its relation to other social categories. They also produce concrete outcomes as they guide the practical implementation of international protection. A related institution is the International Organization for Migration (IOM), an inter-governmental organization that is situated between states and international civil society (Ashutosh and Mountz 2011). IOM acts on many fronts concerning international migration, such as conducting studies and global analysis of global mobilities, providing support to states where national policies are in the making and running campaigns for what is called "voluntary return" for those who wish to or are ordered to return to the countries they left behind. IOM's campaigns against human trafficking are the most explicitly gendered forms of activity of the organization.

MURDEROUS BORDERS

In early October 2013, a migrant boat sunk near the coast of the Italian island of Lampedusa, as a result of which 366 people died. The tragedy was far from being a first or even an isolated event, as there were other incidents of the same kind even immediately after the highly mediatized shipwreck. This tragedy, however, managed to make human mobility across the Mediterranean Sea an extremely topical issue for high-level inter-governmental meetings during weeks to come. The tragedy also incited several working groups to tackle the issue. The Italian Navy initiated the most concrete search and rescue (SAR) activities under the title of Mare Nostrum, which operated for a year after the October 2013 tragedy and saved some 145,000 lives. However, the year 2014 also broke the annual record of recorded deaths despite the enhanced rescue effort. According to data gathered by the IOM Missing Migrants project, over 3,200 people died in the Mediterranean Sea that year, and the number of documented deaths rose again the year after, in 2015, up to 3,770.

At the European level, European leaders shed many "crocodile tears" over the fate of those who died in the October 2013 shipwreck. Nevertheless, the responses provided by state representatives did not alter the focus on strengthening border control and using more technologized, even militarized means to do so. The European border agency Frontex was called to monitor more closely the movements at sea. In the meantime, migrant boats continued their nightly journeys to the European soil in another corner of the Mediterranean, in the Aegean Sea between Greece and Turkey. On board these boats were women and men, families with small babies, many of whom were fleeing conflicts and dictatorial regimes worldwide. They were stopped before landing, and sometimes even after reaching the Greek coasts; their valuables were confiscated, and many were beaten and then returned to the Turkish waters for the coast guards on the other side to come to their rescue (see Pro Asyl 2013, Frontexit 2014). Families and pregnant women did not escape the brutality of these practices, and despite widely expressed concerns over the fate of millions of people fleeing the war in Syria to neighbouring countries, many Syrians trying to reach Europe were denied access. These border control measures are conducted in the name of security.

Preventing such deaths has been on the forefront of the political discourse with the unfolding events over the year 2015 that witnessed a record high number of arrivals, over one million persons, to the EU territory. What began as astonishment over the sudden entries in larger numbers, and continued with the welcoming gestures by the German chancellor Angela Merkel after the iconic death of a little Syrian Kurdish boy Alan Kurdi in September 2015, was brought to a halt by the successive closing of both internal and external borders across the European territory. In its quest for stopping unwanted mobilities that are, to a large extent, undertaken for humanitarian reasons, the EU also engaged in multiple negotiations between other countries and regional entities. The most concrete outcome has been the deal between the EU and Turkey that has basically sacrificed the fundamental right to asylum. In the meantime, these developments provided, at an accelerating speed, a crash course in the mismanagement of human mobility and the security-oriented fortressing of Europe (Kynsilehto 2016, 2017).

A widely developed body of political science and IR literature is the study of the links between migration and security. In critical approaches to security, since the Copenhagen School's formulation of the concept of securitization and its entwinement with mobility that is posited as a security threat, there is burgeoning literature dealing with this nexus at different sites. Often the critical approaches where gender occupies a central place have focused on the level of discourses, studying how security and migration issues are associated with one another in policy documents and political speeches (e.g. Berman 2003, Lobasz 2009). Another tradition within the security-migration nexus is the focus on how security policies are enacted in daily praxis, "practicing security," for example, at border locations and other marginalized spaces (e.g. Agathangelou 2004, Agathangelou and Ling 2004, Long 2006, Segrave 2009, Currah and Mulqueen 2011, Schemenauer 2012, Kynsilehto 2014, 2016). Feminist researchers operating from within critical security studies (e.g. Aradau 2004, 2008) and others more explicitly from feminist security studies perspectives (e.g. Penttinen 2008, Lobasz 2009, Redden and Terry 2013, Freedman 2012, 2016) have problematized gender in relation to security and human mobility.

We need to ask whose security is at stake, when we examine global mobilities from the angle of security. When we respond to this question, we also need to analyse who the subjects and objects of security practices are (Wibben 2011). Do we understand the one "providing security" as a state or perhaps a collective of lay people? Does the security provider we identified seek to secure the state or a supranational entity, or is the goal to safeguard mobile groups or individuals? If we consider the latter as the ones to be secured, we may inquire further after the groups and individuals whom securing should take into account. Are we thinking about air passengers in general; international travellers for business or pleasure? What about the safety of refugees and their access to a first or a subsequent country of asylum? Is their safety even worth asking? Furthermore, asking these questions leads to further inquiries concerning the gendered implications of security-enhancing measures on individuals and families on the move. It is necessary to inquire how these practices affect men, women and children differently (Freedman 2016). How do ethnicity and gender come to matter in these practices? What about the economic status and social class of the persons on the move – is everyone similarly affected? By posing these questions, we begin to think the security-migration nexus from an intersectional angle.

Critical perspectives to states' practices of dealing with unwanted forms of mobility have shown how borders have indeed become murderous and gendered in being so. The most examined border location, in this regard, is the Mexico-US border[2] where many issues culminate, ranging from striking economic disparities between the different sides of the border to the increasing militarization of the border in the quest for keeping the undesirable crossers out. Alongside state-organized border control, unofficial border control is conducted by Minutemen and other vigilante groups coming from different parts of the country to protect the US territory. One familiar trope in the attempts to legitimize official and unofficial border control practices is reference to "coyotes" – human smugglers facilitating crossing at the Mexico-US border – who take advantage of vulnerable individuals, including sexual abuse of persons compelled to rely on their services (Lind and Williams 2013: 110–112). Smuggling can hardly be considered a humanitarian activity that would only be conducted for the benefit of the most vulnerable individuals. What the critiques of profit-seeking smugglers tend to overlook, however, are the ways in which ever-tightening entry and border control measures produce the very problem they seek to resolve (Andrijasevic 2010). That is, in the absence of legal routes to cross the border, shadow routes carve their ways and in so doing constitute shadow-scapes of globalization (Penttinen 2008). Moreover, the emphasis on abusive practices within the shadow networks that facilitate irregular border crossing often forgets that undocumented crossers also fall prey to abuse by official border guard agencies, as testified cases illustrate (Lind and Williams 2013: 110), and which was apparent in the opening narrative on sexual abuse in detention.

Mobile bodies are read and located differently in the scripts on gendered global mobilities at international borders. In other words, the scripts written on certain bodies relate to other scripts, written on the same and other bodies around. The outcome, even if contingent, of the reading draws on a variety of other readings, not only one at the time. Multiple examples can be drawn from foreign nationals entering a country; yet border control practices also address nationals of a given country upon their return. Rachel Silvey (2007) examines one of these sites, Terminal 3 at the Soekarno-Hatta International Airport in Jakarta, Indonesia, which was opened specifically to process the return migration of Indonesian overseas workers upon the termination of their contracts. Silvey argues that this way of channelling return migrants, usually of lower social classes and from rural areas, is part of a process that regulates returning contract workers differently from other international travellers, as they are distanced from other travellers after formally entering the country and picking up their luggage. Drawing on her ethnographic insights, Silvey maintains that returning contract workers are being educated by simplistic methods designed for "their protection," mistreated by the airport personnel and questioned for lengthy periods of time about the details of their departure and return. In so doing, the channel leads to further marginalization of particular groups of returning nationals, despite the stated good intentions in the establishment of the Terminal 3 that would facilitate their return and protect them from robbery and other form of abuse upon their return to the villages.

Passing through a border is rendered increasing difficult for the majority of a given population, such as at the borders between Israel and the Occupied Palestinian Territories (OPTs). The Gaza Strip constitutes an extreme case that resembles a prison. Halting persons at the checkpoints constitutes one of the everyday practices of humiliation, again legitimated by security concerns of Israeli citizens to be protected from terrorist acts. Other practices of humiliation include the construction of the wall in the West Bank that explicitly prohibits passage from one area to another, house demolitions, bombing Palestinian residence areas and shooting at civilians. At the checkpoints, pregnant Palestinian women are kept waiting for hours, as, for example, the case of Rula al-Ghul illustrates (Long 2006). She had already been in labour when arriving at the checkpoint she had to pass through in order to access an ambulance on the other side and continue on to the hospital. For no other reason than being Palestinians, she and her husband were not allowed to pass through and were kept waiting at the border. There she was labouring alone and gave birth to a baby girl who died at birth.

CONTROLLING BODIES AT THE BORDER

Corporeal approach to border control directs our gaze to the ways in which gendered bodies traverse the border control posts. Human bodies are recognized and read through different measures at these sites. Think, for example, debates concerning the identification of persons who wear the full-face veil (niqab, burka) or headscarf (hijab). In Muslim-majority countries, border security posts at airports often direct men and women to different lines, in order to pay respect especially to veiled women's modesty. In some secularly oriented countries – for example, France – the identification has evolved into a political problem where the principle of universality of treatment and even the foundations of the state are claimed to be at stake. The veiled bodies are posited as constituting a security threat, given that the full-face veil does not permit accurate reading of the gendered body, as the body shape is loosely covered by cloth and the eyes and face remain hidden from sight. It is argued that it becomes difficult, if not impossible, to estimate whether the veiled body figures a man or a woman. The full-body veil would mislead the security personnel or any layperson to wrongly identify the gender of the person. Thus, determining the gender of the individual becomes a security issue.

Body-scanning technologies are increasingly used at transport checkpoints especially at international airports. They are legitimized by the quest for more and more precise information on passengers in order to make sure they are not carrying hidden items that would jeopardize the safety of other passengers and the airline personnel. The screening machinery is deployed "to make the invisible visualisable" in order to detect the risky individual among the naked bodies (Amoore and Hall 2009: 444). Critical feminist readings of these technologies pay attention to the ways in which scanning technologies enable the security personnel to see intimate details of mobile women's bodies, such as the exact shape of breasts. These gazing practices can be considered as permitting a futile form of voyeurism that is rendered possible by reference to security-enhancing practices. What is at stake, then, is the dilemma between personal integrity and all-embracing securitization.

These practices of "digitized dissection" (Amoore and Hall 2009) also distinguish bodies that are deemed misfit to normative ideas of body type, body shape or gender identities (Magnet and Rodgers 2012, Currah and

Mulqueen 2011). Transgender individuals identified as mismatches according to the digitized details of their genitalia may be subjected to further physical scrutiny and thus singled out for humiliation that the stopping from the flow of passengers provokes. In local airports of small towns, thus far closeted individuals may be outed against their will, and, as a result, they may risk their jobs and close relationships (Magnet and Rodgers 2012: 111).

The use of scanning technologies has also generated acts of everyday resistance – for example, by avoiding airports where scanning is a recurrent practice. Eventually, this kind of resistance can only be opted by those in a privileged economic and locational position that permits these kinds of choices to be made (Redden and Terry 2013: 240). Other options for resistance would be to undergo a lengthier and no less invasive physical search while talking to the agent who performs the body search in order to raise her awareness on the act and mobilizing with other protesting passengers to render the gender politics of body scanning more visible. Again, these options are not available for everyone, especially to individuals racially profiled as suspect passengers whose passage would be rendered yet again more difficult. Moreover, physical search may be highly traumatizing for persons who have been sexually assaulted at some point in their lives. Practices of resistance also include the use of pasties to cover intimate areas during the screening or the removal of all clothing in a collective flash mob, such as "Fleshmob," performed at the Berlin-Tegel airport in Germany in 2010 (Redden and Terry 2013: 243–247). In this Fleshmob a group of some twenty young Germans paraded in underwear at the airport with critical slogans written on their bare skin. In doing so, they protested the intruding practices of body scans by inverting the quest for exploring more and intimate corporeal details of passing bodies, by exposing as much of their bodies as possible (Zetter 2010).

GENDERING MIGRATION POLICIES

In this second part of the chapter we shift the analytic focus on gendering migration policies. Feminist migration scholars have pointed out that migration policies are gendered and they produce gendered outcomes. According to Piper (2006), political scientists have not been the most active in analysing these multifaceted policies, and especially how gender shapes and is impacted by these politics. Her goal has been to map politics around migration, which enables her to point out three reasons that policies affect men and women differently: (1) the gender-segregated labour markets both at the departure and at the destination channel men and women differently through the migratory flows, (2) gendered socioeconomic power structures and (3) sociocultural definitions of "proper" gender roles at both ends of the migratory channel

(Piper 2006: 139). Furthermore, Piper argues that very little migration research starts from the notion of migrants as political agents and analyse mobile individuals' participation in non-electoral politics (Piper 2006: 155).

Gender indeed shapes different phases of the migration process. The global economic structure and its restructuring bear on men and women in different ways, as we illustrated in the previous chapter. This restructuring then creates the need for individuals and families to look for options outside the area where they were born, also abroad. Emigration policies constitute one policy field that is likely to include gendered dimensions, as they regulate who is allowed to leave. Furthermore, different skills are differently valued drawing on gendered hierarchies. This influences the salaries to be gained by being employed in one field or sector or another, as we discussed in earlier chapters – for example, as regards whether a migrant care worker is employed in a household or in a public care institution (e.g. Huang, Yeoh and Toyota 2012) – or the very way gendered labour market is structured, as we argued in the previous chapter.

Family reunion is a legal channel for migration. It is based on the fundamental right to family life and constitutes an orderly and managed way of receiving people. However, in the present context, these channels are more and more curbed, and it becomes increasingly difficult to bring one's family along when moving from one country to another. Family reunion policies constitute a domain in which gendered outcomes become visible. It is one policy domain in which intersectional feminist analyses are much needed. The objective of an intersectional approach in this case would be to illustrate how the right to family life increasingly depends on nationality, class positioning and migration status (see box 5.1).

Migration policies tend to be written in seemingly gender-neutral language. In practice, this means referring to the migrant as a generic person. In terms of family reunion, policies refer to the reuniting spouse rather than a husband or a wife. Historically, as we have noted several times earlier, the labour migrant has nevertheless been assumed as a male migrant. Hence the reuniting spouse has been understood as the wife joining her husband in migration, although more and more men have moved as family migrants during the past decades and beyond (Kofman 2004: 251).

Since the official closing of borders to labour migration in the mid-1970s, family reunion policies in many European countries have been drafted to allow the entry of family members of those already residing in the country. Yet, as Eleonore Kofman (2004: 244) notes, European policies have been drafted according to a very restrictive definition of family based on the notion of nuclear family with a spouse and dependent children. These policies are in the process of becoming increasingly restrictive, with tightening rules as regards to the required family income and housing. This brings the issue of

---

BOX 5.1

Reshma Bi, referred to as the "runaway grandmother" by the Indian newspaper *The Hindu* (10 January 2013), was able to transgress the heavily militarized state border between India and Pakistan in September 2012. This seventy-year-old woman walked across the line of control (LoC) between the Indian state of Jammu and Pakistan-administered Kashmir in order to join her children and grandchildren living in another state. Her crossing did not go unnoticed, however, but triggered heavier surveillance and the construction of a bunker on the Indian side of the border in order to prevent such crossings from happening again. As the construction went against the terms of the ceasefire establishing the LoC, the protest continued in a violent form, as a result of which three civilian villagers in Charonda and two soldiers died, which again sparked new calls for military retaliation. What started as an elderly lady's wish to spend the final years of her life with her family escalated into a deadly conflict.

Study assignment: Look for other examples of divided communities in contested border areas. How the family life has altered across generations in these communities?

---

social class, or the economic situation of the family, as a crucial factor in determining the ways in which the family can be together. In practice, this means that the requirements concerning accommodation and monthly income of the migrant person who wishes to be reunited with her or his family are set so high that it often becomes practically impossible to fulfil the criteria in regular jobs that are available for migrants. For refugees other than those with the Convention status – that is, refugees recognized within the 1951 Refugee Convention – meeting the criteria may be out of reach (Kofman 2004: 255). This is intensified by the inclination of several European states, including Sweden (which has traditionally been reputed as the country with the highest level of protection), to accord weaker protection statuses to an increasing number of people who would have earlier qualified as Convention refugees.

The incident in box 5.1 shows the arbitrariness of borders that cross villages and tear families apart. Indeed, the politics of family division across newly defined state borders are a recurrent theme, for example, in the narratives on the Partition of India (see Butalia 1998), as elsewhere. At the same time, the story is illustrative of the ways in which a one individual's trajectory may become capitalized for the purposes of militarized security. The story of

Reshma Bi locates also the reasons for her family's dispersion: implicated in cross-border criminal activity, namely a smuggling ring, her sons had crossed the LoC earlier in order to escape charges pressed against them. In their analysis of the case of Reshma Bi, Cons and Sanyal (2013) propose that it is impossible to understand the importance of the nexus of events by simply reflecting on the border alone. Instead, they argue, what is needed is a consideration of the variety of simultaneous histories, spaces and spatial practices that enter into play in this story. These histories negotiate centrality and marginality, as well as nationalism and subalternity.

Feminist and queer scholars have pointed out how some countries, such as Canada, consider queer couples similar to heterosexual couples. However, a closer look at the requirements reveals how the couples are asked to provide guarantees that the joining spouse will not become a burden to social welfare systems. These practices have been taken up with prominent LGBTQI lobby organizations to equip the persons seeking family migration with necessary tools to provide required guarantees. These tools include emphasizing productivity and self-sufficiency, but their use may contribute to drawing and enforcing neoliberal patterns of homonormativity (White 2013).

In addition to changing borders and practices of border enforcement, the requirements for obtaining a visa to enter a given country change, as do the requirements concerning whether passport holders from a particular country need a visa to enter another country. These practices of assessing who may and who may not enter a given country do not cut across lines of nationality only, but they are also gendered and aged. To give an example of changing practices, prior to the handover of Hong Kong to the Chinese authority in 1997, Bangladeshi citizens did not need a visa to enter Hong Kong and they could stay for two weeks with an entrance permit accorded upon arrival at the airport. Despite the absence of a bilateral labour export-import agreement between Bangladesh and Hong Kong, the possibility of entering the country has often meant extending the stay and engaging in irregular work. Ahsan Ullah notes that the sample he surveyed and interviewed for his study with Bangladeshi migrants in Hong Kong is "highly skewed towards male migrants, as cultural constraint and government policies discourage female migration" (Ullah 2013: 171). Gendered and aged assumptions guide also the ways in which particular states treat the nationals of other countries, as is the case of Moroccan women seeking to enter Lebanon. Lebanon does not grant visas to Moroccan women below some forty years of age, due to the assumption that young Moroccan women would seek entry to Lebanon in order to engage in prostitution. Similar assessments capitalizing on ethnicized and gendered fantasies are often linked to Russian women in many countries who find themselves interrogated in their quest to be granted a visa.

Problematizing prioritized mobilities

Feminist research on skilled international mobility has revealed that main-stream research on highly skilled migration mostly focuses on male migrants' experiences and on sectors where men often constitute a majority, such as IT engineering or transnational banking (see, e.g., Beaverstock 2002, 2005). Policy documents are often written in gender-neutral language, which in itself gives little clues as to how to read gender out of these policies. This alludes to the gendered undertone in the construction of skill and being highly skilled as discussed in chapter 2. Arriving at to this conclusion requires meticulous research examining not only the policies themselves but reading them along-side qualitative and quantitative data concerning manifold mobilities and their actual enactments.

Facilitating highly skilled mobility across international borders is a top pri-ority for many countries across the globe. This is a recurrent political priority in different policy documents, such as in Australia, Canada or the European Union (EU). What is taking place can be named as global competition for talent that encompasses various mobility schemes, such as the EU Blue Card that is specifically destined to facilitate the entry of highly skilled migrants from outside the EU to boost the labour-market in Europe. Besides facilitat-ing the mobility of the cardholders, the scheme also sets out to facilitate the mobility of the cardholder's family, including an easier entry for the accom-panying spouse to the labour market. In actual practice, however, the EU Blue Card has been very rarely used over the years, which leaves the provisions accorded within the scheme as empty letters.

Research conducted in Australia and New Zealand has demonstrated a reverse trend too: that of "astronaut families" whose fathers go back to countries of origin in Northeast Asia to work whereas mothers, often highly qualified, stay at home taking care of the children and outside the labour market in the coun-try of immigration (Khoo, Ho and Voigt-Graf 2008: 118). Aihwa Ong (1999: 127–128) explains this as a strategy for the family to earn residence rights in the country of immigration such as the United States and Canada.

The quest of wealthy states in the global North to prioritize the entry of highly skilled migrants has led them to conceive incoming foreign students as potential contributors to the host country's economic growth. States have drafted initiatives to facilitate the transition from student status to a worker status, such as a six-month job-seeker residence permit for the foreign gradu-ates to seek employment in the country where he or she has graduated. Can-ada, for example, issued in 2008 a fast-track permanent residency possibility for foreign graduates through the "Canadian Experienced Class" (McDermott and Sanmiguel-Valderrama 2013: 44) that has also benefitted other highly skilled migrants.

Student migration is one of the most controlled migration schemes, yet the formal status as an individual enrolled in an educational institution usually allows for a legal, albeit limited, entry to labour market in the country that allocated the student visa. International students moving within regional and global exchange programmes as well as degree students constitute a particular form of skilled mobility. It can therefore serve as one channel through which immigration becomes possible (e.g. Pan 2011). The criteria imposed on foreign students in order to receive a student residence permit are however increasingly tightened, and scholarships are becoming rarer in the context of enduring economic crisis. Student migrants also raise families, and family and labour migrants participate in different knowledge acquisition processes before and after they engage in global mobility regardless their migration statuses (Raghuram 2013). Student mobility may also be hindered due to different intersectional factors, such as parenting or disability, which may further hamper, for example, pursuing a career in research (Ackers 2008).

Not everyone gets a long-term student visa, however, nor is everyone seeking to reside in a foreign country for the whole duration of the studies. In these cases as well students may seek to engage in forms of short-term mobility across international borders, such as attending courses, seminars or conferences. However, as Kynsilehto's experience in working with North African academics has shown, students from the global South who plan to attend a course or a conference that takes place in one of the EU member-states, for example, often find their visas refused. This is reasoned by the authorities that administer the allocation of visas by the likelihood of the visa applicant to return to her or his country of departure. Existence of an employment contract and a regular salary are interpreted as signs of the likelihood to return. Yet for students these criteria are difficult to fulfil, which then impedes their possibilities for the short-term global mobility that is widely available for nationals of countries in the global North. Once the diploma is gained and a professional career started, this situation may change, once again, depending on the estimated wealth and income of the visa applicant.

Not all workers migrate in order to stay. Seasonal work is defined as a temporary form of mobility, not as a permanent form of settlement in the host state. For young people from the global North, seasonal work constitutes a form of adventure and discovery of other countries. In the meantime, it provides much-needed income for many families in the global South. Patricia McDermott and Olga Sanmiguel-Valderrama (2013: 44) argue that seasonal work programmes are highly gendered and they produce gendered outcomes based on their research with Mexican workers in Canada and in the United States. The migrant workers in the Seasonal Agricultural Worker Program (SAWP) in Canada, for example, have been over 90 per cent male. The selection criteria for this programme have preferred married men with children assuming that they are more likely to return to Mexico after their contract is over. Married men with children are also deemed less likely to get involved with Canadian women in the rural areas where the seasonal labour force is needed. As the temporary contracts for eight months a year with a relatively low pay would not allow for the whole family to move to Canada, families are left to live separated, that is, children without their fathers and wives without their husbands, for the major part of each year. Amongst Moroccan seasonal workers in Spain the opposite preference has held true: women whose small children stay behind in Morocco have been the preferred labour force in the strawberry fields in southern Spain (Zeneidi 2013), as the mothers are expected to return to live with their children. In this context, however, the economic crisis practically halted the entry of any incoming seasonal workers for jobs that were then to be reserved for unemployed Spanish nationals.

Migration status that is considered temporary, such as seasonal work discussed earlier, is nevertheless not the only way in which family life is being ordered. Huang, Yeoh and Toyota (2012) show how different categories of work visas permit for differential access to family reunion. Based on their study on elderly care provided by migrant workers both at private homes and in institutional settings in Singapore, they show how the level of income correlates with the possibility of bringing dependants. For highly and mid-level skilled workers earning more than S\$ 2,500 a month, it is possible to bring in dependants, whereas family reunion is forbidden for foreign workers categorized as semi- or unskilled workers, such as enrolled nurses, nursing aides, healthcare attendants or foreign domestic workers. Alongside family formation, permanent residency, obtaining citizenship and marrying Singapore citizens is prohibited, and pregnancy will result in immediate deportation. All these issues together show how the care-working bodies are scaled according to migration statuses, and certain nationalities are more targeted than others. These targeted nationalities are deprived of basic rights such as the right to family life. This deprivation of rights may also be explicit, as is the case with Malaysia, where migrant workers are forbidden to bring in their families and also to marry Malaysian citizens (Chee, Yeoh and Shuib 2012). As Chee et al. illustrate, however, the interdiction to marry does not stop people from forming couples regardless of formal regulations, but it produces situations where spouses need to learn to navigate the restrictive practices and at times accept a condition of irregularity they would not have otherwise entered into.

Ordering emigration

Policies that control migration deal not only with immigration – moving into a country – but also emigration – moving out of a country. The ways in which emigration is controlled vary between one country to another, with many countries severely punishing their nationals for an irregular exit. In respect to international human rights commitments, these severe punishments jeopardize the article 13 in the Universal Declaration of Human Rights (1948), which underscores that everyone has the right to leave any country, including one's own. The same right is also granted through the article 12 of the International Covenant on Civil and Political Rights (ICCPR). Gender feeds into these difficulties in exiting one's country as obtaining a passport or an exit permit may be dependent on a male guardian.

Thus far in migration studies, relatively little attention has been paid to the policies of states from where migrants leave when compared to the burgeoning literature analysing migrant receiving countries' policies (Biao 2003). Analysing Chinese government's policies on emigration Biao draws attention to the ways in which emigration is usually managed on a case-by-case basis, which makes the overall picture at the same time coherent and fragmented. Traditionally many areas of mass emigration in China have been located nearby international borders and coastal cities. In the first decennia of the People's Republic of China (PRC), the border areas were considered as highly politicized as they marked the boundary between capitalist and communist worlds. Thus, they were kept under-developed by the central authority. Paradoxically, despite the purposeful under-development of these areas, emigration was seen as betrayal to the ideology of the communist regime.

Due to this under-development, emigration and illicit trade activities across borders became a necessity for the survival of local communities in many border areas. These tendencies have continued since, and the Shanghai Cooperation Organization (SCO) was established in 2000 as a border agreement between China, Kazakhstan, Kyrgyzstan, Russia, Tajikistan and Uzbekistan to facilitate economic cooperation among these countries. In addition, the policy towards Chinese diaspora overseas has changed after the beginning of rapid economic growth from favouring naturalization in the countries of residence to attracting migrants to return to China either permanently or temporarily. The current emphasis on encouraging student migration and the subsequent return of students to China after completing their studies seems a recurrent trend. Several cities such as Beijing, Fujian, Guangdong, Shandong and Shanghai adopted policies that offer skilled returnees high salaries, beneficial tax rates and subsidies for housing and children's education, which favour the return and formation of families, thus entailing explicitly gendered and intersectional aspects. Emigration agencies also interestingly combine activities related to international labour and transnational marriages. Many agencies establish data sets of foreigners, mostly overseas Chinese men looking for Chinese partners, and information on Chinese who seek to emigrate as dependents, with an attempt to make matches (Biao 2003: 34).

Uneven access to nationality

Feminist research pays attention to how citizenship policies that govern also the practices of transmitting nationality to one's children are highly gendered. These policies provide a site through which it is possible to analyse gendered and racialized constructions of a given nation (Yuval-Davis 1997) as they condition the possibility or inability of a gendered citizen to contribute to the continuity of the body of citizenry. In many countries, personal status codes or the family law restrict women's ability to pass the nationality to her children if the father is a foreign national. In many Muslim-majority countries, belonging to a religious community orders especially women's possibility of being legally married; for a Muslim woman, it is not permissible to marry a non-Muslim man.[3] When inscribed into legal codes, this order applies depending on the community in which the person is assumed to belong, regardless of the actual faith of the person.

Obtaining nationality is theoretically divided along two conceptions of the nation: (1) *jus soli*, or birthright to nationality of a given state by being born on its territory, which would correspond to a civic conception of the nation, and (2) *jus sanguinis*, where nationality is transmitted by generational lineage, and it resonates with an ethnic conception of the nation. These principled conceptions rarely exist in their ideal forms, but present nationality codes are composed of a varying mixture of these different principles. During the past decennia, there has also been an increasing turn inwards by many states, which manifests itself in the limitations to access to citizenship.

We introduced the notion of "baby tourism" in chapter 2. Bryan Fanning and Fidele Mutwarasibo (2007) touch on this issue by analysing the process that led to the removal of birthright to nationality in the 2004 Referendum in Ireland. They argue that much of the political support gained for the removal of the birthright exploited the popular imagery of asylum seekers as unproductive scum external to the nation. Prior to the Referendum in 2004 the babies born on the Irish soil were immediately granted Irish nationality by their birthright, and their non-national parents were able to escape deportation and regularize their residence. In the political debate, the migrant mother, and especially her pregnant body, became the threat through which aliens cum non-nationals were to penetrate the Irish nation.

Removals of birthright have become a frequent practice when states have turned into more restrictive, exclusionary practices in keeping the citizenry under control. New gendered enemies emerge as the maternity ward becomes one of the sites in which border can be irregularly crossed simply by being born to a non-citizen mother (Tyler 2010), as already discussed in chapter 2. Feminist research that examines reproductive health practices has shown that migrant women may actually resort to sterilization as part of their contraceptive strategies (O'Leary and Valdéz-Gardea 2013: 88–89). Opting for sterilization may be considered as a way to exert agency in situations where the possibility for sexual abuse and rape is a recurrent fact, such as during undocumented journeys across deserted areas, in order to protect oneself from unwanted pregnancy. Unlike in the prominent narrative of undocumented women accessing residence rights and citizenship through maternity, this suggests that the route to citizenship through maternity is more of a matter of media spectacles creating political urgencies than truly reflective of strategies of those concerned.

GLOBAL GOVERNANCE OF MIGRANTS AND REFUGEES

This third and final part of the chapter examines the global governance of migrants and refugees. In this book, we have argued that it is often difficult to draw clear lines between forced and voluntary mobilities. In migration governance, however, at least a theoretical division of labour exists between international agencies that focus mainly on the global mobility of labour, such as the International Labour Organization (ILO) and the International Organization for Migration (IOM), as opposed to humanitarian migration that is the domain of UN Refugee Agency (UNHCR). We qualify this division of labour as theoretical given that, on one hand, the IOM is implicated in the transportation arrangements of recognized refugees chosen for third country resettlement and "voluntary return" of persons whose asylum applications have received a negative decision. On the other hand, the UNHCR has for several years emphasized "mixed migration" that denotes the simultaneous presence of both refugees and "economic" migrants in different migratory flows, which somewhat blurs the initial focus of the agency.

We begin by the global governance of forced migration, by discussing feminist approaches to refugee status determination (RSD) process. Furthermore, we inquire after the notion of "vulnerable groups," assessing critically a fixed notion of vulnerability that creates solid categories and thereby stabilizes the approach to certain groups and individuals. With this critical assessment, we do not intend to dismantle the practical categorization that works towards facilitating the daily tasks of the organizations involved. In other words, the criteria used for assessing the urgency of the refugee's need to be resettled in a third country is a tool that seeks to facilitate the task of deciding who will access a place in the resettlement quotas, which is difficult to do in practice. This decision-making process is perhaps best referred to as dividing of suffering people to match them with too limited places that are globally available for the resettlement of refugees. However, it is important to examine these categories through feminist lenses in order to lay out the complicated and unintended consequences these matrixes may generate.

Gendering refugee protection

Feminist activists and scholars have criticized the UN Refugee Convention – the UN Convention relating to the Status of Refugees of 1951 and its additional protocol of 1967 – for not recognizing gender-based persecution (Boyd 1999, Freedman 2007, 2008, 2010). These critiques have pointed out how the ideas of "refugee-ness" and "political persecution" have relied on the model of a typical male political dissident. They have thus failed to recognize many other potential positions in which, and situations from which, a person needs to flee. More recently, there have been attempts to conceive the category of refugee more intersectionally. These attempts have produced various guidelines that seek to fill the protection gaps. As Hyndman and de Alwis (2008: 89) point out, gender policies in humanitarian organizations provide a grid of intelligibility for the staff who works with displaced populations. The guidelines are bound to remain incomplete, however, as they are unable to account for variables such as historical context, regional geopolitics, cultural dynamics and existing gender relations, and thus field staff remains in charge of filling in missing information in a given context.

Refugees belonging to vulnerable groups are entitled to special forms of protection. The definition of vulnerable groups includes special needs related to gender, age, disability and medical status. Identified groups that require specific attention and particular protection thus refer to unaccompanied minors, pregnant women, single women as heads-of-household, persons with disabilities, elderly persons and refugees with transmittable diseases, particularly HIV/ AIDS, which that may provoke further discrimination due to the imaginaries attached to this disease.

The UN has produced a plethora of manuals and handbooks to clarify different categories. These handbooks address the issues that are necessary to remember when considering the categories in practical work. In line with the convention of children's rights, there is the *UNHCR Guidelines on Determining the Best Interests of the Child* (2008). To address the specific issues in the work with people with disabilities, there are the *UN Standard Rules on the Equation of Opportunities for Persons with Disabilities* (1993), which acknowledge migrant workers and refugees with disabilities as individuals and groups who need specific attention (art. 15). Standard Rules further specify the term *disability* as summarizing many different functional limitations, permanent or transitory ones, occurring in any population in any country of the world, such as physical, intellectual or sensory impairment, medical conditions or mental illness (art. 17). As for the term *handicap*, it denotes the loss or limitation of opportunities to take part in the life of the community on an equal level with others, that is, the encounter between the person with a disability and the environment (art. 18).

We will now turn to gender and the ways in which it has been addressed within the international protection system in parallel with national legislations. As the large proportion of women among different refugee populations was widely recognized, the interest in women's particular protection needs started to increase in research and activism. Research and advocacy around the ethnic conflicts in the 1990s in the Balkans and Central Africa (Rwanda, ex-Zaire) rendered gendered violence in wars visible to ever-increasing publics. At that time, the use of rape as a weapon of war became internationally recognized. In order to respond to the gender-specific protection needs related to these recently recognized forms of political persecution, the UNHCR issued, in 1995, guidelines under the title *Sexual Violence against Refugees: Guidelines on Prevention and Response* and then, in 2002, the *UNHCR Guidelines on Gender-Related Persecution.*

The 2002 guidelines distinguish three different concepts that refer to violations of fundamental human rights perpetuating sex-stereotyped roles that deny human dignity and the self-determination of the individual and hamper human development: gender-based violence (GBV), violence against women, and sexual violence including exploitation and abuse. The first one, *gender-based violence*, is an umbrella definition drawn from the CEDAW (Convention on the Elimination of All Forms of Discrimination against Women) that covers all forms of violence that target individuals or groups because of their gender or sex. This definition includes acts that inflict physical, mental or sexual harm or suffering, threat of such acts, coercion and other forms of deprivation of liberty. The second one, *violence against women*, denotes private and public acts of gender-based violence that target women and girls, including sexual violence. The third one, *sexual violence*, refers to sexual acts, attempts or threat that result or are likely to result in physical, psychological and emotional harm. In the guidelines, the inclusiveness of the conception of *sexual and gender-based violence* is emphasized in order to recognize boys and men as potential targets of sexual and gender-based violence.

Prior to the publication of the UNHCR guidelines and parallel to similar efforts by this international organization, the chairperson of the Canadian Immigration and Refugee Board (IRB) issued the first guidelines on gender-based persecution, *Guidelines on Women Refugee Claimants Fearing Gender-Related Persecution*, in 1993. These guidelines were the first nationally issued guidelines to address gender-based persecution, and they reflect similar advances by the UNHCR at the international level. That same year Canada also became the first country in the world to recognize gender-based persecution as a legitimate claim for obtaining refugee status (Boyd 1999, Hadjukowski-Ahmed, Khanlou and Moussa 2008).

Gender-based violence includes multiple potential forms – for example, rape, widow burnings (sati), sex-selective abortion, infanticide and neglect of baby girls due to cultural prioritization of boy children over girls. Female genital mutilation (FGM) is a well-known act of violence that targets the female body. According to UNHCR figures, over 90 million women and girls in Africa have been victims of female genital mutilation. FGM is also practised illicitly in diaspora communities in countries where FGM is strictly prohibited. Sometimes it is the state that inflicts gender-based violence, both directly in the form of violations and indirectly by not offering proper protection. In so doing, the state neglects or outright denies women's basic human rights (Boyd 1999: 9).

In parallel with the internationalization of norms and increased attention to gender, there is a tendency in countries where national asylum laws exist to treat gender-based claims under forms of subsidiary protection rather than contributing to the recognition of full refugee status (Freedman 2007: 27–28). This creates paradoxical situations where gender-based persecution is recognized, yet relegated to granting lesser protection than "more real" bases for claiming asylum.

Sexual minorities – lesbian, gay, bisexual, transgender, queer or intersex (LGBTQI) people – encounter specific forms persecution in various countries and contexts worldwide. In up to seventy-eight countries, same-sex sexual acts or gender-variant behaviour is criminalized (Jordan and Morrissey 2013: 13), leading to imprisonment and even the death penalty. In five countries male homosexual acts are penalized by capital punishment, and in four countries sexual acts between women may result in the death penalty (Jordan 2009: 166). Therefore, persecution due to sexual orientation constitutes one of the potential grounds on which a person seeks international protection.

These needs for international protection are, nevertheless, unevenly recognized in different countries, with only a few countries that have over the years profiled themselves as safe havens for LGBTQI refugees. Thanks to active lobbying by various LGBTQI groups and organizations, the first international guidelines that advise on protecting individuals from maltreatment due to sexual orientation were issued by the UNHCR in 2008. In practice, widespread discrimination still persists, which relates both to homophobic and transphobic tendencies in different parts of the world that target LGBTQI people in particular and to the ever-tightening legislations that limit the access to asylum for any individual. Even in countries where persecution on the basis of sexual orientation or gender identity (SOGI) has been recognized since the early 1990s, such as in Canada, tightening regulations concerning

asylum in general have rendered it increasingly difficult to access international protection in practice (Jordan and Morrissey 2013, also Jordan 2009:
173). In detention, LGBTQI detainees, especially transgender individuals, are
particularly visible and easily subjected to abuse by both detention officials
and other detainees (Tabak and Levitan 2013).

Manalansan IV (2006: 231–232, also Jordan 2009: 179), however, warns
against what he calls "Western imperialist bias" in considering cases of
queer asylum. He asserts that an emphasis on the extremely difficult conditions, especially in Muslim-majority and other "non-Western" countries, for
persons who inhabit and express non-heteronormative sexualities may in fact
contribute to demonizing these societies in line with Orientalist imageries. He
argues that there is not enough research that addresses different intersectional
dimensions such as those of social class and race/ethnicity in examining
sexuality and asylum.

Age-specific protection needs constitute another dimension for which
guidelines are issued by UNHCR. Certain categories of refugee children are
identified as particularly vulnerable to sexual and gender-based violence in
chapter 5 of the UNHCR Gender guidelines. These categories are unaccompanied and separated children, children in detention, child soldiers, adolescents,
mentally and physically disabled children, working children, girl mothers,
children born to rape victims/survivors, boys as victims/survivors and child
perpetrators. Prison and detention facilities are reportedly sites of sexual abuse
of children as well. Adult inmates may specifically target children based
on their culturally specific beliefs that sexual contact with a child will cure
HIV/AIDS infections or because of interest in child virgins. For this reason,
the guidelines recommend the separation of children to child-only facilities, unless a careful consideration of the best interests of the child advises
otherwise.

Notwithstanding the fact that the use of detention for people who did not
commit any crime needs to be questioned in general, there are other concerns
specific to children. For example, different ways in which the age of children
is assessed, such as the use of skeletal age assessment, are not flawless. Unaccompanied minors are not always willing to declare themselves as minors
either, due to a lack of trust in the institutional forms of care (if these exist in
a given location). Moreover, even where these child-specific facilities exist,
there is not always enough space to accommodate all undocumented children
and youth that seek asylum. Children may then be directed to facilities that
are designed to host adults only, which potentially exposes them to various
forms of violence, or they are left to survive in the street.

Researchers have also sought to challenge the gloomy picture of unaccompanied refugee children only as ones to be assisted and protected, by
emphasizing refugee children's agency. Christina Clark (2007) describes the

interviews and ethnographic encounters she has had with Congolese children in Uganda. She has been able to show a multifaceted image of the ways in which refugee children indeed take agentive roles vis-à-vis their own lives. These refugee children negotiate even situations that would at the outset seem very likely to lead to sexual abuse, such as living undocumented in a private house. She shows how the category of vulnerability can itself be negotiated, not simply taken at the face value as a fundamental trait of a person socially located in a certain way. The notion of vulnerable categories thus needs to be carefully assessed so as not to victimize but to see the personhood that extends beyond a given category (Penttinen 2016).

Global governance of labour migration

We will last summarize feminist critique of the global governance of labour migration. The UN International Convention on the Protection of the Rights of All Migrant Workers and Members of Their Families from 1990 is a framework comprising wide rights not only for labour migrants but also for their families despite their respective administrative statuses. It is necessary to note the fact that the Convention does not distinguish between regular and irregular migrants. It thus extends the scope of rights to undocumented migrant workers and their families. Currently, however, not one developed country has ratified this Convention. Developed countries argue that the same rights are already covered within the existing national legislations, which is why the ratification of the Convention would not bring any added value. Assessing the Convention from a feminist perspective, Nicola Piper (2008: 12–13) argues that, despite the importance of explicitly extending the scope of rights to all migrants and their families, ratifying and implementing this Convention and ILO's migrant specific instruments would not suffice alone. This is because their ratification would not do away with the gendered structures in labour markets, which contribute largely also to gendered politics of migration. She points out how equity of migrant workers with the natives would not necessarily be sufficient to guarantee full protection of migrants, as there are sectors of labour in different countries in which native workers are not protected either. Thus a wider ratification of the UN Convention as such would not suffice to truly strengthen the existing human rights framework. What is needed are more creative ways of rethinking the overall framework of rights.

International Organization for Migration (IOM) is a central player in the global management of migration. The most visible campaigns of the IOM concern "voluntary return" and the agency's anti-trafficking activities. It is however difficult to decipher exactly its stance when observing the various activities this specific inter-governmental agency is involved in. These activities range from post-disaster reconstruction activities to enhanced support to border management efforts. Ashutosh and Mountz (2011) maintain that IOM is indeed an institution that is strategically placed between the nation-state and international civil society, capable of transforming the state through the language of international humanitarianism.

The practices of the IOM have raised also feminist concerns. Andrijase-vic (2007) has analysed the imagery of IOM's anti-trafficking campaigns in Eastern Europe. Her analysis illustrates how these campaigns deploy erotized and victimized portrayals of women and depict men as the villains, which builds on highly symbolic and stereotypical constructions of femininity and masculinity. She suggests that these portrayals, depicting wounded, muted, partial and dead female bodies, are used as an incentive that would compel women to stay at home (also Andrijasevic 2010). Thereby they seek to restrict women's possibilities, and inclination, to lead a globally mobile life. The posters, combining images with narratives from different situations that have led to forced prostitution, fail to address the issue of restrictive policies that delimit labour migration in general or offer any real alternative apart from staying home. The attempted warning against the real threats women may encounter turns, through critical feminist insight, into a controversial practice that is suggestive of an attempt to contain gendered bodies in place in the country of nationality.

CONCLUDING WORDS

In this chapter, we have discussed the border and the ensuing bordering prac-tices. Influential among these bordering practices are policies that address and seek to regulate and modify global mobilities. We started from the insti-tution of detention that is an extreme way to limit mobility in a prison-like setting. This institution has been designed to contain people whose identity remains to be determined or who are waiting for deportation. In Tanja's case in the opening narrative, the contained space of detention turned into a place where she was sexually abused by those in charge of monitoring her behav-iour. She was brave enough to report on the case.

We then proceeded to examine practices at the border from gendered per-spectives. We did this by presenting various aspects of border control in very concrete border control setting and their intertwined racialized and sexualized dimensions. Many of these dimensions are entangled with the question of whether the person holds appropriate documents for crossing international borders. Intensified control targets particular bodies based on gendered, racialized and sexualized imaginaries.

Included in these interlinked institutional approaches are policies facilitat-ing and hindering global mobilities that seek to channel the global flows of people. It is not far wrong to claim that, globally, policies are increasingly turning towards deploying selective, skills-based criteria for people to be allowed to migrate permanently with full rights to family formation and reunion. On the other side of the coin, there are those who are not deemed qualified for family entitlements, yet whose labour force is crucial for the functioning of economies and sectors of labour that rely on migrant labour, such as care work both in homes and at institutional sites. These individuals are required to choose between a liveable income and family life. Another option is to live, at least in part, in irregularity. For family members, this often means limited or no access to education and decent accommodation, not to mention the constant threat of being deported at any time.

In the following chapter, we continue with abusive practices in gendered globalization by focusing to the issue of trafficking for sexual exploitation.

DISCUSSION POINTS

1. Explain intersectional approach to border control. Give examples.
2. How can the access to cross the border be differentially organized for residents of the same country?
3. How can balance be achieved between the recognition of agency and the care for the fulfillment of basic rights in feminist research on human mobility? How could this be done as regards refugees in particular?

ESSAY QUESTIONS

1. How do feminist security studies theorize border control practices?
2. How does feminist policy analysis enable us to examine seemingly gender-neutral policies? Practice gender policy analysis on a chosen document.
3. What is the role of international organizations in governing global mobilities?

STUDY ASSIGNMENTS

Search for regulations concerning family reunion in different countries across the globe. How do they regulate income needed to bring the family along? Which time limits are imposed for submitting the application for family reunion? How does one's migration status/residence permit facilitate or hinder this process?

Find out which are the grounds for acquiring nationality in the country where you live. Is the process the same for everyone? What happens when a child is born in the territory to parents who are foreign nationals?

EXTRA MATERIALS

M.I.A. (2016) Borders. https://www.youtube.com/watch?v=r-Nw7HbaeWY
Close your eyes and listen to the lyrics of this song. What is its message?
  Then play the clip another time without sound. How is the border figured in
  the clip? How would you interpret gender and sexuality enacted in the clip?
Fortress (2008) is a documentary film directed by Fernand Melgar and
  produced by Climage. The film depicts life in a reception and processing
  centre for asylum seekers in Switzerland. It shows the daily interaction
  between residents of the centre, its personnel and voluntary workers.
What kinds of surveillance mechanisms are in place in the infrastructure of
  the centre that condition everyday mobility?
Special Flight (2011) is a documentary film directed by Fernand Melgar and
  produced by Climage. It presents the life in an immigration detention centre in Switzerland where the detainees are awaiting deportation to different
  countries.
Group exercise: After watching the film, divide the class into four random
  subgroups. Each has a particular positionality and issues to defend (detainees of the centre – personnel of the centre – deportation/removal officials –
  activists opposing detention and deportation). Each group has ten to fifteen
  minutes to draft the main arguments from the given perspectives for a common debate. Finish by unpacking each of these positionalities and ensuing
  argumentation.
Documentary film *Golf Alpha Yankee* shows the struggles of gay men in Iran
  who face abuse, torture and imprisonment. It shows what it is like to live
  as a gay man in exile. http://www.golfalphayankee.com/
What are the diverse effects on a person's well-being when his or her life is
  at risk because of sexual orientation? How does this risk impact the whole
  family?

NOTES

  1. Depicted, for example, in the documentary *Lost in Detention* produced by
Frontline and PBS in 2011 using the case of detention in the United States.
  2. See Doty (2001, 2007), Nevins (2007), Téllez (2008), Morales and Bejarano
(2009), Brown (2010), Weber (2011), Wright (2011, 2013), Lind and Williams (2013)
and Squire (2015).
  3. See Meriem's case as regards the Algerian state in chapter 2.

Chapter 6

Abuse, crime and mobility

In 2001 police officer Kathryn Bolcovac is laid off from her work in UN peacekeeping mission in Bosnia.[1] The reason for being fired was not that she did not do her police work well, but that she disclosed the involvement of her male colleagues organizing trafficking of girls for the purposes of sexual exploitation. During her deployment in Bosnia she discovered that young women and girls were brought to Bosnia from Ukraine and Moldova to service the incoming international clientele. The parties involved in the trafficking ring that Kathryn Bolcovac uncovered were the International Police Task Force (IPTF) members, SFOR (Stabilization Force in Bosnia and Herzegovina) staff, local police, international employees, and local citizens.

Bolcovac had been working on a pilot project on violence against women, which had been initiated by UN High Commissioner Madeleine Rees. During this time, Bolcovac encountered young foreign women in a local women's shelter who all had a similar story to tell: false promises of work abroad, confinement, rape, torture and forced prostitution. These stories motivated Bolcovac to pursue further investigation, which led her to the trail of her co-workers in both buying the sexual services at the local bar, protecting the bar owners from raids, and trafficking women to Bosnia. One of her colleagues actually had confided in her, asking for help as he had realized the girl he had bought for himself for a week had managed to escape. Bolcovac was astounded that this man was troubled by the fact that the girl he had bought had run away, and not by the fact that he had actually committed a crime and human rights violation. During the investigations Bolcovac received continuous threats, was told to take a leave of absence, demoted and later fired. She won the case against the private security corporation for wrongful dismissal but was not hired as a police officer. Currently Bolcovac is a well-known public speaker who speaks for human ethics, trafficking and anti-corruption issues and offers consultancy on code of conduct.[2]

In this chapter our focus is on violence and exploitation of people, which involves moving them from one area or country to another for the purpose of financial gains from unfree labour. This practice is most often referred to as the crime of trafficking. It means exploitation of a person for the purpose of financial gains in the destination country. In this chapter we define the crime of trafficking based on the UN definition. We discuss how trafficking in persons is inextricably linked to processes of globalization, especially in the context of post-9/11 global restructuring, which induces the mobility of military and civilian experts to conflict zones. Simultaneously, ever-tightening immigration regulation and migration policies give power to traffickers to exploit their victims.

Our perspective in this chapter draws from feminist research on violence and feminist security studies. Therefore, we address how military and peacekeeping operations are inextricably linked to flows of trafficking, especially for the purposes of sexual exploitation. Moreover, we recognize how the disruption of societies due to economic restructuring, war and conflict allows organized crime to operate and seek financial gains through trafficking in persons. Our emphasis lies throughout the chapter on what being trafficked entails for the person who is exploited. What does it mean to experience severe violence in the context of global mobility and how is it possible to heal?

We integrate the narrative of a trafficked woman Zara from the novel *Purge* by Sofi Oksanen (2010) as a method of illustrating what the experience of being trafficked entails for the victim. These excerpts are intended to offer a sense of how a person is transformed through traumatic experience. Oksanen presents Zara's story as a fragmented narrative that is representative of a trauma story. The quotes from the novel serve as a way to connect to the experience and feel with the person who has been caught up in an extremely abusive situation and gain understanding of how deeply violence affects the person's sense of self-worth and how the experience of violence continues long after the actual events are over. Therefore, we wish to remind the reader to take breaks if needed and apply safety methods, such as bringing awareness to breathing or a safe place, when appropriate, if the reading or study assignments feel too overwhelming.

In this chapter we focus on trafficking in persons for the purpose of sexual exploitation, because this is reflective of feminist and gender-focused research on trafficking. This does not mean that trafficking in persons for other purposes is less common, but rather that feminists have given more attention to sexual exploitation and neglected other forms of trafficking (Bastia 2006). We acknowledge this bias and emphasize that the trafficking for the purposes of slave labour or for organ trade represents gendered practices of trafficking that are just as exploitative, and even deadly, as trafficking for the purpose of sexual exploitation (see box 6.1). These practices are called new or "neo" forms of slavery (LeBaron 2015). We recognize that the feminist emphasis

---

BOX 6.1

Forced labour of children under age of fifteen in cocoa plantations has been widely documented. Cocoa is the main export product for Cote d'Ivoire and Ghana. Even though the reports that chocolate in M&M's and KitKat bars was produced by children in unfree labour conditions made headlines in 2014, it is estimated that the use of child labour is still on the rise. Children work in hazardous conditions, using machete knives to split the cocoa pods, and they are beaten and locked in at night in order to prevent escape. Traffickers abduct children from neighbouring countries and bring them to cocoa plantations. These children are not able to see their families for years. Currently the means to combat unfree labour in the cocoa production lies with the promotion of certificates such as fair trade and Rainforest Alliance to guarantee for the consumers that cocoa in their chocolate products is not produced by victims of forced labour.

Discussion points: How much do you pay attention to the production of the consumer and food items you use or your family uses? Which items do you select based on fair trade or other labels that indicate fair trade and respect for environment?

If possible, try to trace a food or other consumer item to the production stage. What kind of information is available? What is secret?

---

on trafficking for the purpose of sexual exploitation may turn into political and ideological debates between feminist activists for or against prostitution (Beloso 2012, Penttinen 2008). We are not interested in these debates, as the purpose of this chapter is to focus on how abuse and crime are emerging in the context of globalization of the world economy and how such practices benefit from the tightening border control in post-9/11 global restructuring. Therefore, we also emphasize that trafficking in persons operates through similar patterns and practices despite the purpose for which trafficking takes place. Our focus is on sex trafficking because gender and sexuality are integral to how profits are made in this practice. Sex trafficking services mostly male clientele, and the majority of trafficked persons for the purpose of sexual exploitation are women and girls. Although not all organized prostitution meets the criteria of trafficking in persons, the majority of trafficking in persons takes place for the purposes of sexual exploitation.

The rest of this chapter is divided into three sections. First we discuss how trafficking in persons is configured in the context of globalization. We address how trafficking in persons for purpose of sexual exploitation is connected to economic restructuring, normalization of buying sexual services as well as global mobility of peacekeepers and security experts. In the second section we discuss what constitutes the crime of trafficking based on UN definition. We define the criteria necessary for prosecution and address how traffickers operate in practice to gain and maintain control of their victims. We end the chapter with the discussion on what all of this entails for the victim and what it takes to heal from the experience of violence.

TRAFFICKING IN THE CONTEXT OF GLOBAL MOBILITY

Global inequality constitutes one of the most important factors leading to trafficking of persons for the purposes of prostitution and slave labour. Trafficking flows generally from less affluent societies to more affluent societies. Important here is to recognize how the disruption of societies due to war and conflict, economic restructuring and environmental crisis enables the crime of trafficking. For example, Syrian victims of trafficking were only detected after the violent conflict began in 2011 (UNODC 2014). Similarly, refugee camps for the refugees from environmental crisis such as the tsunami in 2004 and the earthquake in Haiti in 2010 have been areas for recruitment for traffickers. As discussed in chapter 4, transition to market economy in Russia and other former Soviet states lead to increase in mobile prostitution as well as criminal trafficking in persons from former Soviet countries to Europe, the United States and Japan (Penttinen 2008).

The exact number of persons being trafficked for the purposes of sexual exploitation is hard to estimate. This is because trafficking is organized by criminal networks, which obviously avoid detection. In addition, responses against trafficking vary according to country and region. In the European and U.S. contexts, trafficking is considered a more serious problem than in the global South even if the estimated numbers of trafficked individuals are higher in Africa and South-East Asia. Still even in European context, legislation against trafficking is fairly recent (Jyrkinen 2009, Kantola 2010). Indeed, trafficking has been mainly considered a problem of organized crime and irregular migration. In this context the role of the receiving countries cannot be underestimated. Receiving countries also uphold restrictive entry regulations that render the victims all the more vulnerable as they risk being considered irregular migrants and thus face deportation (Andrijasevic 2010). The conceptualization of victims of trafficking as irregular migrants also affects how countries keep track of the number of trafficking victims and whether countries are able or willing to recognize them.

The crime of trafficking functions in the intersections of objective circumstances and subjective choices (UNODC 2012). The objective conditions are poverty, war or environmental destruction, breakdown of societies and lack of social support, whereas subjective choices refer to individual desires to seek opportunities and accept high risks (see box 6.2). The last determining factor is the capacity of traffickers to exploit people in vulnerable situations due to their access to material and financial resources and international networks. The UN Report on Global Trafficking (UNODC 2012) emphasizes that structural reasons alone do not lead into vulnerability of persons and subject them to be victims of trafficking. Trafficking in persons takes place always for a specific purpose, such as sex work, slave labour, organ trade or even ritual purposes, as already briefly mentioned. Therefore, even though trafficking in persons is configured at the intersection of objective conditions and subjective choices, it always takes people who are keen on making a profit through exploitation of others.

The intersections of structural reasons and personal desires are conceptualized in the report in the following way:

> Gender, age, migration status, ethno-linguistic background and poverty . . . are by themselves insufficient explanations of vulnerability, but they tend to become factors of vulnerability if they provide grounds for discrimination from the rest of the community. While anyone could become a trafficking victim, persons who lack protection, who are not integrated in the surrounding community and who are isolated by the national authorities or by the societies where they live are at greater risk of human trafficking. In these areas of discrimination and marginalization, traffickers find the space to exploit the vulnerable situation of potential victims.

(UNODC 2012: 15)

BOX 6.2

An example of established trafficking network is the Balkan organized crime, which was active already before the Balkan wars and was allowed to continue operating after the violent conflict ended. According to EUROPOL (2006), most of the trafficking in women and girls from Central and Eastern Europe to Western Europe and the UK has been operated by Bosnian and Serbian criminal organizations that were active perpetrating and organizing sexualized violence during the war in Bosnia and in Kosovo. The irony of this collaboration is that these criminal syndicates were on the opposite sides of the extremely violent and brutal ethnic conflict but reconciled such political differences in order to conduct the international and regional trafficking in women and girls efficiently and profitably.

Study assignment: Search for a current conflict context where trafficking has been reported. What can we know about the perpetrators and the victims?

As a global criminal activity, trafficking in persons as a crime is often compared to the trafficking in drugs and arms. In this regard trafficking in persons is both more profitable and less risky. One of the explaining factors for the profitability and relative safety for the traffickers to conduct their business is that trafficking for the purpose for sexual exploitation takes place in the context of the overall global sex industry, which includes both licit and illicit activities. Moreover, policing the sex industry may not be a top priority for law enforcement. With regard to traffickers themselves, the EUROPOL report (2006) mentions that these groups are "comfortable with cross border criminality" (EUROPOL 2006: 5). They have already established networks and access to resources that locals in disrupted communities do not have. These resources can be vehicles required for transport, arms and connections. Moreover, trafficking in persons for the purpose of sexual exploitation has been argued to represent a model for how to create a profitable organized criminal activity (e.g. box 6.2). Organized criminal groups take over territory and set up organized prostitution, after which they expand to other criminal activities (Albini 1997, Jyrkinen 2005). They bring locally operating pimps and prostitutes under the control of the organized groups and thus aim for territorial control. For example, in Finland, a police report published in 2002 revealed that Russian and Baltic organized crime had divided the country into three respective sectors that allowed different criminal groups to coexist and operate sex trafficking in their own designated regions and avoid conflict with each other (Leskinen 2003, Penttinen 2008). The curious aspect of this report was that it had taken ten years for the police to reveal that prostitution was actually organized and that the practices the criminal syndicates used met the criteria of trafficking. We will return to the criteria later.

The objective of trafficking is always exploitation for the purpose of financial gains. It is not about charity towards the trafficked persons as providing a means of mobility. Neither is it about providing an affordable service in the context of pleasure industry for a wider range of customers. Trafficking in persons is profitable because there are customers who are willing and interested in buying sexual services. It is often difficult or impossible for clients to discern whether they are buying sex from a victim of trafficking, as it is risky for the victim to let the client know of the conditions. Clients may remain ignorant, or even in denial, of the conditions under which the person they buy sexual services from lives. They may want to believe in the illusion that the woman is into them personally and enjoying the encounter as much as they are (Penttinen 2008).

The crime of sex trafficking is profitable, because there is a demand for commercial sexual services and ignorance of customers in the global North of the constrictive conditions for the women and girls who provide sexual services. Research on clients of sexual services has revealed that the majority of buyers are men regardless of cultural or regional background (O'Connell Davidson 1998). The socio-economic background of men who buy sex does not differ considerably from men who do not use commercial sexual services (Hanmer 2000). However, men use commercial sexual services to fulfil different kinds of needs. For some men, commercial sex is part of sexually compulsive behaviour, others use commercial sex because they are not interested in intimate relationships, some buy sex to replace the intimacy that is lacking in their relationships, and for some men commercial sexual services is the only way to have intimacy (Jyrkinen and Penttinen 2017). However, what is crucial here is that regardless of the need to buy sexual services the clients may not be able to discern whether they are buying sex from a victim of trafficking (Penttinen 2008). Or they may be in denial about the involvement of organized criminal activity with respect to the services they buy. In comparison this ignorance is also telling of how consumers in the global North may not be able to tell whether the cocoa in their chocolate bars, coffee or cheap consumer items have been produced in conditions that include coercion and debt bondage.

The global mobility of peacekeepers, civilian security experts and the military constitute a major factor in increasing trafficking in women and girls for the purpose of sexual exploitation. Peacekeeping and crisis management constitutes a global mobility of scale of mostly men in the context of post-9/11 global restructuring. The institutionalization of long-lasting international missions creates an ongoing flow of military peacekeepers, civilian security experts and private contractors to conflict and post-conflict regions, working in one- or two-year rotations, or hopping from one mission to another one. Peacekeepers and civilian experts often rotate directly from one mission to another and thus can make international peacekeeping even a personal career. It is not a secret that experts in these operations are mostly men. The continuous flow of military and civilian experts in turn creates another current of trafficked persons for the purposes of prostitution and sexual exploitation. The use of sexual services is seen unofficially as rest and relaxation and as means for male-bonding and group cohesion (Whitworth 2007, Belkin 2012). Visiting a brothel is a practice of building trust among the group members, because the secret of unacceptable behaviour now joins the group together.

The life of a trafficked woman for the purposes of sexual exploitation is one of mobility. She is moved from one country to another. Often abuse and torture takes place in the transit country, before the entry to the destination in which she is expected to begin her sex work. In addition, she may be moved to a series of destinations according to seasonal demands as traffickers "chase" prostitution markets such as high seasons of different tourist destinations. Alternatively, she can be moved from one city to another simply in order to make it more difficult for her to establish contacts with locals or seek help. Moving from one city to another is done in order maintain the interests of clients by the supply of different women. She may also be sold again to another pimp or a trafficker and moved to a different country.

The mobility of the victim of trafficking is thus better characterized by the term *friction* rather than *flow*, which can be seen also as an element of the way globalization operates (Tsing 2004). Trafficking in persons is an example of how globalization slows down and limits the mobility of others that are caught into the lure and control of traffickers. In a way, Katherine Bolcovac in the opening narrative also got stuck momentarily in such friction. She won the case against DynCorp (the company that had hired her) for wrongful dismissal. However, for the men guilty for illicit activities and involvement in the trafficking networks, there were no criminal sanctions. The men were dismissed and sent home from the mission. This outcome can be explained by the tolerance and normalization of prostitution in the context of military interventions and peacekeeping. Therefore, sexual exploitation of women and girls or prostitution as such is not seen as a problem, but instead as a normal part of military and peacekeeping operations; after all, "boys will be boys." In fact, her male colleagues told Kathryn Bolcovac time and again to just let the case go and stop the investigations; after all, the girls were just "whores" and Bolcovac should not waste her time on them.

The opening narrative of Kathryn Bolcovac struggling to disclose the involvement of UN peacekeepers shows how deeply embedded the idea that certain men have the right to exploit women and girls, even buy them for their private use. Bolcovac found out that the UN peacekeepers were regular customers at Florida bar, a local brothel-like establishment established to service international clientele.[3] It was the place where Bolcovac had often seen UN vehicles parked outside. During her investigation, Bolcovac and her team raided the place, only to find it empty of customers at the time. Inside she found pictures of international security staff with the girls, stacks of American dollars, passports and seven girls huddled together behind a locked door. She learned that they had been abused, tortured, raped and sold to a trafficker. In order to ensure their continued submission to prostitution they had been compelled to watch the torture and murder of the girls who had rebelled and tried to escape from the confines of the Florida bar.

The girls caught up in the trafficking ring in the Balkans had little chances of escape and had obviously no reason to seek help from the police or trust them. And who could blame them? After all, the international police force was part of the network. Some of the girls had been trafficked in a UN vehicle. The local and international police were involved also in returning escaped girls back to the bar, sharing information warning about prospective raids. Apparently, everyone knew what was going on and it was tolerated, even accepted by the UN officials.

In order to combat the crime of trafficking in persons and other forms of new slavery it is imperative to recognize how these practices are inextricably linked to power hierarchies configured in the globalized world economy, globalization of production (LeBaron 2015) and Western consumer lifestyle. Therefore, the crime of trafficking is not something that is separate from the operation of formal economy, normalized consumer culture or migratory flows. Trafficking in persons is cannot be reduced to "other cultures" that do not value human rights, or red-light districts that service marginalized clientele; instead, the movement of trafficked persons for financial gains takes place in conjunction with the flows of tourists, business travellers and military and humanitarian interventions that increase the demand for sexual services.

THE CRIME OF TRAFFICKING

Right from the start Pasha made it clear that Zara was in debt to him. She could leave as soon as she'd paid him back, but not before! And the only way she could pay him was by working for him – working efficiently, doing work that paid well.

Zara did not understand where the debt came from. Nevertheless, she started counting how much was still left, how many months, how many weeks, days, hours, how many mornings, how many nights, how many showers, how many blow jobs, customers. How many girls. From how many countries. How many times she had to redden her lips and how many times Nina had to give her stitches. How many diseases she got, how many bruises.

(Oksanen 2010: 262)

The UN defines trafficking "as a process by which people are recruited in their community and exploited by traffickers using deception and/or some form of coercion to lure and control them. There are three distinct elements of this crime: the act, the means and the purpose. All three elements must be present to constitute a trafficking in persons offence, although each element has a range of manifestations" (UNODC 2012: 16). The above excerpt from the novel *Purge* exemplifies how the entrapment of trafficking works and how it distorts the reality for the victim. After the trafficker has gained control of the victim a whole new set of rules will apply. If the victim does not comply, there will be repercussions, or the victim may be given false hope for gaining freedom if she complies.

What is notable here is that for the offence to be trafficking it has to include all these three elements (*the act, means and purpose*) in order to be prosecuted as the crime of trafficking. If these three criteria are not met, it can be criminal activity, but it does not constitute trafficking. For example, the crime of trafficking is often differentiated from smuggling of persons. The main difference between the two is that trafficking always has some purpose, such as financial gain, which is acquired by the control of the person and their labour in the *destination* country. Smuggling of persons refers to assistance in illicit crossing of borders and involves financial gains for smugglers; yet the control does not continue in the destination country in a similar way. This distinction is not always as clear in reality, as smuggled persons may also have to work to pay off the debt from smuggling and the smugglers may stay in contact with the smuggled persons.[4]

Trafficking is a complex crime. There is no single way in which the act, means and purpose are constituted. Instead, trafficking practices and purposes vary greatly. According to the UNODC report, the *act* of trafficking refers to "the recruitment, transport, harbouring or receipt of persons intended for trafficking," whereas "the means" refers to the threat or use of force, deception, coercion or abuse of power used to lure the victims. "The purpose" is the form of exploitation to which the traffickers subject their victims, whether sexual exploitation, forced labour, domestic servitude or one of a range of other forms (UNODC 2012: 16). The trafficking in persons (TIP 2016) report also emphasizes trafficking of children for forced begging and child soldiering. The more attention there is to the crime of trafficking, the more areas are discovered in which exploitation of others meets the trafficking criteria.

The EUROPOL (2006) report also includes the process of *grooming* in the act of trafficking. Grooming refers to the period in which a person is approached and lured into trafficking by false promises of work or false promises about working conditions and income in the destination country. Grooming is a descriptive term of the process. Grooming is an expression that is also used to describe sex offenders' tactics towards the child victims. We do not imply here that sexual abuse of children and trafficking are the same type of crime. Instead, we maintain that traffickers actively lure and deceive a person into trafficking and that it takes time to do so. People do not only enter into trafficking accidentally, because poverty or lack of opportunity pushes them into it, or because they are naïve, but they are also actively approached and manipulated into believing that taking the opportunity will be beneficial for them. It takes time and effort to build the trust of the target, and this is done in a systematic way. For example, in the Balkans, a person may be approached by a family member or a relative who is actually working for traffickers. This gives more credibility to the traffickers in the eyes of the target. More importantly, the contact person figures out what it is that the target needs and wants to hear in order to be convinced and uses this information to deceive the person.

In the European context, according to EUROPOL (2006), trafficked persons for sexual exploitation are held in debt bondage ranging from several months up to five to ten years. Being moved around from one country to the next, from one cultural environment to another, makes it difficult for the women to seek help and escape. For many, being trafficked is the only way they believe they can come by restrictive immigration controls. Therefore, they comply with the demands of the trafficker and also reiterate the false story at the border control, a moment at which trafficking at least hypothetically could be detected. The enlargement of the EU has made trafficking easier and less costly for traffickers, as victims travel with their own passports and do not need false documentation.

If trafficking involves also crossing the border with false documents, the control of the traffickers over the trafficked persons is increased. Therefore, the *act* of trafficking, that is, the recruitment and transport is also connected to the *means* of trafficking, which refers to the different forms of force and threat of force that the victims are subjected to during transit and in the destination country. In addition, irregular migrant status results in deportation to country of origin and thus often these women are re-trafficked after return as "the debts" accumulated from trafficking still have to be paid (Thorbek and Pattanaik 2002: 5). Seeking help becomes increasingly difficult in Europe if the victim of trafficking is treated as an irregular migrant or as potential witness against organized crime. Thus, national policies benefit criminal organizations who make business out of exploitation of people in vulnerable positions.

The purpose of trafficking is the financial gains that are made from the persons' labour. Trafficked persons may also be resold to another "pimp" or "owner." The UN and the EU recognize that trafficking in human beings is currently conducted for the following *purposes*: sexual exploitation, forced labour, begging, organ transplants, child soldiers and rituals. Only in the case of trafficking of children for ritual purposes, financial reward is not as direct as trafficking for forced labour and servitude.

International Labour Organization estimated in 2012 that there are 20.9 million people in forced labour, including children and including the victims of trafficking.[5] Although the numbers concerning trafficking are always estimates, it is obvious that the crime of trafficking is global in scope. The UNODC report (2012) was a first attempt to generate a global overview of the crime of trafficking and subsequent report was published in 2014. For the purpose of the first report, the UNODC collected survey data from 132 countries in all different areas of the world and from international governmental organizations as well as non-governmental organizations. The information collected involved national police reports, Ministry of Justice reports and trafficking in persons' reports. In combining this data the report aimed to give an overview of how trafficking operates currently and which parts of the world are the most affected.

Whereas the nation-based survey data varied as different countries responded to the data request and surveys inconsistently, the report is still a useful tool for gaining understanding of both the globality and the severity of the crime. It is clear that in drawing generalizations about where trafficking in persons takes place is Europe and U.S. biased, because in these regions trafficking is approached as a security problem. Conversely, in the European and U.S. contexts legislation that criminalizes trafficking is still fairly recent. Therefore, the report concludes that traffickers have been able to run their activities in relatively risk-free environment.

The UN report explains that regardless of the hype against trafficking in Europe and the United States, the number of convictions of trafficking cases during the period 2010–2012 was very low, equalling the number of convictions for homicide in Iceland, a country whose population is approximately 300,000 habitants. While this comparison with convictions of homicide in Iceland is based on the idea of the Nordic countries as relatively peaceful and low in crime, it also illustrates how, despite the acknowledgement of trafficking as a crime that involves violence, deceit and coercion and is global in scale, not much is being done systematically to detect, prosecute and convict the perpetrators. This may be partly due to sophistication of the traffickers in avoiding detection, but the importance of lack of political will to prevent or prosecute trafficking cannot be underestimated.

Sex trade is usually not the target of governments' efforts locally. Instead, sex industry has been tolerated and the operation of brothels, sex bars and brothel-like establishments has not been controlled (Bales 2008, Penttinen 2008). In Europe, in places such as Amsterdam, prostitution is an accepted part of the city landscape and a tourist attraction. In Finland as well, the working conditions of women in erotic bars was not of public interest (Penttinen 2008). One could easily walk by these places and not care about what was going on inside. Another aspect that enables trafficking for the purposes of sexual exploitation is that countries such as Japan or Cyprus offer entertainment visas or cabaret dancing visas. Traffickers use these visas to bring women to Japan and Cyprus as entertainers, even though the purpose is to provide sexual services, often in controlled environments. However, the control of the traffickers increases when the victim overstays her visa and thus becomes an irregular migrant. This is problematic for the victim, for she risks deportation if she is detected.

The fact that trafficking has been primarily seen in European context as a problem of organized crime and irregular migration (Kantola 2010) has put the victims of trafficking in an increasingly precarious position. In larger European cities projects funded partly by local Deaconess institutes and non-governmental organizations[6] sought out migrant women in sex work in order to offer social, psychological and medical assistance, such as HIV testing, information about safe sex practices for sex workers and condoms and lubricants for the women selling sex. An important part of this work has been informing about the legal rights of the foreign women in sex work in the destination country and thus empowering the women at individual level. These non-governmental organizations would respond to foreign women in prostitution as fellow human beings,[7] recognizing and being attentive to their needs, intentionally building an environment of trust, instead of seeing them as suspect illegal migrants or potential witnesses against organized crime.

EXPERIENCING VIOLENCE AND POTENTIAL FOR HEALING

The powerlessness had knocked Zara to the floor.

The walls were panting, the floor gasped, the floorboards bulged with moisture. The wallpapers crackled. She felt the footsteps of a fly walking across her cheek. How could they see to fly in the dark?

Now Aliide knew.

(Oksanen 2010: 308)

Whether trafficking takes place for the purpose of forced labour, sexual exploitation or other purposes, the common denominator is violence. Violence takes place en route to the destination, or it may continue for years, such as in the cases of children trafficked for domestic servitude or farm work (see Bales 2008). Arguing that trafficking should be studied as violence is not the same as arguing that prostitution in itself is an institution of violence against women and that persons who are seen as forced into prostitution are passive victims. Instead, it is about validating that the violence that takes place in the context of trafficking actually hurts and may do so for a long time afterwards. Traumatic stress that is the result of an overwhelming situation such as trafficking is not a sign of personal weakness or failure, but a normal consequence of violence. Therefore, the discussion of trafficking should also include what the experience of violence feels like for the victim in addition to legal and ethical concerns or structural conditions.

Feminist research on violence is useful as a form of insight into the experience of gendered and gender-based violence (see box 6.3) (McKey 2005). Trafficking can be defined as a form of gender-based violence, because it is based on gender norms and normative notions of gender. Moreover, women and girls are disproportionately affected by trafficking for the purpose of sexual exploitation. Istanbul Convention (ISTA 2011) offers the most comprehensive definition of gender-based violence up to date. First of all, it frames gender-based violence as "a manifestation of historically unequal power relations between women and men, which have led to domination over, and discrimination against, women by men and to the prevention of the full advancement of women" (p. 5). It defines violence against women as "a violation of human

BOX 6.3

Research on violence against women has evolved from the feminist approach in 1970s that focused on domestic violence (i.e. violence against women) to research on sexualized violence, gendered violence and gender-based violence nationally, globally and as a security issue. Sexualized violence refers to the linkage of power and sexuality in the act of violence. Gendered violence refers to the way in which gender gives meaning to violence. Finally, gender-based violence refers to the structure of violence. Feminist research on violence recognizes the complexity of cultural gender roles and hierarchical power structures in the configuration of violence. This means that there are no easy universalizations to be made, such as "men are violent" or that "women are victims." Instead, feminist research on violence calls into question the different levels, the cultural and political contexts in which violence against women takes place and how this violence builds on gender norms and normative notions of gender. The structures of economic, political and social insecurity in which women are often in a disadvantaged position are also central to the study of gender-based violence.

Study assignment: Browse through main news outlets and identify stories of gender-based violence. How would you analyse these stories drawing on feminist approach to violence?

rights and a form of discrimination against women and shall mean all acts of gender-based violence that result in, or are likely to result in, physical, sexual, psychological or economic harm or suffering to women, including threats of such acts, coercion or arbitrary deprivation of liberty, whether occurring in public or in private life" (ISTA 2011: 8).

What is relevant here is that the definition of gender-based violence includes the understanding of the unequal power relations between men and women and comprehensive list of acts of violence that include also psychological and economic harm. Therefore, violence is not limited to acts of physical harm and coercion. In this regard also the practice of grooming and manipulation are already violence and not something that leads to actual violence during transit to destination country. When trafficking is conceptualized only in legal terms as an offence of act, means and purpose, it gives in a way a false sense of trafficking as something that has a clear beginning and a clear end. However, for the victim of trafficking the experience of violence may be something that continues, shapes her experience and sense of self for years to come.

Central to feminist research on violence is to recognize that violence is not something that can be reduced only to the violent event, but instead is something that should be understood as a process that shapes the experience of everyday life long after the actual event or act of violence is over (Ronkainen 2008). Another factor is to gain understanding of the meaning of violence from first person accounts. To understand what violence is, the meaning has to come from the person who has experienced violence, who has been violated and abused. This approach challenges the idea that it is the academic expert who gets to define what violence is. Last, feminist research on violence is a practice of compassionate witnessing (Penttinen 2016). This refers to a practice of turning towards the pain and suffering caused by violence and validating it and thus reducing the sense of shame associated with the experience of violence.

Ronkainen (2008) describes how the experience of sexual abuse at an early age can result in a sense of being "dirty" or "used" which continues way into adulthood. Some women in her study explained how they felt that their own body had changed, it had become unfamiliar to them. Or, they felt that other people were able to tell, just by looking at them, that they have been abused. They were afraid that the experience of abuse made them appear different in the eyes of others, as if it were somehow drawn on their skin for others to discern and judge. Experience of violence impacted their sense of self-worth and capability to trust others. Places once familiar and safe no longer felt so, and mundane things might trigger anxiety and fear. Although abuse was something that had been done to them, they felt shame for being abused. The intensity of this shame is exemplified in the narration of Zara's experience at the moment she hears through the wall that Aliide is informed about Zara's involvement in prostitution. The shame is experienced as an intense sensation of the room enclosing in on her.

Sexual violence is a practice of humiliation. Mollica (2006) explains how humiliation is linked to feelings of shame, uncleanliness and guilt. It is a complex emotion because, "It is primarily linked to how people believe the world is viewing them" (Mollica 2006: 72). Shame is the feeling that makes a person believe that others would not accept or like them, if they knew about the shameful event. Thus, even though a person is target of violence and abuse, it deeply touches their own sense of worthiness through the humiliation. It takes courage to disclose the secret of abuse (Carretta et al. 2016). Violence always carries with it a message of unworthiness; it is a dehumanizing practice that renders the target worthy of violence. The destruction of self-worth results in the feeling that the person has deserved their inhuman treatment or somehow caused it by their own actions. This is especially the case in prolonged abusive relationships, kidnapping and torture, including trafficking in persons.

In the context of trafficking violence is used to break the will of the victim and control her. Rape and other forms of physical abuse often take place during the journey so the victim does not retaliate and accepts her fate in the destination country. These practices indeed are intended to keep the persons under control, in believing they do not deserve anything better, and to make them understand that there are consequences if they try to retaliate or escape. Similarly, children who are trafficked for the purpose of domestic servitude are constantly beaten and treated as inhuman (Bales 2008). As such abuse takes place for a prolonged period of time, it is difficult for the targets of such extreme inhumane treatment to seek help and know that their abuse is not their fault. Thus, violence and threat of violence targets the mind of the victim, what they believe to be true about themselves and others. It breaks the capacity to believe in the goodness of other people, leading the target to ask fundamental questions about good and evil, about human nature, and about one's own sense of self-identity in relation to others (Penttinen 2016).

When violence is understood as a process, an experience that transforms the sense of self and leads into a deep spiritual crisis, it also changes how the healing of the victims can be assisted. Central here is validation of the violence, especially when there is such a strong sense of shame linked to the experience of violence. It is important for the person to hear that it was not their fault and that they are not solely responsible for what has been done to them. This also enables us to share the secret and share the responsibility of the violence with the perpetrators, thus reducing the weight of self-blame (Rothschild 2000). Allowing the person to tell their trauma story also enables them to define what it was that traumatized them. Trauma presents itself in the form of fragmented narrative; it escapes cognitive processing and coherence. Thus, listening and witnessing the trauma story can also be practice that brings coherence and allows the victim of trauma to understand that violence happened to them and they could not have been able to prevent it. This practice of compassionate witnessing (Penttinen 2016) brings coherence to the fragmented trauma story, as happens between Zara and Aliide:

> I didn't have any choice! What they did to girls . . .
>   The way they . . . If you had seen how they . . . They took pictures of everything and they said they would send videos home to Sasha, to everybody, if I tried to get away.

Aliide is able to hear Zara's story from the fragmented sentences and understands deeply what it feels like to be in such a situation and the shame it entails. Zara's story reminds Aliide of her own trauma, which is the shared point of connection between the two women. She responds by describing also her experience of violence:

> And you would never know, when you passed people on the street, if they had seen those pictures. They would look at you and you would never know if you'd been recognized. They would be laughing among themselves and looking in your direction and you would never know if they were talking about you.

(Oksanen 2010: 336)

These narratives also show how the experience of violence does not have a clear ending but continues long after the violent event has ended. A sense of shame can be triggered by the way in which a stranger's look is felt. Triggers, which induce shame and traumatic stress to resurface, could be almost anything, a sound in a distance, a smell, a song on the radio, anything that activates the traumatic memories. Nightmares, intruding memories in the form of flashbacks, panic attacks, hypervigilance and heightened sense of danger can shape the person's life if left untreated (Levine 1997). Healing these symptoms and their causes especially in the case of complex trauma (van der Kolk et al. 1996) takes time and often requires the help of a professional therapist. Whether such services are available for victims of trafficking varies greatly.

Another factor that may hinder the capacity for victims to heal is the difficulty in our contemporary society to accept vulnerability. The experience of violence reminds us that anyone can be violated and hurt (cf. chapter 2 on critical disability studies). Each of us has also the capacity to harm others. In other words, being vulnerable is not about a weakness, but about being human. In contemporary society, especially in countries in the global North that value individualism and "pursuit of happiness" and making it, feeling violated and experiencing traumatic stress can also induce a sense of shame as these can be seen as signs of personal weakness. Ronkainen (2008) explains how in her study the victims of sexualized violence had been told to just "get over it" or "stop thinking about it" by family and friends. Prolonged experience of emotional pain made friends and family feel uneasy around the victim. Close friends did not know how to deal with someone still feeling anxious years after the abuse. In other words, people around the victim of violence were not necessarily always helpful or understanding. Demands placed on the speed and process of healing were often counter-productive, especially because healing requires learning to trust and connect with others. Ronkainen argues that this lack of empathy and compassion is telling of our postmodern culture and society, which values rationality and efficiency and does not allow time for victims to heal. Thus, there is an added experience of suffering for the victims, one that is generated from not recovering fast enough according to societal standards.

In this section we have shown how violence and abuse that takes place in the context of trafficking is not something that can be reduced to any of the three categories – the act, means or purpose. Direct physical, emotional and psychological abuse is integral at all three aspects of the crime of trafficking. Therefore, the deeply harmful effects for the victim of trafficking also need to be acknowledged and validated by the authorities in the host country who potentially try to assist victims of trafficking. In this process non-governmental organizations, women's anti-violence groups, women's shelters and charities (often run by volunteers) have been most active and helpful in meeting victims with the compassion, care and respect they deserve.

CONCLUDING WORDS

In the world-famous TV series and social movement *Half the Sky*, we see the journalist Nicholas Kristof together with Somaly Mam, a Cambodian anti-trafficking activist and a survivor of forced prostitution, raiding a brothel near the northern border. The viewer sees how the big trucks storm to the brothel as if in an action scene in a blockbuster movie. The doors open, and the viewer can see that the walls of the rooms are decorated with pictures depicting baby girls, some even in diapers. The formerly rescued girls now working for Somaly Mam go in and comfort the girls who are in the premises. Later Somaly Mam brings the viewers to the shelter that she runs for the girls rescued from prostitution. Here we see the recovering girls smiling and dancing; they sing their stories of abuse. In this place they are safe and have each other for comfort. We see Somaly Mam holding in her arms a baby girl who was sold to the brothel at the age of two. She explains that the girls in the brothels, whom she goes regularly to rescue, are all the time younger, some even as young as four to five years old when they are sold into prostitution.

Kristof's journalism and the Half the Sky project has received much criticism for the colonialist undertones implicit in the production, especially in the way in which third-world women are represented in his book.[8] He has been accused in the media of making his own career out of the plight of the women and girls who have experienced extreme violence and performing the image of a white rescuer in the action scenes of the documentary.[9] What makes the project more suspect is that it is supported by Hollywood actresses such as Meg Ryan and Susan Sarandon and promoted by Oprah. There is a risk that humanitarianism is used only as a means to advance one's career and gain publicity (Repo and Yrjölä 2011), instead of really finding ways to systematically help the victims or letting the people who are interviewed share their stories in their own terms. Are celebrities truly able to help raise awareness and fight trafficking? Perhaps even curb the demand?

However, regardless of the fierce criticism, Half the Sky brings forth an aspect of trafficking and gender-based violence that is often forgotten and not emphasized in the productions either. This is the continuity of violence against women and girls in war-affected regions in the world such as Cambodia or Sierra Leone. The practices of gender-based violence, and especially institutionalization of brothels and sex trafficking, are not recent cultural phenomena but inextricably linked to the war and military intervention in these areas (Thorbek and Pattanaik 2002). Gender-based violence is thus not a local problem of the third-world countries in the way presented in the films but emerges in connection with the war and security complex. As we have emphasized in this chapter these processes benefit organized criminal syndicates.

The violent conflict and genocide in Cambodia has long been over. Yet the prostitution along the Cambodian northern border continues in the same spaces in which it began with the arrival of tens of thousands of peacekeepers deployed on the UN Transitional Mission in Cambodia (UNTAC) in 1992. Currently these brothels serve local customers but also tourists. The violence and systematic sexual exploitation of young girls continues although the peacekeepers who initiated the demand and organization left the country long ago.

Thus, we are back where we started this chapter – that is, in Bosnia. Similarly, trafficking in women and girls for the purposes of sexual exploitation did not exist in Bosnia before the wars. Yet it still continues after the wars, perhaps with the only difference being that it serves more civilian security experts, tourists and local men. It is estimated that the trafficking to Western Europe from Bosnia will decrease in the coming years and turn towards more regional trafficking within the Balkans. As in the case of Cambodia, in the Balkans the customers are expected to consist mainly of local men and tourists. However, the main reason for more regional trafficking is the institutionalization of EU civilian crisis management missions in Kosovo and Georgia, which provided a continuous flow of mainly male security experts to the Balkans, indeed from Europe. These regions have dropped out of the interest of the media, since the media follows the most recent crisis. The long-term effects on people in war-torn societies do not make the news.

No matter how easy it would be to ignore trafficking in persons for sexual exploitation and distance it as something which exploits mainly people from poor areas and services marginalized groups of men, it has to be remembered that trafficking in persons is a highly profitable activity that goes easily undetected. Victims of trafficking are not somewhere else, but right in the midst of global cities, traffic routes, major sport events and tourists destinations worldwide (Danna 2007). Distancing the problem of trafficking is possible as long as victims of trafficking are treated and perceived as less than human, as exotic others perhaps even deserving their exploitation or suitable for sex work based on their gender and ethnicity. It must be remembered that trafficking is never about providing a service for customers of the Western countries for an affordable price on one hand and provide much needed income for those who live in poverty and without many options. Trafficking takes place always for profit from exploitation of human lives.

Yet focusing on the plight of the victims may be misleading too, for it is perhaps alluring to regard the violence as something that happens to other people in other places, in the war-torn environments or in the red-light districts of the global cities. Instead, we emphasize that trafficking is a practice of abuse and criminality in the context of global mobility. Trafficking in persons is always present at the same time as we see the images of peacekeepers and soldiers deployed on international missions, when we watch the world cup of football on TV or seek inexpensive consumer items in stores.

DISCUSSION POINTS

1. How does normalized consumer culture benefit from unfree labour relations? How are these gendered?
2. How does modern-day slavery differ from slavery before? How is it similar?
3. How are profits generated from trafficking? How are profits made directly and indirectly? List different businesses that can benefit from trafficking in persons.
4. Why is trafficking for the purposes of sexual exploitation or forced labour tolerated? What does this tolerance say about gender, race, culture and class? How is tolerance of sexual exploitation linked to individualism and consumer culture?

ESSAY QUESTIONS

1. What conceptual tools feminist scholarship offers for the analysis of trafficking in persons? You can use any conceptual tool and theoretical perspective presented in this book.
2. Trafficking in Persons (TIP) reports are published annually by the U.S. government. Read through several reports and investigate how the trafficking in persons has changed in recent years. How are the responses to trafficking in persons been enhanced?
3. Find out what organizations in your area provide assistance to trafficking victims. What are their political and ideological backgrounds?
4. Find out what kinds of forms of protection are officially offered if someone is determined as a victim of trafficking? What does victim have to be able to prove to gain the status of victim of trafficking?

EXTRA MATERIALS

The Whistleblower (2010) directed by Larysa Condraki, starring Rachel Weisz, Monica Belucci and Vanessa Redgrave. The film presents the story of Kathryn Bolcovac disclosing the involvement of UN peacekeepers in the trafficking of women and girls to Bosnia. It also portrays the inefficiency and the lack of tools for the UN to protect the victims properly.

Study assignment: Find out how the UN has reacted to the publication of the film. How are the practices for protecting victims of trafficking been improved?

Half the Sky movement: taking oppression into opportunity for all the women worldwide. The DVD portrays a variety of gender-based violence cases and diverse women's organizations helping victims of violence. Celebrities are used as witnesses and commentators for the violence.

See http://www.halftheskymovement.org/. On the website it is possible to find the book, game and DVD for the Half the Sky movement as well as video clips.

Discuss the relevance of celebrities in advancing awareness on gender-based violence globally. What are the advantages? What are the problems?

NOTES

1. Katherine Bolcovac published a book titled *The Whistleblower* in 2010 (Palgrave MacMillan) based on her experiences (see also http://www.bolkovac.com/). The film *The Whistleblower*, starring Rachel Weisz as Kathryn Bolkovac, was released in 2010 (http://www.imdb.com/title/tt0896872/). See also http://www.huffingtonpost.com/lia-petridis/the-whistleblower-author-interview_b_2663231.html and http://www.telegraph.co.uk/culture/film/9041974/What-the-UN-Doesnt-Want-You-to-Know.html.

2. http://www.bolkovac.com/ (last accessed 14 October 2014).

3. Organized prostitution and related crimes have also been reported related to the UN Transitional Authority mission in Cambodia (UNTAC) deployed in 1992, during which prostitution became increased considerably, including child prostitution (Whitworth 2007: 67–68). The increase in prostitution and child prostitution continues to this day (see also Kristof and WuDunn [2010]; *Half the Sky* and the web pages of *Half the Sky movement*, http://www.halftheskymovement.org/).

4. These insights draw on Anitta's ongoing multisited ethnographic research on undocumented mobilities in the Mediterranean.

5. http://www.ilo.org/global/about-the-ilo/newsroom/news/WCMS_181961/lang--en/index.htm.

6. For example, TAMPEP project, http://tampep.eu/.

7. See, for example, global network for sex work, http://www.nswp.org/, and Pro-center in Finland.

8. Sophia Chong writes about the inherent colonialism in Kristof's projects: http://www.e-ir.info/2014/04/07/veiled-colonialism-a-feminist-criticism-of-the-half-the-sky-movement/ (last accessed 28 November 2016).

9. Sunil Batia discusses whether Kristof's projects are about putting his own actions into the forefront and not really about giving a voice to the women he presents in the stories. http://www.thefeministwire.com/2013/03/op-ed-nicholas-kristof-and-the-politics-of-writing-about-womens-oppression-in-darker-nations/.

Chapter 7

Re-imagining global mobilities

In October 2016, much of international media was turned to the town of Calais in Northern France. This site has been highly visible in the European migration agendas for many years due to the fact that it represents a tightly controlled border area in the midst of political Europe. As such, it demarcates the area of free mobility within Europe, the Schengen space, of which the UK is not part. Calais has become famous for its makeshift campsites and for excessive police deployment, including violence that specifically targets undocumented inhabitants. In the meantime, Calais has also become a site of manifold solidarities entwining local and transnational groups and organisations that engage with the people on the move. These acts of solidarity offer a counter-force to the hostile response by successive French governments, strongly backed by the UK, to the people considered as being in transit.

While much of attention is geared to Calais and its surrounding area, it is by far not the only area in France where the official response to the mobile people, many of whom seeking asylum, is insufficient if not lacking completely. Over the years, thousands of people have been camping in the streets of Paris, in particular in the areas around the Gare du Nord and the Gare de l'Est stations. Their stay in the streets may last for weeks or months, and for some the stay in France has consisted of circulation between the street and temporary shelters offered by the municipality as a protection measure against cold weather in the winter. What was initially a phenomenon of lone men and unaccompanied young boys trying to survive the days and nights in parks and in the streets (e.g. Schuster 2011a, b), includes nowadays also an increasing number of women and families with small children. These campsites have emerged in public parks, along the Canal St Martin, and underneath the metro bridge along the line 2, around Stalingrad and Jaures metro stations. This neighbourhood has been also a site of manifold solidarities, the most famous example of which is the St Bernard church that celebrated the twentieth anniversary of occupation and much mediatised campaign by the "sans-papiers" to obtain a formal migration status in 1996. As ever since, in the St Bernard movement, there were people with diverse histories that had led them to an undocumented status, including families with small children. One baby was born in the church during occupation.

Solidarity groups emerge and unfold in the area and across the city, some become more formally recognized associations, and they provide food, clothing and tents, French language teaching, legal information, help in accessing health care, and accommodation especially for those most in need. Most of this support is organised on a voluntary basis and thus alongside any other activities, be they studies, paid work or family commitments. There is space for everyone's competences and capabilities and the needs are huge. Most importantly, these solidarity actors and groups provide much needed human contact by forming friendships and having someone from the local context who cares for the fate of the people on the move that work towards restoring hope in the humanity.

(Anitta's field notes, November 2016)

This book has addressed gender and global mobilities from a variety of viewpoints. We began from categories of migration that constitute a way of organizing research on migration and providing a grid of intelligibility for analysing global mobility in chapter 2, drawing on research on labour migration and forced mobilities. We showed how gendered and sexualized representations are simultaneously enacted and contested in everyday lives of mobile individuals. In chapter 3, we zoomed into addressing how unquestioned heteronormativity guides research questions in migrations studies. We showed how globally mobile life may be lived in non-normative ways and emphasized that recognizing mobile subjects as full human beings enables us to see how hopes, dreams and desires are configured in mobile trajectories. In chapter 4 we turned to feminist economics and global political economy in order to generate understanding of how the gendered functioning of global economy works to enhance and necessitate global mobilities in myriad ways. This analysis enabled us to conceive how the macro level of globalization is built on gendered theories and practices.

Gendered global mobilities cannot, however, be comprehended only by analysing the different categories, unquestioned norms or the objective structural conditions generated by the globalization of world economy. Therefore, in chapter 5, we moved on to borders and policies. Here we discussed the institutional practices that govern global mobilities and that materialize in the institutions of border control and detention, as well as migration management through policies regulating migration and asylum. All these institutional practices entail gendered dimensions, both prior to engaging in mobility and in terms of outcomes of the established policies.

From official institutions we moved on to the question of how violence and abuse concretizes in the context of global mobilities in chapter 6. We focused mainly on the practices of human trafficking for the purpose of sexual exploitation. This theme brought us to see how the connectedness of transitional economies, war and conflict as well as peacekeeping contributes to the phenomenon of trafficking and what this entails for the victim. The discussion touched upon the structural, historical as well as intimate violence, bringing together the themes that travel throughout this book, ranging from the economy, politics, border control, policies and institutions governing global mobilities to intimate experience of violence and possibilities for healing.

The narrative of the book, this journey if you may, has traversed not only through several geopolitical locations but also through many disciplines, as we have shown how analysing and understanding global mobilities cannot be comprehensive by leaning on one discipline or even a particular multidisciplinary subset only. In turn we have sought to generate an overview of literatures and approaches that deal with and try to make sense of gender, global and mobilities in their own terms.

Now we wish to turn the gaze towards the future by asking what might be the conclusions of all these aspects: what do these insights indicate in terms of future academic work in studying mobilities? What kinds of political implications and possible policy suggestions could we draw on the presented and discussed insights? In this concluding chapter, we propose a move toward sketching the possibility for imagining the ethics of a postcapitalist world, building on posthumanist ethics of worlding and the ethics of homelessness. As the introductory narrative on the context in Paris suggests, and as became more widely visible and publicly acknowledged over the year 2015, there are many ways to transcend intersectional divides that demarcate people along the lines of ethnicity, nationality and migration status. Put shortly, there are ways to enact oppositional, resistant agency to the structures that seek to impede encounters and to political contexts that grow evermore hostile. At this point in time, with populism, racist and sexist ideologies gaining support at the level of political representation that transpires into groups and individuals who seem to conceive everyday violence against migrants and ethnic and religious minorities as more legitimate than before, there is a crucial need to put these alternative ways of thinking and acting into practice.

However, before we continue with this conversation, let us now turn and look at how the entwinement of global economy and securitizing practices of globalization – the economy-security complex – concretizes at borders and beyond. Laying out this context paves the way for asserting the necessity for creative ways of thinking and acting differently.

PARADOXICAL SIMULTANEITY: LOSS OF
CONTROL, QUEST FOR CONTROL

Since the 9/11 and the war on terror that followed, politics governing global mobilities have become ever more severe. Chapter 5 demonstrated how policies regulating entry and stay of foreign nationals have been tightened, despite the global capital's need for flexible labour on one hand and enhanced mobility for the privileged on the other. Also the biopolitical control investigating the most intimate details of mobile bodies is increasingly imposed through different surveillance systems (Amoore and Hall 2009). Walls and fences have been built since mid-1990s across various borders around the globe, and the war on terror has offered useful legitimation for the endorsement of these fences and walls by leaning on the argument of enhanced security for their citizens within the confines of state sovereignty. Rights-based and human security arguments get easily lost within these practices, remaining at the level of discourse, as was witnessed, for example, after the deadly shipwreck nearby the island of Lampedusa in the Mediterranean in early October 2013. One year later, in October 2014, political leaders, family members of the few survivors and civil society activists gathered in Lampedusa to commemorate the loss of human lives. A major tension that emerges in such encounters are the ways in which the collective mourning over the lost lives that everyone seems to share does not result in a collective way of learning from such tragedies. The year after, 2015, was even deadlier in terms of recorded deaths at the Mediterranean Sea, and the following year, 2016, again broke the previous record by early October.

There is no shared understanding on what is necessary to be done in order to prevent such losses of human lives in the future. For the European political leaders, the response is to tighten the border control measures to block departures further away from the actual border areas, whereas migrants' rights organizations and activists demand a real access to the European territory as the only way to prevent people in need from risking their lives at sea. Family members of survivors join the latter in their call for easier access, as, for example, the very possibility of attending the commemoration event depended on an existing migration status and documents in order to board a flight or passenger ship to Lampedusa. For family members and friends elsewhere, participation in the collective mourning of the tragedy as such does not necessarily constitute an adequate reason for regular travel in the eyes of the border control authorities.

Examining the practices of walling and fencing in different locations across the globe, Wendy Brown (2010) argues that the erection of walls can be seen as a symptom of nation-states' quest for asserting their powers in a global context where state sovereignty is in fact fading away – waning, as

Brown puts it. As chapter 4 illustrated, our time is characterized by the context of global economic restructuration and neoliberal capitalism, in which no one seems to be in control, or even capable, of predicting what might happen in the nearest future. In addition, not only is the global economy volatile and unpredictable, but in the postcapitalist, post-9/11 world, there seem to be uncontrollable threats such as environmental changes and enemies such as home-grown terrorism that cannot be easily located.

In this context, states and their coalitions are struggling to appear as capable of protecting citizens, or at least a privileged strata of them, while seeking to exclude those who could in one way or another be discerned from those "better off" (also Benhabib 2011: 102–116). Brown analyses the elusiveness of sovereignty in the face of global capitalism that manifests itself in the desperate quest for walling and fencing at different sites to block unwanted forms of mobility. She shows that this quest does not relate only to international borders. One of her examples is a gated community in Padua, Italy, which was walled in order to uphold a class-based distinction between groups living not far from each other. Seyla Benhabib (2011), in turn, centres her argument on the potentiality of international norms to circulate and offer safeguards for locally based, yet transnationally networked, groups. She argues that international norms continue to be morally stronger than only nationally endorsed legal guarantees. In our view, both of these viewpoints hold true. We need to keep in mind both increasing tensions between the global economy and a nation-state's pursuit of holding onto what remains of its sovereignty by exclusionary practices (Brown) and the ways in which states are still needed for guaranteeing international legal norms, where transnational activist networks may seek to exert their influence to push for the enactment of these norms (Benhabib). Highlighting this parallel is crucial in analysing global mobilities so as to account for the agentive capacities of differently mobile persons, be they those who need to move, those who are impeded from moving and those who stay put.

In line with Brown's analysis earlier, the security approach endorsed by 9/11 and the subsequently reiterated war on terror, with related attempts to control and contain the global flows, seem to have come to a dead end, as it is unable to respond to the challenges ahead. If this widely endorsed approach is in reality becoming a dead end road, we should think of something else, taking into account the results of the research conducted in different parts of the world that we have presented in the previous pages. What if we tried to visualize, or at least begin to imagine, approaching global mobilities in a fundamentally different manner?

The first move, for us, would indicate a departure from the prevailing security orientation of policies regulating global mobilities. It would accept, honestly and open-mindedly, the slipping away of the feeling of being in control, acknowledging the interconnections and fragility of the constellations named as *global* and national institutions and their derived impacts.

In doing so, the policy orientations would necessarily become more humble in their quest for regulating the incontrollable, and accepting that control and orderly management may just not be within reach in the contemporary world marked by intensified change and indeed movement. As such, the policies would rather facilitate and enhance the circulation of persons in such a way that the porousness of borders would become an ideal, not threatening, as has been the case during earlier times of nomadic lifestyles in different corners of the globe.

If the terrorizing enemy is already among us, indeed within us, taking different shapes, forms, genders and skin colours and deploying different means to provoke fear that do not necessitate physical proximity, there is not much that can be achieved through erecting visible boundaries that pretend to block the wrongdoers (cf. Brown 2010). At the same time, more and more jobs have already been outsourced to cheaper locations and thus left people unemployed, retraining to work in some other field, or required people to move nearer or further away in various locations of the global North.

These moves are rendered more possible for some bodies than others, depending on nationality and class privileges that can both enable the move towards better opportunities and ease the actual practice of crossing borders. However, other intersectional dimensions such as gender, age, dis/ability, class or positioning in the life cycle or family come to matter in the possibilities and means that people move. The options that were available to Maria (chapter 4) and Meriem (chapter 2) to engage in a globally mobile life were very different. Yet it was their positioning in the family that prompted the necessity to move across international borders.

Albeit from different perspectives, for both of them the acts of mobility were shaped by considerations from outside, reflected through others' readings of these acts. As for Meriem, it was the reading encoded in the family law in Algeria that became a veritable hindrance to her social mobility in that country, eroding her legal existence. Her marriage to a Frenchman was considered an illegitimate act. Maria, on the other hand, negotiated her choice of joining her husband in France within the scripts of accepted gender roles for a highly educated Nordic woman, to become a full-time mother of their children. Both of them were able to engage in the acts of mobility with a relative ease given their class and nationality statuses, which was not the case with the detained Nigerian man encountered in Greece (chapter 1), or for the Eastern European woman Tanja detained in the UK (chapter 5). For both of them, their acts of mobility were halted and resulted in unwanted immobility in the confined spaces of extended waiting (Conlon 2011, Mountz 2011). For the Nigerian man, his undocumented status combined with him being a male and coming from a country (Nigeria) that gets often located in a script of an outcast in the international scene, famous for being very rich, yet where the wealth is highly unequally distributed and, simultaneously, a country permeated with violence. A similar story is told in the novel *Americanah* (2013), in which Adichie illustrates how the post-9/11 security measures have rendered it increasingly difficult for male Nigerians to access a visa to the United States or a residence permit to an EU country. She tells the story of Obinze, son of a university professor, who has dreamt of the United States during all his youth, devouring American literature. After finishing his BA studies in Nigeria he hopes to join his teenage love Ifemelu in the United States but is refused a visa simply on the basis of his sex and nationality. So he redirects his itinerary and travels to the UK, living undocumented after his visa expires until he is caught and deported back to Nigeria.

In parallel with a change of direction from methodological nationalism rendered visible through walling and fencing, we would suggest parting from the individualistically oriented approach to mobile subjectivity. Methodological individualism, in terms of policy making, is also embedded in the policies regulating family reunion that connect the mobile individual to her or his nuclear family, often justified and proved by biological kinship ties and DNA testing when there is a doubt concerning the nature of the family ties. This approach refuses to acknowledge mobile subjects' manifold relationalities. It takes one family model as the universal one, failing to consider the actual contacts and interdependences between families that can be considered in a very different manner, including those that are being reconfigured while *en route*. A departure from this prevailing line of drawing family reunion policies thus implies rethinking the foundations of how families and family unity are conceived in the drafted policies.

Indeed, could we actually dare to ask for more professionalism in migration management? With this question we intend, for example, insights gained through critical studies that engage with asylum decision making. In the asylum processes, surprisingly, specialized knowledge of asylum officers concerning the workings of the traumatized mind and its (in)ability to formulate coherent autobiographical stories seems to be lacking. It has been noted how this lack of coherence occurs, namely, because of the trauma that has violated the mind (Caruth 2001, Shuman and Bohmer 2004, Bohmer and Shuman 2007). What is sought for via asylum interviews leading to granting or withholding the applicant's right to asylum, instead, are coherent and chronologically ordered narratives of events and facts. These narratives should balance neatly between an "objectively" factual account that can be verified by country-of-origin information reports and a personalized story that would truly convey the sense of "having been there." Insights from trauma studies may thus be outright rejected or, to say the least, left out of consideration.

As one of us has argued elsewhere, this results in a failure of acknowledging equal incoherence that characterizes both asylum decision making as asylum seeking, even if the former is usually understood as pertaining to the domain of "objective knowledge" (Kynsilehto and Puumala 2015). More importantly, this failure results in grave, even fatal, consequences in the lives of those denied asylum on these grounds.

Hence, it would be necessary to consider critically the foundations and existing practices of current policies. This critical assessment would benefit from a wide scope of research, such as studies on family formation, or research on the impact of trauma, as was illustrated earlier. To begin rethinking these foundations and ensuing practices building an ethical commitment, a different vision of the world and its ultimate relatedness is the first task.

POTENTIAL OF POSTHUMANISM AS NEW INSIGHT ON GENDER AND GLOBAL MOBILITIES

So, in a deep enough view, we in our act of observation are like that we observe: relatively constant patterns of abstracted movement from the universal field movement, and thus merging ultimately with all other patterns that can be abstracted from this movement.

(Bohm 1996: 94)

In this last section we turn towards addressing new ways of understanding gender and global mobilities in the light of the recent move in feminist theorizing. Throughout the chapters we have raised the concern of how our conceptualizations and ideologies guide our perception. The themes that have been raised revolve around the question of freedom versus force and rationality and predictability versus irrationality and uncertainty. The recent move in feminist theorizing, posthumanism and new materialism addresses these same questions and presents new kinds of answers. The objective of this line of theorizing is to rework the fundamental unquestioned assumptions and question the ontology of metaphysical individualism and the conceptualization of subjectivity, agency and ethics that follow.

Although we cannot develop the posthumanist contribution to social and cultural studies at full length here, due to space restrictions, we want to just propose this line of inquiry as a possibility for questioning fundamental assumptions we often hold onto unknowingly or simply out of habit. We propose a possibility of studying mobilities from the starting point of ontological connectedness and entanglement of human beings; natural forces; and social, cultural, political and economic forces, in line with imagining an approach to mobility and ensuing policies that build on the ontology of uncertainty and continuous change. This approach could overcome the limitations of the analysis of push and pull factors that have informed migration studies.

Posthumanist (feminist) theory investigates the philosophical implications of new biology and second-wave quantum mechanics[1] for social sciences. Posthumanism builds on especially feminist poststructuralism and queer theory and reopens the questions of nature and the nature of matter. It challenges the status quo in academia; that is, natural sciences study the natural world and social sciences study the social or cultural world. The basic premise of posthumanism is that the nature-culture distinction is fundamentally flawed. It is therefore critical of the linguistic turn in social sciences that has turned our attention to language, discursive communities, narratives and semiotics as a sphere in which we see the formation of subjectivity and agency in the social world. In turn, nature and physical matter are seen as passive and mute. For example, Bennett (2010) argues that post-structuralist anti-foundational approaches have enforced the separation between social and natural worlds. Moreover, the established scepticism against naïve realism and representationalism as well as Marxist and critical realism has influenced the overall move toward more abstraction, dismissing matter and materiality as irrelevant in social interactions and workings of power and thus reinforcing the nature-culture distinction. However, the post-structuralist and anti-foundationalist perspectives still share metaphysical individualism, which sees human beings as singular subjects situated in the world. More importantly, all these approaches share an anthropocentric view of knowledge.

Anthropocentric view of knowledge refers to the conceptualization of human being as the knowing subject. In other words, humans have a birthright to knowledge, which separates them from the rest of the natural world. The distinction between nature and culture, thoughts and things are based on this idea. In accordance with metaphysical individualism, it is presumed that subjects and the world pre-exist before their interaction or relations with others and perhaps even that they remain the same. The pre-existing separate individual gains knowledge of the world and makes decisions based on this information. Moreover, the trust in ontological separation between the self and the world positions the knowing subject as a mediator of knowledge of the world. Knowledge is, in this framework, a matter of mediation of information from the world to other separate pre-existing knowing subjects.

Barad (2003) calls this approach as "habit of the mind" – a way of perception that is reminiscent of Cartesian thought even in constructivist and also poststructuralist approaches, which seek openly to criticize such stances. The dualist conceptualizations of self-other, thought and things are so deeply ingrained in us that we reiterate them out of habit (of the mind). What is at stake here is indeed the paradigm "I think, therefore I am." The question becomes: What if the thinking "I" is an illusion, or simply a habit, and we as human beings are not in the world as singular separate subjects, but intra-active parts in the world's continuous reconfiguration? This is the question that Barad proposes as she designs her framework of agential realism. In this framework, humans are put off their pedestal of knowing subjects and instead seen as agential parts of the world.

Indeed, posthumanism, as the name implies, is *post*humanism. It is therefore critical of the anti-humanist stance, which sees human beings as machines or simply subject to outside forces and thus inherently vulnerable and weak. Yet posthumanism is *post*humanism; it is critical of the humanist subject of the enlightenment, who is understood as having exclusive birthright to knowledge. Instead, it reconfigures nature and matter as active participants in the process of knowledge. As Barad argues, knowing is a process of intra-activity of the world between its parts, where different parts become differentially intelligible to each other, and these parts need not be human.

Therefore, posthumanist intervention is more than just showing how social sciences unquestioningly reiterate outdated conceptualization of matter and nature, as they continue in line with nature-culture distinction. It is about investigating how this new understanding of matter based on second-wave quantum mechanics, which shows that also matter is alive and unpredictable, affects our core assumptions about the relationship between human beings, nature and complex relationships. It is about accounting for the inherent aliveness of interactions and creating a scholarship that builds on the ideas of pluripotency and emergence and thus reframes the structure and agency problematic in fundamentally new ways than naïve realist, constructivist or post-structuralist social theorizing have enabled. Indeed, the main thesis of the posthumanist and new materialist approaches is to claim that there is no ontological duality between nature and human-made cultures but that the material world is active in the ways in which the (social) world unfolds. The cells of bodies regenerate, and matter may take unpredictable forms and present agential qualities that shape our world (Bennett 2010).

In this framework, agency has to be understood in new ways superseding metaphysical individualism and hierarchical structure. Barad explains: "Crucially, agency is a matter of intra-acting; it is an enactment, not something someone has" (2007: 235). Thus the starting point for subjectivity and agency is not the individual but *agentiality* within the whole of the phenomenon. In other words, the world is not an idea that exists only in the human mind; instead, the mind is a specific material configuration of the world, and this mind does not have to be configured as a human brain. Similarly, *"embodiment is a matter not of being specifically situated in the world, but rather being of the world in its dynamic specificity"* (Barad 2007: 377, italics in the original).

We have discussed throughout this book how intersections of gender, class, dis/ability, race/ethnicity and sexuality come to matter in the context of global mobility in terms of what kind of possibilities, opportunities or constraints specific individuals face and take advantage of. In such framework, subjectivity, agency and freedom to choose and act are often unquestioningly seen as properties belonging to that specific individual in relation to an outside world. Grosz (2010) argues how both libertarian and deterministic approaches as well as most feminist theorizing still share such an understanding although they differ on what constitutes or determines the relation between individual agency and the world.

In other words, cause and effect are seen as something that is either internal or external to the self. Liberalist understanding sees the human being as inherently free and thus responsible for rationally navigating the complex word. External causes that enable or constrict individual freedom are, for example, changes in political and economic structures or environmental disasters, war and conflict, which obviously constitute the objective reality in which people live. These internal and external causes and their effects are still very much part of the conversation that seeks to explain and understand the ways in which gender and global come to matter in the context of mobility. They are also the source of heated debates as we have seen throughout the chapters.

What posthumanist or new materialist approach would bring to these debates is a way of calling off the fight by asking whether the inherent metaphysical individualism is the trouble that prevents us from moving beyond the binary logic. As posthumanist notion of human being points towards recognizing that human beings are part of the aliveness of the continuous reconfiguration of the world, it also challenges the ontological cynicism in contemporary anti-humanist social theorizing, which sees the human being as somehow stuck in the exploitative structures and forces of the world, having very little freedom, or either as privileged, enjoying the world and indeed having all the freedom in the world.

Drawing on Bergson's theorizing, Grosz (2010) maintains that freedom is not something that can be owned or something that pre-exists action, but instead is something that can be discerned only in the context of specific actions and situations. Freedom, as Grosz seeks to explain, is more than just a property to be had or lost but rather should be understood as a capacity to act fully as oneself in a given interaction with others and the world. In other words, freedom does not pre-exist as a property prior to the interaction but can be discernible and experienced only at the moment of the action. If freedom is the capacity to act fully as oneself in a specific situation, then it is not something that is determined either by internal or external conditions. In other words, freedom is not something that is reserved for the privileged tourist who has the freedom to roam and explore the world freely, whereas the labour migrants, refugees and sex workers are forced to do so. Instead, freedom becomes an integral aspect of being, which can or cannot be enacted regardless of the situation or persons' background and social status.

This brings us to the core of what posthumanist understanding of human being is and that is an understanding of human being as a part of the world, not as a singular separate subject that is in the world. At its most radical form, this means that there is no speaking "I," no subject, no ego-self, which exists prior to its interaction or intra-actions with the world and others in it. Being is therefore a matter of inter-being, or being in-between selves. In this way, posthumanist understanding of human being comes close to relational Buddhism (Kwee 2012) and Buddhist psychology (Brown, Ryan and Creswell 2007). That which we experience as the "Me – Self" is rather the thinking mind. Thinking itself cannot be trusted; thoughts, emotions and feelings seem to have a life of their own. They are like the weather; they arise and then they go away. Buddhist psychology maintains that humans have the capacity to cultivate mindful action, mindful listening and mindful communication. The difference that mindful action makes is that it is responsible and arises out of the present moment. There is a difference between reactivity and responsibility and recognition of the ontological uncertainty. This uncertainty is not a negative thing, but rather a matter of befriending the present moment, knowing that nothing ever stays the same. Posthumanist feminist theorizing points to the aliveness of all these elements – time, space and body-mind – in the process of the world's ongoing reconfiguration.

It is not only the world that is being transformed through the process of *space-time-mattering*, but also the human subject is reconfigured with every act, every choice and every interaction (Grosz 2010). We also change, as we interact with others, the choices we make and experiences we have. We get older and the experiences we have alter our perceptions about the self and others. Perhaps we do not make the same choices again even though our gender, class and social status stay the same. Or perhaps, we are changed through the interactions with the others who enter into our familiar spaces. This leads us also to the question of ethics: what does it mean to meet the others and respond to them if we let go of the idea of separate selves?

Posthumanist ethics of worlding

Letting go of metaphysical individualism also means that we have to reconceptualize ethics. If humans are intra-active parts in the whole of space-time-mattering, then ethics is not only about right response toward ontologically separate others, human or non-human, but rather about the acknowledgement that our actions and reactions are already entangled with the whole of the world. Our actions and reactions have real consequences that defy the logic of linearity. These ripple out like diffracting waves, creating unpredictable and unprecedented outcomes. For Barad, this means asking "do I dare to disturb the universe?" as the acknowledgement of how deeply ingrained we are in this world and how the multiple effects of our actions cannot be predicted. For Bennett, this means treading on this planet lightly and being mindful of the imprints left behind our footprints and how we decide to consume. Barad uses the *intimate* to grasp at how closely, and indeed intimately, humans are part of the world, more so than models of cause and effect ever suggest.

Intra-active parts of the world and our actions and reactions not only impact the world but also contribute to the continued emergence of the world continuous unfolding. Barad (2007: 392–393) explains:

The very nature of materiality is an entanglement. Matter itself is already open to, or rather entangled with, the "Other." The intra-actively emergent "parts" of phenomena are co-constituted. Not only subjects but also objects are permeated through and through with their entangled kind; the other is not just in one's skin, but in one's bones, in one's belly, in one's heart, in one's nucleus, in one's past and future. . . . Just as human subject is not the locus of knowing, neither is it the locus of ethicality. . . . Ethics is therefore not about the right response to a radically exterior/ized other, but about responsibility and accountability for the lively relationalities of becoming which we are part.

This understanding of human beings as part of the world, and not in the world as singular subjects, resonates with the way in which Khosravi (2010) frames the ethics of homelessness as a solution to overcome the reiteration of the mobile subjects as strangers, or as the Others who are either accepted or denied entry. The concept of home country is in itself problematic because it simultaneously frames the others who come into our home as strangers who invade our space or invited guests who must leave when the time comes. If we were all home-less on this planet earth, then the category of strangers could not be sustained.

Khosravi explains how the understanding of national identity and citizenship is based on a botanical or territorial worldview. Thus, our identity and belonging is often framed by using the language of having *roots* in a specific territorial and/or cultural place. In other words, the place of birth, or origin, implies that we belong to this place perhaps more naturally than to other places. The people who enter this sphere can be, on the other hand, seen as having been uprooted from another place – perhaps a place that they should return to. In accordance with such a botanical worldview, it is possible to respond to mobile subjects in a hostile way. After all, they are invading our space, or they naturally belong to their place of origin and are out of place. Contemporary right-wing sentiments in the EU member states, Fortress Europe and anti-immigration policy in the United States and Australia resonate with this worldview. It is as if people stemming from a particular place should stay there or return to their country of origin, home, to their roots.

The ethics of homelessness that Khosravi proposes resonates with how Barad conceptualizes posthumanist ethics of worlding. Ethics of homelessness is a matter of non-territorial ethics. Similarly, posthumanism ethics of worlding sees that the human subject is not the locus of ethicality. As long as we hold onto the idea of separate selves, with territorial roots, the mobile subject will always be the other, out of place. Homelessness, Khosravi maintains, is our ontological condition, and therefore the idea of territorial or cultural home is an illusion. This is in line with posthumanism, which sees intra-activity as the moment in which the self and the other emerge, and dismisses the idea of pre-existing separate subjects. Ethical action is therefore not about right action toward an ontologically separate other. Instead, the ethics of our actions should arise from the acknowledgement of our shared humanity and a shared planet and from the recognition of the multitude and unpredictability of our actions. It is this realization that leads to the recognition of a new level of responsibility. We are already part of the world, entangled with it, and our actions have real material consequences.

Ethics of worlding means a responsibility and accountability to the whole of the world, and not only to the immediate others in close proximity. Events and actions have "consequences" and create transformations, which impact and change the world in unpredictable ways. This means that things and people that seem far off and distant, such as different parts of the world or distant planets, are seen as already entangled with our actions.

Posthumanist ethics of worlding transforms the anti-humanist notions of human beings as specks of dust in a meaningless and cold universe that has been left to run on its own. Being of the world in its continuous becoming challenges the habit of the mind in thinking itself into being as a separate self (Brown et al. 2007). But, if we are part of the continuous reconfiguration of the world, and not separate selves in the world having subjectivity and agency, would this entail that we should not care about how things go? If there is no "I" in the world, but only intra-activity of the world's parts that need not even be human, then should we just give up? Or if we already are homeless on this planet earth, then how to make sense of needing to belong and form an identity with respect to one's own community?

The acknowledgement of our intra-activity in the whole of movement calls for even deeper responsibility than individualist ethics. Perhaps this can also offer more meaning to our lives than anti-humanist or anti-foundationalist approaches suggest. Ethics of worlding begins with the understanding that it is not so much that we are in this world as individual subjects, but it is the world that is alive in us. In the spirit of Khosravi's ethics of homelessness, we can see ourselves in those who are not yet familiar to us and recognize we are not so different after all, and that these regions on Earth were not for us to own.

CONCLUDING WORDS: A RENEWED CALL TO IMAGINE

Throughout this book we have proposed an invitation to imagine what global mobility means for the people on the move. This is a call we continue to insist upon. To take the call seriously implies, for us, rendering ourselves vulnerable to be able to touch and be touched by the manifold mobilities we are surrounded by, to allow ourselves the luxury of occupying the space of vulnerable observers (Behar 1996). It is indeed the recognition of our ultimate existential vulnerability that could make us strong, to stand up even if, as we bend, we are shaped by the currents around our existence.

At the level of action, this existential vulnerability could also entail something that goes beyond individual feelings of empathy, to understand multiple entanglements and work towards collective engagement on burning issues. This may take the shape of, for example, engaging in organizations, signing online petitions against forced labour, going out to the streets arguing for the rights of detained migrants or becoming a friend for a newcomer in the community where one is based. As the year 2015 manifested very vividly, this may also mean travelling long distances to engage in voluntary work and solidarity action outside and beyond formal frameworks in the most exposed sites where day-to-day survival is at stake. There is space for everyone, for all skills and contributions, and each act counts.

Tools for conceptualizing different forms of entanglement are already abundant within feminist theory. Postcolonial feminists have advocated solidarity across borders that necessitates a dismantling of hierarchies and taking differences between us seriously (Mohanty 2003). Feminist ethicists have developed the notion of care ethics (Robinson 2011, Raghuram 2016) or solidarity as a form of social empathy (Gould 2007), which is an encompassing notion that enables us to transgress distances and overcome limitations of existing human rights frameworks. These insights chime with the ethics of homelessness and the posthumanist ethics of worlding in that they call for a vision of coexistence based on a relational, not atomistic, view of the world.

Social empathy does not require a notion of solidarity as identity of singular selves but rather "identification with the lived situation of others and with an appreciation of the injustices to which they may be subject" (Gould 2007: 156), which emerges in "relations of responsibility and care for particular others" (Robinson 2011: 847). What is needed, then, is a notion of solidarity as "a disposition to act toward others who are recognized as *different from* oneself, by way of being differently situated" (Gould 2007: 156–157). This solidarity across differences in an entangled coexistence would help conceiving what is at stake in encountering multiple others and building bridges, indeed engaging in collective struggles, in an increasingly complex world.

Across the chapters of this book we have discussed gender and global mobilities by drawing attention to how our perceptions, assumptions, hidden ideologies and beliefs may guide our perception in framing and understanding what gender, global and mobilities are. In this endeavour we have followed feminist curiosity, which means a practice of asking questions, even unsettling ones – the kinds that challenge our positions of privilege.

Feminist theorizing is therefore not for the faint-hearted. It does not allow the kind of safety and security that can be seen in mainstream, or malestream, approaches. Contemporary feminist theorizing means being open-hearted, being curious and having the capacity to not only hear but listen to others. In closing this conversation and journey on gender and global mobilities, we wish to plea for taking the demands of ethical communication seriously. This kind of communication begins from mindful listening, acceptance and presence in the moment now, that is, really the only moment we ever have. And this matters because we are already part of the pluripotency of the world. Indeed, the future is yet to be determined.

DISCUSSION POINTS

1. Why are states so fervently seeking to tighten border control? In which ways this works or doesn't work?
2. Do you have experience in any form of solidarity action? Which kinds of practices would you feel the most comfortable with?
3. How could the posthumanist ethics of worlding and the ethics of homelessness be enacted in the everyday life and encounters with various others?

NOTE

1. David Bohm (2008) has suggested that quantum mechanics should result in at least a germ for developing a new worldview that could account for the ontology of non-fragmentation or the world as the "whole of movement." In this setting the evidence of quantum mechanics challenges humanist understanding of knowing and being and therefore challenges the metaphysical individualism shared by both disembodied and embodied epistemologies.

Bibliography

Ackerly, Brooke, and Jacqui True. 2010. *Doing Feminist Research in Political and Social Science*. Basingstoke: Palgrave MacMillan.

Ackers, Louise. 2008. "Internationalisation, mobility, and metrics: A new form of indirect discrimination?" *Minerva* 46: 411–435.

Adichie, Chimamanda Ngozi. 2013. *Americanah*. London: Fourth Estate.

Agathangelou, Anna M. 2004. *Global Political Economy of Sex: Desire, Violence and Insecurity in Mediterranean Nation States*. Gordonsville, VA: Palgrave Macmillan.

Agathangelou, Anna M., and L. H. M. Ling. 2004. "Power, borders, security: Lessons of violence and desire from September 11." *International Studies Quarterly* 48: 517–538.

Ahmad, Ali Nobil. 2009. "Bodies that (don't) matter: Desire, eroticism and melancholia in Pakistani labour migration." *Mobilities* 4: 309–327.

Ahmed, Sara. 1998. *Differences That Matter: Feminist Theory and Postmodernism*. Cambridge: Cambridge University Press.

Ahmed, Sara. 2000. *Strange Encounters: Embodied Others in Post-Coloniality*. London: Routledge.

Ahmed, Sara. 2004. "Affective economies." *Social Text* 22: 117–139.

Ahmed, Sara. 2006. *Queer Phenomenology: Orientations, Objects, Others*. Durham: Duke University Press.

Ahmed, Sara. 2012. *On Being Included: Racism and Diversity in Institutional Life*. Durham: Duke University Press.

Al-Ali, Nadje. 2002. "Gender relations, transnational ties and rituals among Bosnian refugees." *Global Networks* 2: 249–262.

Albini, Joseph L. 1997. "The mafia and the devil: What they have in common." In *Understanding Organized Crime in Global Perspective. A Reader*, edited by George E. Rush and Patrick J. Ryan, 63–70. London: Sage.

Amnesty International. 2013. *The Dark Side of Migration. Spotlight on Qatar's construction sector ahead of the World Cup*. https://www.amnesty.org/en/documents/mde22/010/2013/en/ (last accessed 18 January 2017).

Amoore, Louise, and Alexandra Hall. 2009. "Taking people apart: Digitized dissection and the body at the border." *Environment & Planning D: Society and Space* 27: 444–464.

Anani, Ghida. 2013. "Dimensions of gender-based violence against Syrian refugees in Lebanon." *Forced Migration Review* 44: 75–78.

Andrijasevic, Rutvica. 2007. "Beautiful dead bodies: Gender, migration and representation in anti-trafficking campaigns." *Feminist Review* 86: 24–44.

Andrijasevic, Rutvica. 2010. *Agency, Migration and Citizenship in Sex Trafficking.* Basingstoke: Palgrave MacMillan.

Aradau, Claudia. 2004. "The perverse-politics of four-letter words: Risk and pity in the securitization of human trafficking." *Millennium: Journal of International Studies* 33: 251–277.

Aradau, Claudia. 2008. *Rethinking Trafficking in Women: Politics out of Security.* Basingstoke: Palgrave Macmillan.

Archambault, Caroline. 2010. "Women left behind? Migration, spousal separation, and the autonomy of rural women in Ugweno, Tanzania." *Signs: Journal of Women in Culture and Society* 35: 919–942.

Ascencio, Marysol, and Katie Acosta. 2009. "Migration, gender conformity, and social mobility among Puerto Rican sexual minorities." *Sexuality Research & Social Policy* 6: 34–43.

Ashutosh, Ishan, and Alison Mountz. 2011. "Migration management for the benefit of whom? Interrogating the work of the International Organization for Migration." *Citizenship Studies* 15: 21–38.

Bach, Jonathan. 2011. Remittances, gender and development. In *Gender and Global Restructuring*, edited by Marianne H. Marchand and Anne Sisson Runyan, 129–142. London: Routledge.

Bakker, Isabella, and Rachel Silvey. 2008. *Beyond States and Markets: The Challenges of Social Reproduction.* London: Routledge.

Bales, Kevin. 2008. *Ending Slavery: How We Free Today's Slaves.* Berkeley: University of California Press.

Barad, Karen. 2003. "Posthumanist performativity: Toward an understanding of how matter comes to matter." *Signs: Journal of Women in Culture and Society* 28: 801–831.

Barad, Karen. 2007. *Meeting the Universe Half-Way: Quantum Physics and the Entanglement of Matter and Meaning.* Durham: Duke University Press.

Bastia, Tania. 2006. "Stolen lives or lack of rights? Gender, migration and trafficking." *Labour, Capital and Society* 39: 20–47.

Bastia, Tania. 2011. "Migration as protest? Negotiating gender, class, and ethnicity in urban Bolivia." *Environment and Planning A* 43: 1514–1529.

Beaverstock, Jonathan. 2002. "Transnational elites in global cities: British expatriates in Singapore's financial district." *Geoforum* 33: 525–538.

Beaverstock, Jonathan. 2005. "Transnational elites in the City: British highly-skilled inter-company transferees in New York City's financial district." *Journal of Ethnic and Migration Studies* 31: 245–268.

Behar, Ruth. 1996. *The Vulnerable Observer: Anthropology That Breaks Your Heart.* Boston: Beacon Press.

Belkin, Aaron. 2012. *Bring Me Men: Military Masculinity and the Benign Façade of American Empire 1898–2001.* New York: Columbia University Press.

Beloso, Brooke Meredith. 2012. "Sex, work, and the feminist erasure of class." *Signs: Journal of Women in Culture and Society* 38: 47–69.

Benhabib, Seyla. 2011. *Dignity in Adversity. Human Rights in Troubled Times.* Cambridge: Polity Press.

Bennett, Jane. 2010. *Vibrant Matter: A Political Ecology of Things.* Durham: Duke University Press.

Berman, Jacqueline. 2003. "(Un)popular strangers and crises (un)bounded: Discourses of sex-trafficking, the European political community and the panicked state of the modern state." *European Journal of International Relations* 9: 37–86.

Biao, Xiang. 2003. "Emigration from China: A sending country perspective." *International Migration* 41: 21–48.

Biggs, John. 2003. *Teaching for Quality Learning at University.* Berkshire: The Society for Research into Higher Education & Open University.

Bohm, David. 1996. *On Creativity.* London: Routledge.

Bohm, David. 2008. *Wholeness and the Implicate Order.* London: Routledge.

Bohmer, Carol, and Amy Shuman. 2007. "Producing epistemologies of ignorance in the political asylum application process." *Identities: Global Studies in Culture and Power* 14: 603–629.

Bolcovac, Kathryn. 2010. *The Whistleblower: Sex Trafficking, Military Contractors, and One Woman's Fight for Justice.* New York: Palgrave MacMillan.

Boyd, Monica. 1999. "Gender, refugee status and permanent settlement." *Gender Issues* 17: 5–25.

Brown, Kirk Warren, Ryan, Richard M., and J. David Creswell. 2007. "Addressing fundamental questions about mindfulness." *Psychological Inquiry* 18: 272–281.

Brown, Wendy. 2010. *Walled States, Waning Sovereignty.* New York: Zone Books.

Butalia, Urvashi. 1998. *The Other Side of Silence: Voices from the Partition of India.* New Delhi: Penguin Books.

Butler, Judith. 1990. *Gender Trouble: Feminism and the Subversion of Identity.* London: Routledge.

Cabezas, Amalia L. 2006. "The eroticization of labor in Cuba's all-inclusive resorts: Performing race, class and gender in the new tourist economy." *Social Identities* 12: 507–521.

Carretta, Carrie M., Burgess, Ann W., and Rosanna DeMarco. 2016. "To tell or not to tell." *Violence against Women* 22: 1499–1518.

Carrillo, Héctor. 2004. "Sexual migration, cross-cultural sexual encounters, and sexual health." *Sexuality Research and Social Policy* 1: 58–70.

Caruth, Cathy. 2001. "Parting words: Trauma, silence and survival." *Cultural Values* 5: 7–26.

Casier, Marlies, Heyse, Petra, Clycq, Noel, Zemni, Sami, and Christiane Timmerman. 2013. "Breaking the in-group out-group: Shifting boundaries in transnational partner choice processes of individuals of Moroccan, Tunisian, Algerian, Turkish, Punjabi Sikh, Pakistani and Albanian descent in Belgium." *The Sociological Review* 61: 460–478.

Castles, Stephen. 1984. *Here for Good. Western Europe's New Ethnic Minorities*. London: Pluto Press.

Castles, Stephen, and Mark J. Miller. 2003. *The Age of Migration: International Population Movements in the Modern World*. Revised and updated third edition. Basingstoke: Palgrave Macmillan.

Chang, Kimberly A., and L.H.M. Ling. 2011. "Globalization and its intimate other: Filipina domestic workers in Hong Kong." In *Gender and Global Restructuring*, edited by Marianne H. Marchand and Anne Sisson Runyan, 30–47. London: Routledge.

Chee, Heng Leng, Yeoh, Brenda S.A., and Rashidah Shuib. 2012. "Circuitous pathways: Marriage as a route toward (il)legality for Indonesian migrant workers in Malaysia." *Asian and Pacific Migration Journal* 21: 317–344.

Chow, Esther Ngan-Ling, Fleck, Chadwick, Fan, Gang-Hua, Joseph, Joshua, and Deanna Lyter. 2003. "Exploring critical feminist pedagogy: Infusing dialogue, participation, and experience in teaching and learning." *Teaching Sociology* 31: 259–275.

Clark, Christina R. 2007. "Understanding vulnerability: From categories to experiences of young Congolese people in Uganda." *Children & Society* 21: 284–296.

Collins, Dana. 2009. "'We're there and queer': Homonormative mobility and lived experience among gay expatriates in Manila." *Gender and Society* 23: 465–493.

Collins, Patricia Hill. 1990. *Black Feminist Thought. Knowledge, Consciousness, and the Politics of Empowerment*. London: Routledge.

Conlon, Deirdre. 2011. "Waiting: Feminist perspectives on the spacings/timings of migrant (im)mobility." *Gender, Place & Culture* 18: 353–360.

Conlon, Deirdre, and Nancy Hiemstra, eds. 2016. *Intimate Economies of Immigration Detention: Critical Perspectives*. London: Routledge.

Cons, Jason, and Romola Sanyal. 2013. "Geographies at the margins: Borders in South Asia – An introduction." *Political Geography* 35: 5–13.

Crabtree, Robbin D., and David Alan Sapp. 2003. "Theoretical, political and pedagogical challenges in the feminist classroom." *College Teaching* 51: 131–140.

Crenshaw, Kimberlé. 1991. "Mapping the margins: Intersectionality, identity politics, and violence against women of color." *Stanford Law Review* 43: 1241–1299.

Currah, Paisley, and Tara Mulqueen. 2011. "Securitizing gender: Identity, biometrics, and transgender bodies at the airport." *Social Research* 78: 557–581.

Danna, Daniela. 2007. "'Buying sex is not a sport' – A campaign against trafficking in women." *Societies without Borders* 2: 243–259.

Dauphinee, Elizabeth. 2010. "The ethics of autoethnography." *Review of International Studies* 36: 799–818.

Dauphinee, Elizabeth. 2013. *The Politics of Exile*. London: Routledge.

Davis, Lennard J. 2013. *The Disability Studies Reader*. London: Routledge.

De Genova, Nicholas. 2010. "The queer politics of migration: Reflections on 'illegality' and incorrigibility." *Studies in Social Justice* 4: 101–126.

De Haas, Hein, and Aleida van Rooij. 2010. "Migration as emancipation? The impact of internal and international migration on the position of women left behind in rural Morocco." *Oxford Development Studies* 38: 43–62.

Denzin, Norman K., and Yvonna S. Lincoln. 1998. "The fifth moment." In *The Land-scape of Qualitative Research: Theories and Issues*, edited by Norman K. Denzin and Yvonna S. Lincoln, 407–429. California: Sage.

Doty, Roxanne Lynn. 2001. "Desert tracts: Statecraft in remote places." *Alternatives: Global, Local, Political* 26: 523–543.

Doty, Roxanne Lynn. 2007. "States of exception on the Mexico-U.S. border: Security, 'decisions,' and civilian border patrols." *International Political Sociology* 1: 113–137.

Doty, Roxanne Lynn. 2010. "Autoethnography – making human connections." *Review of International Studies* 36: 1047–1050.

Dyer, Sarah, McDowell, Linda, and Adina Batnitzky. 2010. "The impact of migration on the gendering of service work: The case of a West London hotel." *Gender, Work and Organization* 17: 635–657.

Ehrenreich, Barbara, and Arlie Russell Hochchild, eds. 2003. *Global Woman: Nannies, Maids and Sex Workers in New Economy*. London: Granta.

Eisenstein, Zillah. 2004. *Against Empire: Feminisms, Racism, and the West*. New York: Zed Books.

Eisenstein, Zillah. 2007. *Sexual Decoys: Gender, Race and War in Imperial Democracy*. London: Zed Books.

Elias, Juanita. 2005. "Stitching-up the labour market: Recruitment, gender and ethnicity in the multinational firm." *International Feminist Journal of Politics* 7: 90–111.

Elias, Juanita. 2013. "Foreign policy and the domestic worker: The Malaysia-Indonesia domestic worker dispute." *International Feminist Journal of Politics* 15: 391–410.

Ellis, Carolyn, and Arthur P. Bochner. 1992. "Telling and performing personal stories: The constraints of choice in abortion." In *Investigating Subjectivity. Research on Lived Experience*, edited by Carolyn Ellis and Michael G. Flaherty, 79–101. London: Sage.

Elshtain, Jean Bethke. 2003. *Just War against Terror: The Burden of American Power in a Violent World*. New York: Basic Books.

Elson, Diane. 2010. "Gender and the global economic crisis in developing countries: A framework for analysis." *Gender & Development* 18: 201–212.

EMHRN – Euro-Mediterranean Human Rights Network. 2013. *Violence against Women, Bleeding Wound in the Syrian Conflict*. http://www.wluml.org/sites/wluml.org/files/Euromedrights-VAW-Syria-Nov-2013.pdf (last accessed 9 March 2017).

Enloe, Cynthia. 1996. "Margins, silences and bottom rungs: How to overcome the underestimation of power in the study of international relations." In *International Theory: Positivism and Beyond*, edited by Steve Smith, Ken Booth, and Marysia Zalewski, 186–202. Cambridge: Cambridge University Press.

Enloe, Cynthia. 2004. *The Curious Feminist: Searching for Women in a New Age of Empire*. Berkeley: University of California Press.

Ennaji, Moha, and Fatima Sadiqi. 2008. *Migration and Gender in Morocco. The Impact of Migration on the Women Left Behind*. Trenton, NJ: The Red Sea Press.

Espiritu, Yen Le. 2001. "'We don't sleep around like white girls do': Family, culture and gender in Filipina American lives." *Signs: Journal of Women in Culture and Society* 26: 415–440.

EUROPOL. 2006. *Trafficking of Women and Children for Sexual Exploitation in the EU: The Involvement of Western Balkans Organised Crime, Crimes against Persons Unit.* http://edz.bib.uni-mannheim.de/daten/edz-min/hum/02/Western_Balkans_THB_Threat_Assessment.pdf (last accessed 19 January 2017).

Faber, Stine Thidemann, and Helene Pristed Nielsen. 2015. "Centering the periphery." In *Remapping Gender, Place and Mobility: Global Confluences and Local Particularities in Nordic Peripheries*, edited by Stine Thidemann Faber and Helene Pristed Nielsen. London: Routledge.

Fanning, Bryan, and Fidele Mutwarasibo. 2007. "Nationals/non-national: Immigration, citizenship and politics in the Republic of Ireland." *Ethnic and Racial Studies* 30: 439–460.

Feigenbaum, Anna. 2007. "The teachable moment: Feminist pedagogy and the neoliberal classroom." *Review of Education, Pedagogy, and Cultural Studies* 29: 337–349.

Freedman, Jane. 2007. *Gendering the International Asylum and Refugee Debate.* Basingstoke: Palgrave Macmillan.

Freedman, Jane. 2008. "Women's right to asylum: Protecting the rights of female asylum seekers in Europe?" *Human Rights Review* 9: 413–433.

Freedman, Jane. 2010. "Mainstreaming gender in refugee protection." *Cambridge Review of International Affairs* 23: 589–607.

Freedman, Jane. 2012. "Analysing the gendered insecurities of migration: A case study of female Sub-Saharan African migrants in Morocco." *International Feminist Journal of Politics* 14: 36–55.

Freedman, Jane. 2016. "Engendering security at the borders of Europe: Women migrants and the Mediterranean 'Crisis.'" *Journal of Refugee Studies.* doi:10.1093/jrs/few019

Frohlick, Susan. 2009. "Pathos of love in Puerto Viejo, Costa Rica: Emotion, travel and migration." *Mobilities* 4: 389–405.

Frontexit. 2014. *Frontex between Greece and Turkey: The Border of Denial.* http://www.frontexit.org (last accessed 19 April 2016).

Frontline and PBS. 2011. *Lost in Detention.* http://www.pbs.org/wgbh/pages/frontline/lost-in-detention/ (last accessed 16 December 2013).

Giordano, Cristiana. 2008. "Practices of translation and the making of migrant subjectivities in contemporary Italy." *American Ethnologist* 35: 588–606.

Gittings, Lesley. 2016. "'When you visit a man you should prepare yourself': Male community care worker approaches to working with men living with HIV in Cape Town, South Africa." *Culture, Health & Sexuality* 18: 936–950.

Gopinath, Gayatri. 2005. "Bollywood spectacles: Queer diasporic critique in the aftermath of 9/11." *Social Text* 23: 157–169.

Gould, Carol C. 2007. "Transnational solidarities." *Journal of Social Philosophy* 38: 148–164.

Griffin, Penny. 2010. "Gender, governance and the global political economy." *Australian Journal of International Affairs* 64: 86–104.

Grosz, Elizabeth. 2010. "Feminism, materialism and freedom." In *New Materialisms: Ontology, Agency and Politics*, edited by Diana Coole and Samantha Frost, 139–157. Durham: Duke University Press.

The Guardian. 2016. "Six teenage boys arrested over death of a Polish man in Essex." *Guardian*, 30 August 2016. https://www.theguardian.com/uk-news/2016/aug/30/five-teenage-boys-arrested-after-man-dies-following-attack-in-essex (last accessed 27 October 2016).

Guevarra, Anna. 2006. "Managing 'vulnerabilities' and 'empowering' migrant Filipina workers: The Philippines' Overseas Employment Program." *Social Identities* 12: 523–541.

Hadjukowski-Ahmed, Maroussia, Khanlou, Nazilla, and Helene Moussa, eds. 2008. *Not Born a Refugee Woman: Contesting Identities, Rethinking Practices.* New York: Berghahn Books.

Halberstam, Judith. 2012. *Gaga Feminism: Sex, Gender, and the End of Normal (Queer Action/Queer Ideas)*. Massachusetts: Beacon Press.

Hancock, Ange-Marie. 2007. "When multiplication doesn't equal quick addition: Examining intersectionality as a research paradigm." *Perspectives on Politics* 5: 63–79.

Hanmer, Jalna. 2000. "Buying sex: Responding to Kerb-Crawlers." In *Expert Meeting on Violence against Women, 8–10 November 1999, Jyväskylä, Finland: Recommendations of the E.U.*, edited by Juha Lavikainen and Laura Keeler, 98–104. Helsinki: Sosiaali- ja terveysministeriö.

Hanson, Susan. 2010. "Gender and mobility: New approaches for informing sustainability." *Gender, Place & Culture* 17: 5–23.

Henry, Leroi. 2007. "Institutionalized disadvantage: Older Ghanaian nurses' and midwives reflections on career progression and stagnation in the NHS." *Journal of Clinical Nursing* 16: 2196–2203.

The Hindu. 2013. "Runaway grandmother sparked savage skirmish on LoC." *The Hindu*, 10 January 2013. http://www.thehindu.com/news/national/runaway-grandmother-sparked-savage-skirmish-on-loc/article4291426.ece (last accessed 2 December 2013).

Hochchild, Arlie Russell. 2000. "Global care chains and emotional surplus value." In *On the Edge: Living with Global Capitalism*, edited by Will Hutton and Anthony Giddens, 130–146. London: Jonathan Cape.

Hondagneu-Sotelo, Pierrette, and Ernestine Avila. 2003. "I'm here, but I'm there: The meanings of Latina motherhood." In *Gender and U.S. Migration: Contemporary Trends*, edited by Pierrette Hondagneu-Sotelo. Berkeley: University of California Press.

hooks, bell. 1994. *Teaching to Transgress: Education as a Practice of Freedom.* London: Routledge.

Huang, Shirlena, Yeoh, Brenda S.A., and Mika Toyota. 2012. "Caring for the elderly: The embodied labour of migrant care workers in Singapore." *Global Networks* 12: 195–215.

Hussein, Shereen, Ismail, Mohamed, and Jill Manthorpe. 2016. "Male workers in the female-dominated long-term care sector: Evidence from England." *Journal of Gender Studies* 25: 35–49.

Hyndman, Jennifer. 2010. "Introduction: The feminist politics of refugee migration." *Gender, Place & Culture* 17: 453–459.

Hyndman, Jennifer, and Malathi de Alwis. 2003. "Beyond gender: Towards a feminist analysis of humanitarianism and development in Sri Lanka." *Women's Studies Quarterly* 31: 212–226.

Hyndman, Jennifer, and Malathi de Alwis. 2008. "Reconstituting the subject: Displaced women and humanitarian assistance in Sri Lanka." In *Not Born a Refugee Woman*, edited by Maroussia Hadjukowski-Ahmed, Nazilla Khanlou and Helene Moussa, 83–96. New York: Berghahn Books.

Hyndman, Jennifer, and Wenona Giles. 2011. "Waiting for what? The feminization of asylum in protracted situations." *Gender, Place & Culture* 18: 361–379.

Iredale, Robyn. 2005. "Gender, immigration policies and accreditation: Valuing the skills of professional women migrants." *Geoforum* 36: 155–166.

Isaksen, Lise Widding. 2002. "Masculine dignity and the dirty body." *NORA* 10: 137–146.

Istanbul Convention (ISTA) 2011. *Council of Europe Convention on Preventing and Combating Violence against Women and Domestic Violence*. Council of Europe, published April 12, 2011. http://www.coe.int/en/web/istanbul-convention/home (last accessed 3 November 2016).

Jansen, Stef. 2008. "Misplaced masculinities: Status loss and the location of gendered subjectivities amongst 'non-transnational' Bosnian refugees." *Anthropological Theory* 8: 181–200.

Jordan, Sharalyn. 2009. "Un/convention(al) refugees: Contextualizing the accounts of refugees facing homophobic or transphobic persecution." *Refuge* 26: 165–182.

Jordan, Sharalyn, and Chris Morrissey. 2013. "'On what grounds?' LGBT asylum claims in Canada." *Forced Migration Review* 42: 13–15.

Jureidini, Ray. 2010. "Trafficking and contract migrant workers in the Middle East." *International Migration* 48: 142–163.

Jyrkinen, Marjut. 2005. *The Organisation of Policy Meets the Commercialisation of Sex – Global Linkages, Policies, Technologies*. Helsinki: Hanken School of Economics.

Jyrkinen, Marjut. 2009. "Discourses on the sex trade: Implications for policies and practice." *Politics & Policy* 37: 73–100.

Jyrkinen, Marjut, and Elina Penttinen. 2017. "Organisoitunut prostituutio ja seksikauppa." In *Sukupuolistunut väkivalta. Oikeudellinen ja sosiaalinen ongelma*, edited by Johanna Niemi, Heini Kainulainen and Päivi Honkatukia. Helsinki: Vastapaino.

Kantola, Johanna. 2010. "Gender and violence in the European Union." In *Gender and the European Union*, edited by Johanna Kantola, 148–167. New York: Palgrave MacMillan.

Karkulehto, Sanna. 2011. *Seksin mediamarkkinat*. Helsinki: Gaudeamus.

Keys, Angela, Masterman-Smith, Helen, and Drew Cottle. 2006. "The political economy of a natural disaster: The Boxing Day tsunami, 2004." *Antipode. A Radical Journal of Geography* 38: 195–204.

Khoo, Siew-Ean, Ho, Elsie, and Carmen Voigt-Graf. 2008. "Gendered migration in Oceania. Trends, policies and outcomes." In *New Perspectives on Gender and Migration. Livelihood, Rights and Entitlements*, edited by Nicola Piper, 101–136. London: Routledge.

Khosravi, Shahram. 2010. *"Illegal" Traveller: An Auto-Ethnography of Borders*. Basingstoke: Palgrave Macmillan.

King, Russell, and Anastasia Christou. 2011. "Of counter-diaspora and reverse transnationalism: Return mobilities to and from the ancestral homeland." *Mobilities* 6: 451–466.

Kofman, Eleonore. 1999. "'Birds of passage' a decade later: Gender and immigration in the European Union." *International Migration Review* 33: 269–299.

Kofman, Eleonore. 2000. "The invisibility of female skilled migrants and gender relations in studies of skilled migration in Europe." *International Journal of Population Geography* 6: 45–59.

Kofman, Eleonore. 2004. "Family-related migration: A critical review of European studies." *Journal of Ethnic and Migration Studies* 30: 243–262.

Kofman, Eleonore. 2007. "The knowledge economy, gender and stratified migrations." *Studies in Social Justice* 1: 123–135.

Kofman, Eleonore, and Gillian Youngs, eds. 1996. *Globalization: Theory and Practice*. London: Pinter.

Kofman, Eleonore, and Parvati Raghuram. 2006. "Gender and global labour migrations: Incorporating skilled workers." *Antipode* 38: 282–303.

Kristof, Nicholas, and Sheryl WuDunn. 2010. *Half the Sky: Turning Oppression into Opportunity for Women Worldwide*. New York: Random House.

Kunz, Rahel. 2008. "'Remittances are beautiful'? Gender implications of the new global remittances trend." *Third World Quarterly* 29: 1389–1409.

Kwee, G. T. Maurits. 2012. "Relational Buddhism: Wedding K.J. Gergen's relational being and Buddhism to create harmony in-between-selves." *Psychological Studies* 57: 203–210.

Kynsilehto, Anitta. 2011a. "Negotiating intersectionality in highly educated migrant Maghrebi women's life stories." *Environment and Planning A* 43: 1547–1561.

Kynsilehto, Anitta. 2011b. *The Politics of Multivocality. Encountering Maghrebi Women in France*. Tampere: University of Tampere Press.

Kynsilehto, Anitta. 2014. "Irregularity as a securitized phenomenon in the hubs of transit migration: Practicing security at the EU's external and internal borders." In *Binaries in Battle: Representations of Division and Conflict*, edited by Marja Vuorinen, Aki Huhtinen and Noora Kotilainen, 141–163. Newcastle-Upon-Tyne: Cambridge Scholars Publishing.

Kynsilehto, Anitta. 2016. "Resisting borders: Mobilities, gender, and bodies crossing the mediterranean." *Refugee Watch: A South Asian Journal of Forced Migration* 47: 10–19.

Kynsilehto, Anitta. 2017. "Mobilities, politics and solidarities." *Peace Review: A Journal of Social Justice* 29. doi:10.1080/10402659.2017.1272303

Kynsilehto, Anitta, and Eeva Puumala. 2015. "Persecution as experience and knowledge: The ontological dynamics of asylum interviews." *International Studies Perspectives* 16: 446–462.

LeBaron, Genevieve. 2015. "Unfree labour beyond binaries." *International Feminist Journal of Politics* 17: 1–19.

Leskinen, Jari. 2003. "Organisoitu paritus ja prostituutio Suomessa." In *Rikostutkimus 2002*, 9–30. Helsinki: Keskusrikospoliisi.

Levine, Peter A. 1997. *Waking the Tiger: Healing Trauma*. Berkeley, CA: North Atlantic Books.

Likupe, Gloria. 2006. "Experiences of African nurses in the UK National Health Service: A literature review." *Journal of Clinical Nursing* 15: 1213–1220.

Lind, Amy, and Jill Williams. 2013. "Engendering violence in de/hypernationalized spaces: Border militarization, state territorialization, and embodied politics at the US-Mexico border." In *Feminist (Im)Mobilities in Fortress(ing) North America: Rights, Citizenships, and Identities in Transnational Perspective*, edited by Anne Sisson Runyan, Amy Lind, Patricia McDermott, and Marianne H. Marchand, 95–114. Farnham, Surrey: Ashgate.

Lobasz, Jennifer K. 2009. "Beyond border security: Feminist approaches to human trafficking." *Security Studies* 18: 319–344.

Long, Joanna C. 2006. "Border anxiety in Palestine-Israel." *Antipode* 38: 107–127.

Luibhéid, Eithne. 2008. "Queer/Migration: An unruly body of scholarship." *GLQ: A Journal of Lesbian and Gay Studies* 14: 169–190.

MacMahon, Martha. 1995. *Engendering Motherhood: Identity and Self-Transformation in Women's Lives*. New York: Guilford Press.

Madianou, Mirca. 2012. "Migration and the accentuated ambivalence of motherhood: The role of ICTs in Filipino transnational families." *Global Networks* 12: 277–295.

Madianou, Mirca, and Daniel Miller. 2011. "Mobile phone parenting: Reconfiguring relationships between Filipina migrant mothers and their left-behind children." *New Media and Society* 13: 457–470.

Magnet, Shoshana, and Tara Rodgers. 2012. "Stripping for the State: Whole body imaging technologies and the surveillance of othered bodies." *Feminist Media Studies* 12: 101–118.

Mahdavi, Pardis. 2013. "Gender, labour and the law: The nexus of domestic work, human trafficking and the informal economy in the United Arab Emirates." *Global Networks* 13: 425–440.

Mai, Nicola, and Russell King. 2009. "Introduction: Love, sexuality and migration: Mapping the issue." *Mobilities* 4: 295–307.

Malkki, Liisa. 1996. "Speechless emissaries: Refugees, humanitarianism, and dehistoricization." *Cultural Anthropology* 11: 377–404.

Manalansan IV, Martin F. 2006. "Queer intersections: Sexuality and gender in migration studies." *International Migration Review* 40: 224–249.

Marchand, Marianne H., and Anne Sisson Runyan. 2011. "Introduction: Feminist sightings of global restructuring: Old and new conceptualizations." In *Gender and Global Restructuring: Sightings, Sites and Resistances*, edited by Marianne H. Marchand and Anne Sisson Runyan. 2nd edition. London: Routledge.

McCall, Leslie. 2005. "The complexity of intersectionality." *Signs: Journal of Women in Culture and Society* 30: 1771–1800.

McDermott, Patricia, and Olga Sanmiguel-Valderrama. 2013. "(Im)mobilizing unskilled migrant labor post-NAFTA: Racialized and gendered legal barriers to the human rights of migrant Mexicans in Canada and the US." In *Feminist (Im)Mobilities in Fortress(ing) North America. Rights, Citizenships, and Identities in Transnational Perspective*, edited by Anne Sisson Runyan, Amy Lind, Patricia McDermott and Marianne H. Marchand, 39–55. Farnham, Surrey: Ashgate.

McEvoy, Jamie, Petrzelka, Peggy, Radel, Claudia, and Birgit Schmook. 2012. "Gendered mobility and morality in a South-Eastern Mexican community: Impacts of male labour migration on the women left behind." *Mobilities* 7: 369–388.

McGregor, JoAnn. 2007. "'Joining the BBC (British Bottom Cleaners)': Zimbabwean migrants and the UK care industry." *Journal of Ethnic and Migration Studies* 33: 801–824.

McKey, Linda. 2005. *Families, Violence and Social Change*. Maidenhead: Open University Press.

Mirhady, Vera. 2011. "Canadian perspective on queer migration." *Undercurrent Journal* 8: 55–62.

Mohanty, C.T. 2003: *Feminists without Borders. Decolonizing Theory, Practicing Solidarity*. Durham: Duke University Press.

Mollica, Richard F. 2006. *Healing Invisible Wounds: Paths to Hope and Recovery in Violent World*. Orlando: Harcourt.

Morales, Maria Cristina, and Cynthia Bejarano. 2009. "Transnational sexual and gendered violence: An application of border sexual conquest at a Mexico-US border." *Global Networks* 9: 420–439.

Morokvaśic, Mirjana. 1984. "Birds of passage are also women." *International Migration Review* 18: 886–907.

Morokvaśic, Mirjana. 2015. "La visibilité des femmes migrantes dans l'espace publique." *Hommes & Migrations* 1311: 7–13.

Moukarbel, Nayla. 2009. *Sri Lankan Housemaids in Lebanon: A Case of "Symbolic Violence" and "Everyday Forms of Resistance"*. IMISCOE Dissertations. Amsterdam: Amsterdam University Press.

Mountz, Alison. 2011. "Where asylum-seekers wait: Feminist counter-topographies of sites between states." *Gender, Place & Culture* 18: 381–399.

Murray, David A.B. 2013. "Identity, performativity and queer immigrant bodies: A Dominican perspective." *GLQ: A Journal of Lesbian and Gay Studies* 19: 131–133.

Näre, Lena. 2010. "Sri Lankan men working as cleaners and carers: Negotiating masculinity in Naples." *Men and Masculinities* 13: 65–86.

Nash, Jennifer. 2008. "Re-thinking intersectionality." *Feminist Review* 89: 1–15.

Nevins, Joseph. 2007. "Dying for a cup of coffee? Migrant deaths in the US-Mexico border region in a neoliberal age." *Geopolitics* 12: 228–247.

Noiriel, Gérard. 1988. *Le creuset français. Histoire de l'immigration XIXe–XXe siècle*. Paris: Seuil.

O'Connell Davidson, Julia. 1998. *Prostitution, Power and Freedom*. Ann Arbor, MI: University of Michigan Press.

Oksanen, Sofi. 2010. *Purge*. L. Rogers (trans.). London: Atlantic Books.

O'Leary, Anna Ochoa, and Gloria Ciria Valdéz-Gardea. 2013. "Neoliberalizing (re)production: Women, migration, and family planning in the peripheries of the state." In *Feminist (Im)Mobilities in Fortress(ing) North America: Rights, Citizenships, and Identities in Transnational Perspective*, edited by Anne Sisson Runyan, Amy Lind, Patricia McDermott and Marianne H. Marchand, 75–93. Farnham, Surrey: Ashgate.

Ong, Aihwa. 1999. *Flexible Citizenship: The Cultural Logics of Transnationality.* Durham: Duke University Press.

Osezua, Clementina O. 2011. "Cross-border sex trade, transnational remittances and changing family structures among *Benin* people of Southern Nigeria." *Gender & Behaviour* 9: 4276–4297.

Pajaron, Marjorie. 2016. "Heterogeneity in the intra-household allocation of international remittances: Evidence from Philippine households." *Journal of Development Studies* 52: 854–875.

Pan, Darcy. 2011. "Student visas, undocumented labour, and the boundaries of legality: Chinese migration and English as a foreign language education in the Republic of Ireland." *Social Anthropology* 19: 268–287.

Pande, Amrita. 2010. "Commercial surrogacy in India: Manufacturing a perfect mother-worker." *Signs: Journal of Women in Culture and Society* 35: 969–992.

Pande, Amrita. 2013. "'The paper that you have in your hand is my freedom': Migrant domestic work and the sponsorship (Kafala) system in Lebanon." *International Migration Review* 47: 414–441.

Parreñas, Rhacel. 2005a. *Children of Global Migration: Transnational Families and Gendered Woes.* Stanford: Stanford University Press.

Parreñas, Rhacel. 2005b. "Long distance intimacy: Class, gender and intergenerational relations between mothers and children in Filipino transnational families." *Global Networks* 5: 317–336.

Penttinen, Elina. 2008. *Globalization, Prostitution and Sex Trafficking: Corporeal Politics.* London: Routledge.

Penttinen, Elina. 2012. "Nordic women in international crisis management: A politics of hope." In *Making Gender Making War: Violence, Military and Peace-Keeping Practices*, edited by Annica Kronsell and Erika Svedberg. London: Routledge.

Penttinen, Elina. 2013. *Joy and International Relations: A New Methodology.* London: Routledge.

Penttinen, Elina. 2015. "Taking advantage of peripherality: Gendered and racialized mobilities in the context of post-911 globalization." In *Remapping Gender, Place and Mobility: Global Confluences and Local Particularities in Nordic Peripheries*, edited by Stine Thidemann Faber and Helene Pristed Nielsen. London: Routledge.

Penttinen, Elina. 2016. "Compassionate witnessing of trauma as a potential practice for security studies scholarship." *Critical Studies on Security* 4: 129–132.

Pessar, Patricia R. 2003. "Engendering migration studies: The case of new immigrants in the United States." In *Gender and U.S Immigration: Contemporary Trends*, edited by Pierrette Hondagneu-Sotelo, 20–42. Oakland: University of California Press.

Peterson, V. Spike. 2003. *A Critical Rewriting of Global Political Economy.* London: Routledge.

Peterson, V. Spike. 2012. "Rethinking theory: Inequalities, informalization and feminist quandaries." *International Feminist Journal of Politics* 14: 5–35.

Petrozziello, Allison J. 2011. "Feminised financial flows: How gender affects remittances in Honduran–US transnational families." *Gender and Development* 19: 53–67.

Piper, Nicola. 2006. "Gendering the politics of migration." *International Migration Review* 40: 133–164.

Piper, Nicola. 2008. "International migration and gendered axes of stratification." In *New Perspectives on Gender and Migration. Livelihood, Rights and Entitlements*, edited by Nicola Piper, 1–18. London: Routledge.

Piper, Nicola. 2015. "Democratizing migration from the bottom up: The rise of the global migrants rights movement." *Globalizations* 12: 788–802.

Preibisch, Kerry, and Evelyn Encalada Grez. 2013. "Between hearts and pockets: Locating the outcomes of transnational homemaking practices among Mexican women in Canada's temporary migration programmes." *Citizenship Studies* 17: 785–802.

Pro Asyl. 2013. *Pushed back: Systematic human rights violations against refugees in the Aegean Sea and the Greek-Turkish land border*. https://www.proasyl.de/wp-content/uploads/2015/12/PRO_ASYL_Report_Pushed_Back_english_November_2013.pdf (last accessed 9 March 2017).

Puar, Jasbir. 2002. "Circuits of queer mobility: Tourism, travel and globalization." *GLQ: A Journal of Lesbian and Gay Studies* 8: 101–137.

Puar, Jasbir. 2005. "Queer times, queer assemblages." *Social Text* 23: 122–139.

Puar, Jasbir. 2012. "'I would rather be a cyborg than a goddess': Becoming-intersectional in assemblage theory." *Philosophia* 2: 49–66.

Puumala, Eeva, Väyrynen, Tarja, Kynsilehto, Anitta, and Samu Pehkonen. 2011. "Events of the body politic: A Nancian reading of asylum-seekers' bodily choreographies and resistance." *Body & Society* 17: 83–104.

Raghuram, Parvati. 2004. "The difference that skills make: gender, family migration strategies and regulated labour markets." *Journal of Ethnic and Migration Studies* 30: 303–321.

Raghuram, Parvati. 2013. "Theorising the spaces of student migration." *Population, Space and Place* 19: 138–154.

Raghuram, Parvati. 2016. "Locating care ethics beyond the Global North." *ACME: An International Journal for Critical Geographies* 15: 511–533.

Raghuram, Parvati, and Eleonore Kofman. 2004. "Out of Asia: Skilling, re-skilling and deskilling of female migrants." *Women's Studies International Forum* 27: 95–100.

Redden, Stephanie M., and Jillian Terry. 2013. "The end of the line: Feminist understandings of resistance to full-body scanning technology." *International Feminist Journal of Politics* 15: 234–253.

Repo, Jemima, and Riina Yrjölä. 2011. "The gender politics of celebrity humanitarianism in Africa." *International Feminist Journal of Politics* 13: 44–62.

Richardson, Laurel. 1997. *Fields of Play: Constructing Academic Life*. New Brunswick, NJ: Rutgers University Press.

Robinson, Fiona. 2011. "Stop talking and listen: Discourse ethics and feminist care ethics in international political theory." *Millennium: Journal of International Studies* 39: 845–860.

Rohrer, Judy. 2005. "Toward a full-inclusion feminism: A feminist deployment of disability analysis." *Feminist Studies* 31: 34–63.

Ronkainen, Suvi. 2008. "Intiimi loukkaus ja haavoittuvuus: Seksuaalinen väkivalta ja pornografisoivat narratiivit." In *Paljastettu intiimi: Sukupuolistuneen väkivallan dynamiikka*, edited by Suvi Ronkainen and Sari Näre, 43–83. Rovaniemi: Lapland University Press.

Roos, Hannelore. 2013. "In the rhythm of the global market: Female expatriates and mobile careers: A case study of Indian ICT professionals on the move." *Gender, Work and Organization* 20: 147–157.

Rothschild, Babette. 2000. *The Body Remembers: The Psychophysiology of Trauma and Trauma Treatment*. New York: W.W. Norton & Company.

Ruddick, Sara. 1996. *Maternal Thinking: Towards a Politics of Peace*. Boston: Beacon Press.

Salih, Ruba. 2001. "Moroccan migrant women: Transnationalism, nation-states and gender." *Journal of Ethnic and Migration Studies* 27: 655–671.

Sarti, Raffaella, and Francesca Scrinzi. 2010. "Introduction to the special issue: Men in a woman's job, male domestic workers, international migration and the globalization of care." *Men and Masculinities* 13: 4–15.

Sassen, Saskia. 2000. "Women's burden: Counter-geographies of globalization and the feminization of survival." *Journal of International Affairs* 53: 503–524.

Schemenauer, Ellie. 2012. "Victims and vamps, madonnas and whores: The construction of female drug couriers and the practices of the US security state." *International Feminist Journal of Politics* 14: 83–102.

Schuster, Liza. 2011a. "Dublin II and Eurodac: Examining the (un)intended(?) consequences." *Gender, Place & Culture* 18: 401–416.

Schuster, Liza. 2011b. "Turning refugees into 'illegal migrants': Afghan asylum seekers in Europe." *Ethnic and Racial Studies* 34: 1392–1407.

Scrinzi, Francesca. 2010. "Masculinities and the international division of care: Migrant male domestic workers in Italy and France." *Men and Masculinities* 13: 44–64.

Segrave, Marie. 2009. "Order at the border: The repatriation of victims of trafficking." *Women's Studies International Forum* 32: 251–260.

Shackelford, Jean. 1992. "Feminist pedagogy: A means for bringing critical thinking and creativity to the economics classroom." *Alternative Pedagogies and Economic Education* 82: 570–576.

Sheller, Mimi, and John Urry. 2006. "The new mobilities paradigm." *Environment and Planning A* 38: 207–226.

Sherry, Mark. 2004. "Overlaps and contradictions between queer theory and disability studies." *Disability & Society* 19: 769–783.

Shildrick, Margrit. 2012. *Dangerous Discourses of Disability, Subjectivity and Sexuality*. Basingstoke: Palgrave MacMillan.

Shrewsbury, Carolyn. 1997. "What is feminist pedagogy?" *Women's Studies Quarterly* 25: 166–173.

Shuman, Amy, and Carol Bohmer. 2004. "Representing trauma: Political asylum narrative." *Journal of American Folklore* 117: 394–414.

Siddle, Julian. 2013. "Kiribati island: Sinking into sea?" *BBC*, November 25, 2013. http://www.bbc.com/news/science-environment-25086963 (last accessed 21 October 2014).

Silvey, Rachel. 2007. "Unequal borders: Indonesian transnational migrants at immigration control." *Geopolitics* 12: 265–279.

Sjoberg, Laura. 2006. *Gender, Justice and the Wars in Iraq: A Feminist Reformulation of the Just War Theory*. London: Lexington Books.

Skjelsbaek, Inger. 2006. "Therapeutic work with victims of sexual violence in war and post war: A discourse analysis of Bosnian experiences." *Peace and Conflict: Journal of Peace Psychology* 12: 93–118.

So, Christine. 2006. "Asian mail-order brides, the threat of global capitalism, and the rescue of the U.S. nation-state." *Feminist Studies* 32: 395–419.

Spivak, Gayatri. 1988. "Can the subaltern speak?" In *Marxism and the Interpretation of Culture*, edited by Cary Nelson and Lawrence Grossberg, 271–313. London: Macmillan.

Squire, Vicki. 2015. *Post/humanitarian Border Politics between Mexico and the US: People, Places, Things*. Basingstoke: Palgrave MacMillan.

Steans, Jill. 1998. *Gender and International Relations: An Introduction*. Cambridge: Polity Press.

Sylvester, Christine. 1994. *Feminist Theory and International Relations in a Postmodern Era*. Cambridge: Cambridge University Press.

Tabak, Shana, and Rachel Levitan. 2013. "LGBTI migrants in immigration detention." *Forced Migration Review* 42: 47–49.

Taylor, Edward J. 1999. "The new economics of labour migration and the role of remittances in the migration process." *International Migration* 37: 63–88.

Téllez, Michelle. 2008. "Community of struggle: Gender, violence, and resistance on the U.S./Mexico border." *Gender and Society* 22: 545–567.

Teofilovski, Ognen. 2016. "Hundreds of migrants march out of Greek camp, cross to Macedonia." *Reuters*, 14 March 2016. http://www.reuters.com/article/us-europe-migrants-march-idUSKCN0WG1J7 (last accessed 19 April 2016).

Thorbek, Susanne, and Bandana Pattanaik. 2002. *Transnational Prostitution: Changing Global Patterns*. New York: Zed Books.

TIP. 2016. *Trafficking in Persons Report 2016*. Department of State, United States of America. http://www.state.gov/documents/organization/258876.pdf (last accessed 19 January 2017).

Tolentino, Roland. 1996. "Bodies, letters, catalogs: Filipinas in transnational space." *Social Text* 14: 49–76.

Toyota, Mika, and Leng Leng Thang. 2012. "'Reverse marriage migration': A case study of Japanese brides in Bali." *Asian and Pacific Migration Journal* 21: 345–364.

Truong, Thanh-Dam. 1990. *Sex, Money and Morality: Prostitution and Tourism in Southeast Asia*. London: Zed Books.

Tsing, Anna. 2004. *Friction: An Ethnography of Global Connection*. Princeton: Princeton University Press.

Twigg, Julia. 2004. "The body, gender, and age: Feminist insights in social gerontology." *Journal of Aging Studies* 18: 59–73.

Twigg, Julia, Wolkowitz, Carol, Cohen, Rachel Lara, and Sarah Nettleton. 2011. "Conceptualising body work in health and social care." *Sociology of Health & Illness* 33: 171–188.

Tyler, Imogen. 2010. "Designed to fail: A biopolitics of British citizenship." *Citizenship Studies* 14: 61–74.

Ullah, A. K. M. Ahsan. 2013. "Bangladeshi migrant workers in Hong Kong: Adaptation strategies in an ethnically distant destination." *International Migration* 51: 165–180.

UN. 1993. *The UN Standard Rules on the Equation of Opportunities for Persons with Disabilities.* http://www.un.org/disabilities/documents/gadocs/standardrules.pdf (last accessed 19 January 2017).

UNHCR. 2003. *Sexual and Gender-Based Violence against Refugees, Returnees and Internally Displaced Persons. Guidelines for Prevention and Response.* Geneva: UNHCR.

UNHCR. 2008. *UNHCR Guidelines on Determining the Best Interests of the Child.* http://www.unhcr.org/4566b16b2.html (last accessed 13 December 2013).

UN-INSTRAW. 2006. *Gender, Migration, Remittances and Development.* http://www.un.org/esa/population/meetings/fifthcoord2006/P02_INSTRAW.pdf (last accessed 27 October 2014).

UNODC. 2012. *Global Report on Trafficking in Persons 2012* (United Nations publication, Sales No. E.13.IV.1). New York: United Nations.

UNODC. 2014. *Global Report on Trafficking in Persons.* UN Office on Drugs and Crime. New York: United Nations. https://www.unodc.org/documents/data-and-analysis/glotip/GLOTIP_2014_full_report.pdf.

Urry, John. 2007. *Mobilities.* Cambridge: Polity Press.

van der Kolk, Bessel A., McFarlane, Alexander C., and Lars Weisaeth, eds. 1996. *Traumatic Stress: The Effects of Overwhelming Experience on Mind, Body and Society.* New York: Guilford Press.

Vogel, Katrin. 2009. "The mother, the daughter, and the cow: Venezuelan *transformistas'* migration to Europe." *Mobilities* 4: 367–387.

Waitt, Gordon, and Andrew Gorman-Murray. 2011a. "Journeys and returns: Home, life narratives and remapping sexuality in a regional city." *International Journal of Urban and Regional Research* 35: 1239–1255.

Waitt, Gordon, and Andrew Gorman-Murray. 2011b. " 'It's about time you came out': Sexualities, mobility and home." *Antipode: A Radical Journal of Geography* 43: 1380–1403.

Walby, Silvia, Jo Armstrong, and Sofia Strid. 2012. "Intersectionality: Multiple inequalities in social theory." *Sociology* 46: 224–240.

Wang, Hong-zen. 2007. "Hidden spaces of resistance of the subordinated: Case studies from Vietnamese female migrant partners in Taiwan." *International Migration Review* 41: 706–727.

Weber, Cynthia. 2011. "Design, translation, citizenship: Reflections on the virtual (de)territorialisation of the US-Mexico border." *Environment and Planning D: Society and Space* 30: 482–496.

White, Melissa Autumn. 2013. "Governing queer intimacies at the US-Canada 'border.' " In *Feminist (Im)Mobilities in Fortress(ing) North America: Rights, Citizenships, and Identities in Transnational Perspective*, edited by Anne Sisson Runyan, Amy Lind, Patricia McDermott, and Marianne H. Marchand, 147–163. Farnham, Surrey: Ashgate.

Whitworth, Sandra. 2007. *Men, Militarism & UN Peacekeeping: A Gendered Analysis*. London: Lynne Rienner Publishers.

Wibben, Annick T.R. 2011. *Feminist Security Studies: A Narrative Approach*. New York: Routledge.

Wise, J. MacGregor. 2000. "Home: territory and identity." *Cultural Studies* 14: 295–310.

Wright, Melissa W. 2011. "Necropolitics, narcopolitics and femicide: Gendered violence on the Mexico–US border." *Signs: Journal of Women in Culture and Society* 36: 707–731.

Wright, Melissa W. 2013. "Feminicidio, narcoviolence, and gentrification in Ciudad Juárez: The feminist fight." *Environment and Planning D: Society and Space* 31: 830–845.

Yeates, Nicola. 2004. "Global care chains." *International Feminist Journal of Politics* 6: 369–391.

Yeates, Nicola. 2012. "Global care chains: A state-of-the-art review and future directions in care transnationalization research." *Global Networks* 12: 135–154.

Yeoh, Brenda S.A., and Katie Willis. 2005. "Singaporeans in China: Transnational women elites and the negotiation of gendered identities." *Geoforum* 36: 211–222.

Yuval-Davis, Nira. 1997. *Gender and Nation*. London: Sage.

Zeneidi, Djemila. 2013. *Femmes/Fraises: Import/Export*. Paris: Presses Universitaires de France.

Zetter, Kim. 2010. "German 'Fleshmob' Protests Airport Scanners." *Wired*, 12 January 2010. http://www.wired.com/threatlevel/2010/01/german-fleshmob/ (last accessed 27 January 2014).

Index

About the Authors

Elina Penttinen is a university lecturer in gender studies, University of Helsinki. She has published widely on globalization and sex trafficking, new security agency in the context of civilian crisis management, gendered experience of war and compassion-based methodology. She leads a multidisciplinary research project on experience of violence and develops feminist analysis on healing trauma. She is the author of *Joy and International Relations: A New Methodology* (2013) and *Globalization, Prostitution and Sex Trafficking: Corporeal Politics* (2008). She teaches courses on feminist methodology, scientific writing and gender studies and supervises doctoral thesis projects in the Gender, Culture and Society doctoral programme. Her areas of expertise are feminist methodology, creative analytic writing, contemplative pedagogy and research on violence.

Anitta Kynsilehto works at the Tampere Peace Research Institute, University of Tampere, Finland. Kynsilehto's research focuses on human mobility, intersectionality, borders and solidarity activism, with an ongoing project studying corporeal forms of resistance and relational knowledge formation between undocumented migrants and solidarity activists in North Africa, the Middle East and Europe. Her work has been published, for example, in *Environment and Planning A, Body & Society, International Studies Perspectives* and *European Journal of Cultural Studies*. Alongside her academic interests, she takes part in civil society networks that deal with the above topics, for example, by serving in the executive committee of the EuroMed Rights as the political referent on migration and asylum.